P9-CQH-547

THE SEXUAL REVOLUTION IN MODERN AMERICAN LITERATURE

by

CHARLES I. GLICKSBERG

*Brooklyn College
of the City University
of New York*

MARTINUS NIJHOFF / THE HAGUE / 1971

ISBN 90 247 5036 9

PRINTED IN THE NETHERLANDS

To Paul

TABLE OF CONTENTS

PART ONE

SEX, RELIGION, SCIENCE, AND LITERATURE

INTRODUCTION

1. The Dialectic of the Sex-Motif in Literature

Sex is a function of culture; in literature today it plays only a small though aggressively righteous part. Nature, long held in bondage, periodically breaks out in revolt, but its victory is never complete. In every society, primitive as well as modern, the sexual instinct is for good or evil always subject to some measure of regulation and restraint. In literature, where the battle between love and sex, spirit and flesh, is fought out in terms of symbolic action, the writers support their cause, for or against sexual freedom, with varying degrees of evangelical ardor and outspokenness. On this issue there is no unanimity for the simple reason that American culture is not unified in its beliefs concerning the nature of man. The central conflict between instinctual needs and the claims of the ideal, between physical desire and the inner check, between Dionysus and Christ, goes on all the time. Sublimation is the cultural process whereby sexual energy is deflected from its biological source and diverted into spiritually "higher" and socially more useful channels.

But sublimation is for most men hard to achieve. As civilization grows more complex, the individual is exposed to a series of increasingly severe moral strains. Pitted against Nature while subject to its laws, he must henceforth be governed in his behavior by inner as well as outer controls. Thus he forfeits his original spontaneity of being and becomes a house divided against itself. As he seeks to subjugate the unbridled pressure of instinct, he begins to suffer from a corrosive sense of guilt. He strives to live up to the prescribed ideal of conduct, his own or that of the community, struggling hard to make "good" prevail over "evil," but the more strenuously he endeavors to tame the mutinous flesh the more grievously is he afflicted with neurotic symptoms. The clamorous voice of instinct will not be silenced.

The twentieth century gave rise, especially in the United States, to a number of movements designed to redress the balance and cure man of his sexual neurosis. The strident call for a return to primitivism was accompanied by the glorification of instinct and then, later, by the apotheosis of the orgasm. The revolt initiated in the twenties by the members of the lost generation was carried out in a more thoroughgoing militant fashion by the beat generation during the fifties. Rebelling against the institutionalized force of custom and convention, the spokesmen of the beat generation scoffed at all talk of sublimation, spirituality, and moral values. The quest for the apocalyptic orgasm, they contended, was motivated by the highest morality. The rest was so much bourgeois hypocrisy and cant. As Norman Mailer, the prophet of the hipsters, declared in an interview: "After all, if my generation of writers represents anything, if there's anything we've fought for, it's a sexual revolution."[1] And he cites the fact that what was forbidden fare twenty years ago – books like *Lady Chatterley's Lover* and *Tropic of Cancer* – is now published without fuss or hindrance and allowed to circulate freely. For better or worse, sex was liberated, and the liberation brought about a greater inclination on the part of American writers to explore the full potentialities of the sexual theme, including the phenomenon of sexual aberration.

The sexual revolution that Norman Mailer says his generation fought for and won had its antecedents in the contribution made by such iconoclastic figures as Sherwood Anderson, Dreiser, and Eugene O'Neill, all of whom warred against the repressions imposed by the Puritanic ideal. Literary naturalism achieved its end, but the Christian conception of the spiritual self still retained its hold on the American character. Though the doctrine of original sin had ceased to oppress the conscience of modern man, the Christian stress on the primacy of spirit over the flesh was still a potent restraining influence. Despite the orgasmic credo of Norman Mailer, the human spirit finds it difficult to glory in the role of the beast with the double back. If sexuality is a puissant god, as Dylan Thomas lyrically proclaimed, it is tormented by a haunting awareness of death. Thus, even in the libertarian atmosphere of the twentieth century, the old dualism persists. The desire for uninhibited sexual indulgence is held back by the realization that sex is not enough.

For the fundamental principle of Christian theology is based on the assumption that love must be viewed from the contrasting – and yet complementary – perspectives of the body and the spirit. The two must not be confounded. But the Christian prescription in the field of sexual morality, even when not carried to ascetic extremes, could not be followed in a culture

[1] *The Realist*. No. 40. December 1962, p. 15.

in which religious faith had drastically declined. Those who echoed Nietzsche's belief that God was dead would reject the sexual morality formulated by the Church, and they rejected it categorically on the ground that it violated the law of Nature.

The literary sex-rebels were supported in their position by the science of psychoanalysis. Freudianism refutes the idea of original sin, which is associated primarily with the sexual act.[2] It explodes the fiction that sex exists, or should exist, exclusively for the purpose of perpetuating the species. Once faith in God was abandoned, the spiritualized version of love was debunked and modern American literature dedicated itself to the worship of the Common rather than the Heavenly Aphrodite. After the dethronement of the gods, biology was crowned king.

But the sensational success of the sexual revolution, the sudden scandalous breakdown of age-old taboos, did not bring about the anticipated fulfillment of happiness. The zoological perspective does as much violence to the nature of man and proves in practice as frustrating as the ascetic one. Here, in essence, is the heart of the conflict that grips modern man, in Europe as well as the United States, and finds expression in the literature he produces.

Though modern man rebels against the Judaeo-Christian heritage in the sphere of sexuality, he cannot entirely cut himself off from his cultural and spiritual roots. In the name of Nature and Reason, he launches his revolt against the ascetic doctrine of Christianity, but he remains restless and unhappy in this new bondage to his instincts. He glorifies the body electric and then, swinging to the other extreme, he rejects the fate of carnality, the enslavement of the flesh. He wishes to transcend his fallen state and rise above his biological limitations. The metaphysical passion for transcendence that wars against the ignominious compulsion of sex, is not to be gainsaid. He is of the earth earthy but he would fain rise to heaven, soar upward to the realm of the Absolute, become transformed into pure Spirit. It is the prison of this body of death that renders his aspirations absurd and makes his spiritual passion seem useless. The flesh impels him and the flesh defeats him. The woman that gave him birth dooms him to death; the womb is also the gateway to the tomb. As Simone de Beauvoir says in *The Second Sex:* "Wherever life is in the making – germination, fecundation – it always arouses disgust because it is made only in being destroyed; the slimy embryo begins the cycle that is completed in the putrefaction of death."[3] That

---

[2] Some critics argue that Freudianism has virtually rehabilitated the Christian dogma of original sin. Norman O. Brown makes the sweeping statement that "the doctrine of the universal neurosis of mankind is the psychoanalytical analogue of the theological doctrine of original sin." Norman O. Brown, *Life Against Death*. Middletown, Connecticut: Wesleyan University Press, 1959, p. 6.

[3] Simone de Beauvoir, *The Second Sex*. Translated by H. M. Parshley. New York: Alfred A. Knopf, 1953, p. 146.

is the familiar and poignant cry of transcendence the Christian fathers uttered again and again in battling against the inexorable decree of Nature.[4]

The appeal to Nature as the final arbiter of sexual destiny arouses as much resistance on the part of man as his baffled attempt to transmute the flesh into pure spirit. In the light of this conflict, it is not surprising that the treatment of the sexual motif in American literature is beset by a number of seemingly irreconcilable contradictions. Shall the writer defy the regnant social conventions and run the risk of not having his work accepted for publication? Then, too, since he belongs to American history and the tradition it has built up, he must reckon with the residual but still active force of Puritanism that has shaped his mind as well as the mind of his people. He is part of Nature and yet is able to stand apart from it and even in opposition to it. *Human* nature is nature humanized and spiritualized, though never to the degree where culture is permitted to throttle the life of instinct. Thus the nature of man is largely shaped – or misshaped – by his culture. The sexual attitudes and behavior of the Trobriand Islanders differ strikingly from those of American men and women. Though man resembles the animals in that he must satisfy his biological needs, the way in which he satisfies these is determined by the cultural compulsives of his age. Therein lies his uniqueness: he is bound to Nature and yet must strive in some measure to transcend Nature.

The literary interpretation of sexuality in the United States runs the whole gamut from asceticism to Dionysian affirmation, from the anguish of sin as delineated in the plays of T. S. Eliot to the unabashed varietism of Theodore Dreiser. More concretely, the struggle is waged between an "immoralism" or amorality that is sanctioned or at least not forbidden by Nature and the countervailing Christian ethic of abnegation. Indeed, there is no American writer of our time, no matter how rebellious his stance, who is completely free of this existential conflict, though each writer will present it in a manner congruent with his individual temperament and his *Weltanschauung*. The point is that in the context of our pluralistic culture no single code of morality prevails. More than a century ago Whitman had insisted that it is false to postulate an unavoidable dualism between Eros and Agape, higher and lower, soul and body. The body is not an inferior and shameful incarnation of the higher self. Even an apostle of untrammeled sexuality like Henry Miller depicts the metaphysical malaise that drives his rutting males in search of sexual consummation. Even the beat and hipster

---

[4] Charles I. Glicksberg, "Eros and the Death of God," *The Western* Humanities Review, Autumn, 1959, XII, p. 359. Reprinted in Charles I. Glicksberg, *Modern Literature and the Death of God*. The Hague: Martinus Nijhoff, 1966, pp. 39—40.

heroes are impelled in their copulatory activities by a confused desire for a heightened form of consciousness.

Most modern American writers avoid falling into the trap of dealing with sexuality as an end in itself. There is no justification, on artistic grounds alone apart from other considerations, for the writer to concentrate on the sexual motif to the exclusion of other activities and aspirations that make up the life of man. If he is to render a faithful report of human experience, a mature and balanced criticism of life, he must not drag in sex for its own sake. But some literary mavericks refuse to pay heed to such cautionary wisdom. They will go the whole hog, they will hide nothing that pertains to the *vita sexualis*. They persist in describing in considerable detail the various techniques of sexual intercourse. They have, in effect, sexualized the universe and ransack the world of Nature for properly evocative sexual symbols. As Edmund Fuller points out, a flourishing school of orgasm symbolism has arisen that gives a violently distorted picture of the actual relationship between men and women. For no normal person devotes all his energies to sex.

On the other hand, the old Adam is still very much alive. The *Kinsey Report* has disclosed the flagrant discrepancy that exists in the United States between morality and instinct. The disconcerting statistical facts are there, not to be discounted. Whereas Eros among the Greeks was looked upon as one of the oldest gods, the Puritanic tradition forbade such a pagan cult of love from taking root. The God of Love had to be spiritualized and the effect of such a restrictive conception of love led native writers in the nineteenth century to deal with the subject by means of genteel indirection. But love, however disguised its manifestations may be under a cloud of euphemisms or the rhetoric of romance, remains a central and, if repressed, obsessive concern in the lives of people. The pursuit of sex or the search for love may not be the acknowledged theme of a novel, yet these may operate behind the scenes as a dominating influence. The fear of the flesh lives on in the Puritan conscience, as is shown in the character of Arthur Dimmesdale in *The Scarlet Letter* and in that of Joanna Burden in *Light in August*. Even by the prophets of the new sexual dispensation, woman is still regarded as the dangerous sex. Henry Adams comments astringently on the ambivalent and anomalous position woman occupied in American life:

The Woman had been supreme .... Why was she unknown in America? For evidently America was ashamed of her, and she was ashamed of herself, otherwise they would not have strewn fig-leaves so profusely all over her. When she was a true force, she was ignorant of fig-leaves, but the monthly-magazine-made American female had not a feature that would have been recognized by

Adam. The trait was notorious, but any one brought up among Puritans knew that sex was sin.[5]

Why, Henry Adams wondered, had no American artist possessed the courage to insist on the power of sex? "American art, like the American language and American education, was as far as possible sexless."[6]

2. Literature and the Sexual Theme

Henry Adams died in 1918 before the sexual revolution really got under way. During the twenties new attitudes toward human nature and its biological needs were making themselves strongly felt in American literature. The Puritan ethic, furiously assailed by the champions of modernism, gradually gave way to a more liberal and enlightened outlook. The writer no longer feared that if he took up the sexual theme he would be accused of being obsessed with the subject.[7] Whitman has been amply vindicated in his fight against prudery. In fact, today there is, if anything, an undue preoccupation with the sexual problem. Strongly influenced by such diverse figures as the Marquis de Sade, Freud, and Wilhelm Reich, contemporary American literature has unleashed a moral revolution which defines the sexual instinct, whatever form it takes, as "natural" and therefore "good." The full truth of sex must be revealed without apology and without the discreet use of asterisks. The American house of letters now prides itself on having exorcised the bogey of Puritanism. The naturalistic revolt was carried forward in this country by such writers as Dreiser, Sherwood Anderson, Hemingway, John O'Hara, Faulkner, Henry Miller, and Norman Mailer. In defending himself against the charge that in *A Rage to Live* he portrayed a heroine who was promiscuous and immoral in her married life, John O'Hara wrote: "The author who writes a novel without introducing sex has automatically limited the extent of his responsibility and is thus not entitled to full artistic consideration."[8]

A study of the ways in which patterns of love and codes of sexual behavior are reflected in modern literature is under no obligation to determine such formidably complex problems as what is right and wrong. Who, after

[5] Henry Adams, *The Education of Henry Adams*. Boston and New York: Houghton Mifflin Company, 1918, p. 384.

[6] *Ibid.,* p. 385.

[7] In 1929 Bertrand Russell pointed out: "The writer who deals with a sexual theme is always in danger of being accused, by those who think that such themes should not be mentioned, of an undue obsession with his subject." Bertrand Russell, *Marriage and Morals.* New York: Liveright, 1929, p. 288.

[8] Irving Stone, John O'Hara, and MacKinlay Kantor, *Three Views of the Novel.* Washington, D.C.: U.S. Library of Congress, 1957, p. 29.

all, is to prescribe what constitutes the "proper" sexual morality?[9] It is legitimate, however, to trace, eliminating or reducing as far as possible the impact of moral value-judgments, the pattern of change, as interpreted in the body of modern American literature, that has taken place in the love ethic and sexual behavior of different generations. The task of tracing this pattern is by no means an easy one. Literature, prophetic or rebellious in its insights, is often a harbinger of values that are only gradually and reluctantly accepted by society at large. Because he tries to be uncompromisingly honest in his reading of life, the writer frequently offends the taste of his time and is reviled, as was the case with Ibsen's *Ghosts*, as an "enemy of the people." Then, too, critics are notoriously fallible, as Henri M. Peyre has shown in *Writers and Their Critics*, in estimating the importance of the work of their contemporaries. It is a fact "that an innovator has to create his own public and to mold the very taste which will enable future generations to borrow his own lens or listen with his own ears."[10] Not that all writers play, or are willing to play, such an iconoclastic and prophetic role. Like William Dean Howells, they may prefer to compromise with the existing moral standard and concern themselves with the smiling, sunny aspects of life. Bolder spirits, however, fought doughtily for the right to uncensored freedom of expression in the field of sexual love. Their primary aim was not to shock the susceptibilities of the respectable or to bait the bourgeoisie but to report what they believed was the whole truth, however unpleasant, about the nature of man.

If the practise of sexual freedom for the lost generation of the twenties ended time and again disastrously – the pathetic story of this failure is recounted in Scott Fitzgerald's *The Crack-Up* – it was because the sexual problem was vastly more complex than the libertarians of that gaudy and irrepressible decade realized. Sexual love transcends the physiological basis of instinct; it is a metaphysical as well as physical passion. Thielicke rightly speaks of the mystical component in the sex urge, "which exists alongside the physiologically determined libido: the mystery can be unveiled along with another person."[11] The spirit enters into the mystery of the sexual

---

[9] Kathleen Nott sees no reason why a natural, human instinct should be condemned as inherently evil. "I am simply stating that physical sexual relations normally cause intense enjoyment and that no person, otherwise ignorant, would learn this fact from the works of our most influential novelists from the early nineteenth century to the present day." Kathleen Nott, *The Emperor's Clothes*. London: Heinemann, 1954, p. 304.

[10] Henri M. Peyre, "The Criticism of Contemporary Writing," in Elliot Coleman (ed.), *Lectures in Criticism*. New York: Harper & Brothers, 1961, p. 135.

[11] Helmut Thielicke, *The Ethics of Sex*. Translated by John Doberstein. New York, Evanston, and London: Harper & Row, 1964, p. 74.

encounter. Sex is a mystery because it is not a function of organs specially reserved for this purpose; it involves the whole man. Though the biological basis of sex is common to all men, the experience is psychologically and spiritually differentiated for each individual. What distinguishes the human from the animal world is love rather than sex.

The manner in which a writer interprets the function of sex will be determined by his conception of human nature and his philosophy of love. The naturalistic novelists, unlike their Victorian predecessors, portrayed man as a child of Nature. Whatever is "natural" is "right." That was the formulated faith they believed in and more or less consistently applied. The facts that science had made known about the character of man must be realistically faced. Creative wholeness, these writers felt, is to be achieved through instinctual fulfillment. The revolt of the literary naturalists and those who came after them was conducted in the august name of science.

CHAPTER II

THE SCIENCE OF PSYCHOANALYSIS AND SEXUALITY

Anyone who considers sex as something mortifying and humiliating to human nature is at liberty to make use of the more genteel expression "Eros" and "erotic". I might have done so myself from the first and thus have spared myself much opposition. But I did not want to, for I like to avoid concessions to faint-heartedness. One can never tell where that road may lead one; one gives way first in words, and then little by little in substance too. I cannot see any merit in being ashamed of sex . . . .[1]

1. The Psychoanalytic Outlook and Its Impact on American Literature

I cannot see any merit in being ashamed of sex: it was this attitude that the younger literary generation of the twenties adopted as their battlecry. Psychoanalysis was one of the sciences that wrought far-reaching changes in the entire structure of sexual morality. The explorations of biologists, anthropologists, psychologists, and social scientists helped to trigger the sexual revolution of our time. Not that the revolution was won without a bitter struggle, and the struggle, though with diminishing force, is still going on. Some writers adamantly refused to accept the new sexual gospel. But on the whole the formidable influence of science on the minds of the American literati and their attitude toward the love of the sexes was not to be withstood. Psychoanalysis in particular appealed to many free spirits and furnished a ready-made rationale for their revolt against institutionalized monogamy and their quest for a more satisfying sexual relationship.[2]

Though writers made discoveries in their own right, without benefit of psychoanalytic doctrine, that anticipated the findings of science and necessitated a revaluation of the traditional ethic of love, science seemed to

---

[1] Sigmund Freud, *Group Psychology and the Analysis of the Ego.* Translated by James Strachey. London and Vienna: International Psycho-Analytic Press, 1922, p. 33.
[2] See Frederick J. Hoffman, *Freudianism and the Literary Mind.* New York: Grove Press, Inc., 1959, pp. 63–65 *passim.*

justify their vital concern with the issue of the function of sex in life. The science of psychoanalysis taught them a great deal about the subliminal working of sexual desire, the interdependence of body and mind, the role of the unconscious, the significance of dreams, the vagaries of instinct and how it is shaped or twisted out of shape by culture. Like Whitman, they boldly affirmed their belief in the flesh and the appetites:

I do not press my fingers across my mouth;
I keep as delicate around the bowels as around the head and heart;
Copulation is no more rank to me than death is.

Science performed a notable service for the twentieth-century writer in the United States in that it forced him to question and then to revise his attitude toward morals, society, religion, and the nature of man. To be sure, there were profound individual differences in the way writers interpreted the scientific outlook and put it to use in their work. In general, however, what united the literary naturalists, despite marked divergencies in their reaction to the scientific *Anschauung,* was their belief that Nature was indifferent to the operation of the moral law. Dreiser presented this point of view consistently in his fiction. The spread of the scientific enlightenment led to the weakening of religious faith and the undermining of the absolute morality based on the supernatural. In 1902, Bertrand Russell defiantly stated his atheistic position in "A Free Man's Worship."[3] The death of God that Nietzsche proclaimed led to disturbing consequences for the future of sexual morality.[4] The naturalistic ethic that dominates much of modern American literature stems from the belief that man is a part of Nature that is completely indifferent to human weal or woe.

Dreiser, who had read Nietzsche as well as Tyndall, Herbert Spencer, and Thomas Henry Huxley, formulated a radically revised conception of the nature of man and his place in the universe. Man responds as he must because of his instinctual endowment. A militant determinist, Dreiser saw no hint of an ultimate purpose manifesting itself in the physical universe. Why then postulate the existence of a fixed moral order? If man is but the result of chance, the fortuitous product of the evolutionary flux of biological

[3] Bertrand Russell defined religion as "the desire to believe a lot of nonsense to make yourself comfortable . . . ." Alan Wood, *Bertrand Russell: The Passionate Skeptic.* London: Allen & Unwin, 1957, p. 233.

[4] In *The Genealogy of Morals,* Nietzsche castigates the "bad conscience," the haunting consciousness of sin that Christianity implanted in its deluded followers. In *Ecce Homo* he wrote: "All deprivation of the sexual life, all sullying of it by means of the concept of 'impure,' is *the* crime against life – is the veritable sin against the Holy Ghost of Life." Quoted in F. A. Lea, *The Tragic Philosopher.* London: Methuen & Co., 1957, p. 144.

energy, then religion stands condemned. As a mechanist viewing himself as an atom in a greater machine, Dreiser rejected all talk of soul or spirit as so much superstitious nonsense. That is the philosophical framework he employed in *Sister Carrie*, when dealing with the problem of sexual morality.

Furthermore, science provided modern American writers with an elaborate rationale of sex. Though culture had the power to shape the character and conduct of the individual, there were physiological limits beyond which the process of sublimation could not be carried. Every culture must make liberal provisions for the satisfaction of instinctual needs. The physical organism is rooted in biology; though all human beings live in and are influenced by their culture, which constitutes their uniquely human environment, culture cannot be severed from its biological matrix. As one psychoanalytically-oriented anthropologist declares: *"Man's 'human nature' derives from the kind of body he has."* [5] In his field study of life among the Trobriand Islanders, Bronislaw Malinowski showed that they looked upon sex as a legitimate and wholesome source of pleasure. Since no cruel prohibitions were placed on the sexual freedom of the Trobrianders, their sex life was singularly free from perversion. [6] The growing popularity of psychoanalysis further served to discredit the Christian sex ethic. A number of poets, novelists, dramatists, and critics became deeply absorbed in the work of Freud; some even underwent psychoanalytic treatment, convinced that here was the scientific road to mental health and creative fulfillment.

2. The Influence of Freud, Jung, and the Revisionists

The American writers of the twenties were attracted to Freud for a variety of reasons, one of which was his radical reinterpretation of the nature and function of sexuality. Waldo Frank, like Dreiser, harped insistently on the traumatic impact of Puritanism, the sinister sex repressions from which American culture suffered. Floyd Dell, an aggressive leader during the twenties in the cause of sexual freedom, found in Freudianism another mighty weapon to be used in his fight against bourgeois morality. During this decade, Freudianism was converted into a veritable crusade. By utilizing the Freudian discoveries of dream displacement and the dynamic role of the unconscious, writers were able to arrive at a better understanding of

[5] Weston La Barre, *The Human Animal*. Chicago: The University of Chicago Press, 1954, p. xiv.

[6] Malinowski declares: "In Melanesia there is no taboo on sex in general; there is no putting of any veils on natural functions, certainly not in the case of a child." Bronislaw Malinowski, *Sex and Repression in Savage Society*. New York and London: Harcourt, Brace and Company, 1927, pp. 54–55.

the self and its relation to reality. The novelist, for example, could gain a deeper insight into the irrational components of human motivation. As Frederick J. Hoffman notes: "Thus it is quite possible that Freud influenced the writing of our time more radically than other theorists because the subject matter with which he dealt was more intimately related to aesthetic interests." [7] The seminal ideas of Freud brought out into the open the fundamental conflict between Eros and civilization. What made his theories so potent an influence was their supposed scientific grounding. What is more, psychoanalysis, in refraining from passing moral judgment on neurotic victims or the sexual perversions, pointed up the need for a new evaluation of what constitutes the "normal" sexual life.

As a scientist, Freud was surprised by the furore of indignation his work aroused, especially his psychology of sex, yet he reported his findings on the sexual factors responsible for the outbreak of neuroses as if he were writing a clinical report on the love life of the paramecium or the amoeba. Ernest Jones, his biographer, declares that Freud displayed

less than average *personal* interest in what is often an absorbing topic. There was never any gusto or even savor in mentioning a sexual topic. He would have been out of place in the usual club room, for he seldom related sexual jokes and then only when they had a special point illuminating a general theme. He always gave the impression of being an unusually chaste person – the word "puritanical" would not be out of place – and all we know of his early development confirms this conception.[8]

The persecution to which he was subjected, instead of discouraging his zeal, made him more convinced of the truth of his theory that sex played an all-important part in the etiology of the neuroses. On one point he would not yield an inch of ground: he would not avert the wrath of the prudish by the semantic dodge of calling sex by some other, less offensive name. As he wrote to Jung in 1917, the best kind of defence is to spring to the attack. "What is demanded of me is after all that we deny the sexual instinct. So let us proclaim it." [9] He refused to employ a face-saving euphemism like "love." Forthrightly he announced: "The nucleus of what we mean by love naturally consists . . . in sexual love with sexual union as its aim." [10] Like Schopenhauer, he would not spare man any of his deep-seated and fondly cherished illusions. And like Schopenhauer, he indicated how on the biological level the individual leads a double existence:

[7] Frederick J. Hoffman, *Freudianism and the Literary Mind,* p. 91.

[8] Ernest Jones, *The Life and Work of Sigmund Freud.* New York: Basic Books, Inc., 1953, I, p. 271.

[9] Ernest Jones, *The Life and Work of Sigmund Freud.* New York: Basic Books, Inc., 1955, II, p. 436.

[10] Sigmund Freud, *Group Psychology and the Analysis of the Ego,* p. 37.

one designed to serve his own purposes and another as a link in a chain, in which he serves against, or at any rate without, any volition of his own ends; while from another point of view he is only an appendage to his germ-plasm....[11]

It is not at all surprising that Freud, in the United States as well as Europe, was fiercely attacked for violating the taboo of silence and secrecy surrounding the subject of sex. He disclosed the secrets hidden behind the multifarious disguises assumed by the sexual instinct. In his essay on "Moral Responsibility for the Content of Dreams," he took up the difficult question whether people were to be held responsible for the dreams they have, so many of which are outrageously "immoral." Freud would not absolve the dreamer from blame. "Obviously one must hold oneself responsible for the evil impulses of one's dreams. In what other way can one deal with them? Unless the content of the dream (rightly understood) is inspired by alien spirits, it is a part of my own being." [12] It was this outspokenness on Freud's part which called forth emotional resistance to his theories, both in the United States and abroad, and prompted the charge that psychoanalysis was guilty of pansexualism, though Freud had never recommended unrestricted sexual indulgence. What psychoanalysis advised was a reduction in the moral strictness which kept the sexual instinct repressed. Actually, as Freud argued, "culture is acquired essentially at the cost of sexual component-instincts," and "these instincts must be suppressed, restrained, transmuted, directed towards loftier goals, for civilized psychical achievements to take place." [13] In fact, as we shall see, it was this emphasis on the necessity for sublimation which led the beat writers to reject psychoanalysis as a means of therapy.

At any rate, here was the scientific ammunition the writers could use with deadly effect in their assault on the moral conventions of their culture. If the sexual impulses are not easily controlled by the higher centers, if sublimation is more honored in the breach than in the observance, then there can be no question of imputing guilt to those who violated the prescribed moral code. The aberrant sexual behavior of people can be understood without belaboring them with charges of degeneracy. As writers like Sherwood Anderson were to discover, only a thin line separates the normal from the so-called abnormal. "In no normal person," according to Freud, "does the normal sexual aim lack some designable perverse element, and this uni-

---

[11] Sigmund Freud, *Collected Papers*. Translated by James Strachey. London: The International Psycho-analytical Press, 1925, IV, pp. 35–36.
[12] *Ibid.*, V, 156.
[13] *Ibid.*, II, 109.

versality suffices in itself to prove the inexpediency of an opprobious application of the name perversion." [14]

Unquestionably American writers of the twentieth century benefited greatly (the full measure of their indebtedness has not yet been assessed despite the numerous studies that have appeared analyzing the impact of psychoanalysis on American literature) from the science of psychoanalysis. Not only was the taboo on the sexual theme lifted but the fear of sex, which generated the taboo in the first place, was removed. Henceforth American writers felt free to portray sexual abnormalities in their work, regardless of the moral or legal condemnation of the community they might incur. The literary revolt against the entrenched Puritan ethic was both salutary and inescapable. In his essay on "'Civilized' Sexual Morality and Modern Nervousness," Freud had warned of the dangerous consequences that ensued from denying the sexual demands of the body for too long a time. A morality which insisted upon sexual abstinence culminates in some form of neurosis. "All who wish to reach a higher standard than their constitution will allow, fall victim to neurosis. It would have been better for them if they could have remained less 'perfect.'" [15] Here is the substance of the theme O'Neill worked out in Diff'rent, written in 1920.

Emboldened by this scientific evangel, the literary rebels on the American scene proceeded to draw up their manifesto of sexual freedom. In his plays O'Neill unsparingly diagnosed the disease of romantic idealism and attacked the Puritanic cult in America. Men like Sherwood Anderson and Floyd Dell revealed what they had learned, partly from Freudianism and partly from direct observation and personal experience, about the amazing contradictions of sexual behavior. The Freudian doctrine spread rapidly in the twenties and from then on there was no stopping its advance. A generation of writers sprang up who were by sex obsessed. The "back-to-sex" movement steadily gained momentum.

The protest against such excesses in interpreting the significance of sex in life and literature was bound to come. The quarrel over the implications to be drawn from the conception of the libido broke out in the inner circle of Freudian disciples long before psychoanalysis became a popular cult. Freud had accused Jung of suppressing the sexual factor in psychoanalysis as a concession to the prejudices of a prudish-minded public. [16] Jung de-

[14] Sigmund Freud, Three Contributions to the Theory of Sex. Translated by A. A. Brill. New York and Washington: Nervous and Mental Disease Publishing Co., 1939, p. 24.

[15] Sigmund Freud, On War, Sex and Neurosis. New York: Arts & Science Press, 1947, p. 172.

[16] As Freud pointed out: "All the changes that Jung has wrought in psycho-analysis

sexualized the libido whereas for Freud the libido was electrically charged with the elemental force of sex, the instinctual energy that motivates all human striving. Jung, on the contrary, contended that sex is but one of the forms this energy can take. Sex, he felt, was not the central, sustaining power in the psyche. No society, primitive or modern, permitted the sexual instinct uninhibited modes of expression. Why, Jung asked, should all cultural manifestations, including art, be interpreted in terms of the sexual drive? Though Jung did not deny the importance of sexuality in psychic life, he sought

to set bounds to the rampant terminology of sex which threatens to vitiate all discussions of the human psyche. I wish to put sexuality itself in its proper place. Common-sense will always return to the fact that sexuality is only one of the life-instincts – only one of the psycho-physical functions – though one that is without doubt very far-reaching and important.[17]

Jung wished to put sexuality itself in its proper place, but what is its proper place? That is the question to which not only psychologists but writers of all kinds earnestly addressed themselves. Increasingly Jung came to feel that this disproportionate emphasis on the power of sex was symptomatic of the spiritual malaise of his time; the age had gone mad on the subject, enough to indicate that the sexual life of modern man was profoundly disturbed. Only a change of heart, an allegiance sworn to the kingdom of the spirit, could save man from this biological bondage. "It is not the children of the flesh, but the 'children of God' who know freedom."[18] In short, according to Jung, there is much between heaven and earth not included in the Freudian philosophy of sexuality. Reproaching Freud for overestimating the dark, brutish aspects of the unconscious, Jung endeavored to redress the balance:

As a matter of fact, no moral condemnation could make sex as hateful as the obscenity and blatant vulgarity of those who exaggerated its importance. The intellectual crudeness of the sexual interpretation makes a right valuation impossible. Thus, probably very much against the personal aspirations of Freud himself, the literature that has followed in his wake is effectively carrying on the work of repression. Before Freud nothing was allowed to be sexual, now everything is sexual.[19]

flow from the ambition to eliminate all that is disagreeable in the family complexes, so that it may not evidence itself again in ethics and religion. For sexual libido an abstract term has been substituted, of which one may safely say that it remains mystifying and incomprehensible to fools and wise alike." Sigmund Freud, *Collected Papers*, I, 353.

[17] C. G. Jung, *Modern Man in Search of a Soul*. Translated by W. S. Dell and Cary F. Baynes. London: Kegan Paul, Trench, Trubner & Co., 1941, p. 138.

[18] *Ibid.*, p. 140.

[19] C. G. Jung, *The Development of Personality*. Translated by R. F. C. Hull. New York: Pantheon Books, 1954, p. 84.

Now everything is sexual! Whether or not Freud was principally to blame for this untoward development, that was virtually the situation which prevailed in much of the literature of the twenties. Not that the Freudian interpretation of sexuality was allowed to pass unchallenged. Some writers began to question the validity of the Freudian thesis that every neurosis is without exception conditioned by some abnormality in the *vita sexualis.* Even more objectionable to them was Freud's conception of the artist as deriving his inspiration fundamentally from neurotic roots. In his monograph on Leonardo da Vinci, Freud had maintained that the sexual impulse has "the power to change its nearest aim for others of higher value which are not sexual." [20] The all-consuming sexual curiosity that governs the child is sublimated into new channels of science or philosophy or literature or art. Though Freud frankly admitted that the psychoanalytic method failed to make clear why an artist suffering from a neurotic handicap should attain greatness in his field, he would not abandon his conviction that the productions of the artist are an expression, however disguised in form and content, of his sexual desires.

If the mystique of sex encountered spirited resistance in some quarters, it found one redoubtable champion who withdrew from the psychoanalytic school on the ground that Freud did not go far enough in his psychology of sex. Wilhelm Reich called for a world-wide sexual revolution. In *The Sexual Revolution,* he charged that capitalist society was engaged in a vast conspiracy to frustrate the sexual needs of the young and rob them of mental independence and creative originality. Rejecting wholesale the Freudian theory of sublimation, he denied that repressions are either necessary or desirable. Insisting that the full gratification of the sexual instinct would result not only in the integration of the individual but also in the salvation of society, Reich assails the idea of lifelong monogamous marriage as a species of enslavement not to be borne. Sex thus emerges as the new religion of life – a religion which the hipsters and the members of the beat generation have enthusiastically taken over. Reich went far beyond Freud in tracing all our troubles – social disorders, political strife, the outbreak of Fascism, the eruption of war – to disturbances in the sexual life of man. All of culture, in fact, is essentially governed by sexual needs.

This Reichian psychology of sexual revolution elicited a sympathetic response from various literary groups in the United States. Paul Bowles describes William Burroughs, the author of *Naked Lunch,* sitting doubled

---

[20] Sigmund Freud, *Leonardo da Vinci*. Translated by A. A. Brill. New York: Nervous and Mental Disease Publishing Co., 1932, p. 26.

up in a Reich orgone box that he had made himself, "smoking kif."[21] Those writers who had lost their faith in Marxist eschatology found the Reichian summons to full sexual freedom especially meaningful. The politically disaffiliated, the rebels, and the deviants discovered in Reich scientific confirmation for their belief that the goal of life was to give unconditional expression to their sexual energies.

It is the signal distinction of Erich Fromm, whose work had a marked influence on a whole generation of American writers, that, in opposition to the scientific and statistical approach to sex, he highlighted those elements in the experience of love which are not included in the Freudian or Kinsey outlook. The aim of love is to break down the walls of isolation that hem us in, to achieve a deep feeling of intimacy and union. It is more than that; it is an art that calls for sensitiveness, insight, and a readiness to give generously of oneself. Instead of analyzing sexual love in physiological and instinctual terms, he looks upon it as a quest for union with another person. Physical desire is not to be confused with the complex feeling of love. He makes the point that every theory of love grows out of a theory of human nature. When love inspires the desire for sexual union, it is always blended with the element of tenderness.

If the desire for physical union is not stimulated by love, if erotic love is not also brotherly love, it never leads to union in more than an orgiastic, transitory sense. Sexual attraction creates, for the moment, the illusion of union, yet without love this "union" leaves strangers as far apart as they were before – sometimes it makes them ashamed of each other ... because when the illusion has gone they feel their estrangement even more markedly than before.[22]

Fromm criticizes Freud's theory not only on the ground that it overemphasized sex but that it failed "to understand sex deeply enough."[23] Love must be viewed within a larger frame of discourse, a context that transcends the instinctual.

3. Some Literary Implications

To what extent each of these men – Freud, Jung, Reich, and Fromm – influenced twentieth-century American literature in its portrayal of the sex motif is still an open question. Undoubtedly the major influence was that of Freud. Psychoanalysis made it possible for the writer to explore new, hith-

[21] Paul Bowles, "Burroughs in Tangier," in Thomas Parkinson (ed.), A Casebook on the Beat. New York: Thomas Y. Crowell Company, 1961, p. 115.
[22] Erich Fromm, The Art of Loving. New York: Harper & Brothers, 1956, pp. 54–55.
[23] Ibid., p. 37.

erto tabooed areas of experience, unconscious as well as instinctual. He could utilize the stream-of-consciousness technique and the interior mono- logue, break up the sequence of time in the ordering of the narrative, exploit the rich resources of dream symbolism, and, finally, uncover traits of human nature that had until then not been allowed to be discussed in literature. He could rely on biology and psychology for many of his controlling insights. Whatever was "natural" was not only "normal" but "moral" as well and perfectly legitimate material for literary presentation.

The sexual revolution in literature gained momentum during the twenties. Hemingway's heroes affirm that any experience which made one feel good afterwards was "good." Mrs. Evans in *Strange Interlude* sounds the same naturalistic ethic when she advises Nina, her daughter-in-law, to abort the child she is bearing (there is a strain of insanity in the family) and have a child with another man, without her husband's knowledge. "Being happy," she says, "that's the nearest we can ever come to knowing what's good! Being happy, that's good!"[24] Like Sherwood Anderson, American writers in the twenties, heeding Emerson's call for self-reliance, depended on Nature as the source of inspiration, the origin of beauty and of art, the touchstone of value. What had he to do, Emerson asked, with the sacredness of tradi- tion if he lived wholly from within? When his friend suggested that these impulses to which he responded might come from below and not from above, Emerson replied: "They do not seem to me to be such; but if I am the Devil's child, I will live then from the Devil."[25] Like Emerson, but without any relation to his transcendentalism, the literary rebels of the twenties were resolved that no law would be sacred to them but that of their own nature. Back to Nature – that was their concerted and impassioned cry, and they derived support for their moral revolt in the findings of psycho- analysis. Sherwood Anderson fervently preached his gospel of liberation from the trammels of sex-repression. In *Dark Laughter* he declared cate- gorically: "If there is anything you do not understand in human life consult the works of Dr. Freud."[26]

The scientific outlook, moreover, helped to develop an attitude of tolerance toward all forms of sexual behavior. The existence of sexual ab- normality could be accepted without branding it with the stigma of moral corruption. The knowledge and improved practice of birth control served to emancipate woman from her oppressive fear of pregnancy outside the

[24] Eugene O'Neill, *Nine Plays*. New York: The Modern Library, 1952, p. 546.
[25] Ralph Waldo Emerson, *Selected Prose and Poetry*. New York and Toronto: Rinehart & Co., Inc., 1950, p. 168.
[26] Sherwood Anderson, *Dark Laughter*. New York: Liveright Publishing Corpora- tion, 1960, p. 230.

covenant of marriage. All these influences contributed to the revaluation of the traditional Victorian attitude toward sex. Now that sex had become an object of enlightened scientific inquiry, there was no good reason why writers should not deal honestly with this experience in their work. As John O'Hara wrote:

There is no responsible author who gratuitously introduces sex. The author who does so is irresponsible and foolish, since it somehow becomes apparent even to the layman that it has been gratuitous and that the author hasn't much else to offer. The author who writes a novel without introducing sex has automatically limited the extent of his responsibility and is thus not entitled to full artistic consideration.[27]

The universality of the sex impulse, however, does not prescribe that he must make it, in the manner of Henry Miller, his central, all-absorbing theme. The writer's imagination, his philosophy of life as well as his creative method, will determine in large measure what he wishes to stress. Each writer will portray the sexual motif in accordance with his individual temperament, his *Weltanschauung,* his religious or irreligious leanings, his aesthetic predilections. In the visionary cosmos that is shaped by the religious imagination of Claudel, the flesh is a grievous burden to bear; for Henry de Montherlant, as for the Russian Rozanov, sex is transformed into a virtual religion. Gide, after throwing off the Christian ethic, affirmed as "good" the "evil" of inverted sex in his being, the natural laws which governed his homosexuality. Once his Puritanism collapsed, he ceased to fight against his taste for perversion and yielded to the pull of instinct. He sought the fulfillment of the senses as an authentic way of coming close to Christ. Indeed, he invoked Christ to "justify this sensual self-abandonment . . . ."[28]

The past forty years or so have witnessed in the United States an increasing literary interest in the psychology of inversion. Whatever the underlying cause or causes may be, the rate of sexual maladjustment in our time is steadily growing. There seems to be a direct connection between the hypertrophied development of industrialism and the spread of sexual frustration – a correlation Sherwood Anderson was among the first to bring out in his fiction. In a technological society that is depersonalized, the individual cannot function spontaneously as a sexual being. The result is that sexual abnormality becomes a dominant theme in much of modern American

[27] Irving Stone, John O'Hara, and MacKinlay Kantor, *Three Views of the Novel.* Washington, D.C.: U.S. Library of Congress, 1957, p. 29.
[28] Lawrence Thomas, *André Gide: The Ethic of the Artist.* London: Secker & Warburg, 1950, p. 85.

literature. Writing in 1951, John W. Aldridge declares in *After the Lost Generation:*

A strong preoccupation with homosexuality as a literary theme runs through all the novels the young writers have produced, and it has become one of their most distinguishing characteristics as well as the most curious.[29]

In the theater, the playwright is no longer under the embarrassing necessity of disguising a homosexual theme in terms of a heterosexual situation.[30] The theme is treated with great sympathy and insight, based on the understanding that sexual perversions spring out of a frustration of the sense of life. On the whole, science, particularly the science of psychoanalysis, gave the American writer a heightened awareness of the complexities and anomalies of sex in all its ramifications: the conflict between love and hate, between Eros and Thanatos, between prescriptive social norms and the outbreak of abnormality.

[29] John W. Aldridge, *After the Lost Generation.* New York and London: McGraw-Hill Book Company, Inc., 1951, p. 100.

[30] In 1961 the then dramatic critic of *The New York Times* declared: "The taboos are not what they used to be. Homosexuality is not a forbidden theme." *The New York Times,* November 5, 1961.

PART TWO

THE NATURALISTIC EROS IN AMERICA

CHAPTER III

THE FORERUNNERS OF REVOLT

1. Howells and the Genteel Tradition

Though the theme of love is universal and appears in world literature from Homer and Cervantes to Henry James and William Faulkner, the closely related theme of sexuality has, in the past history of American culture, been glossed over with genteel circumlocutions or been discreetly omitted. It is these euphemistic evasions or strategic omissions that point to the moral taboos of a given age and to the values society ostensibly abides by. Not that writers are as a profession inclined to be mealy-mouthed Puritans. The shades of Rabelais, Fielding, Robert Burns, Jonathan Swift, Baudelaire, and Flaubert bear eloquent witness to the contrary. The history of literature is replete with accounts of stormy rebels who formulated new standards of conduct based on what they considered to be a truer conception of man. But in the main literature reflects the mores and conventions of its age.

Though literature incorporates the cultural compulsives of the milieu in which it arises, it does not promulgate a set of officially approved sentiments or beliefs; modern culture, in the United States as in Europe, does not subscribe to a homogeneous body of moral values. Moreover, literature as a form of symbolic action is not, whether in the realm of love or sex, presented as a series of sociological or ethical propositions. Literature is always concrete and particular. As a rule it avoids not only the didactic but the abstract. It focuses on the vagaries, the uniqueness, of individual characters; it reveals, it does not state, but its individualized revelations nevertheless radiate a network of intrinsic social meanings.

Just as the novel and the drama project an image of man in relation to his culture, so do they embody significant insights about the experience of love and sex, for this experience is a universal datum of human nature. If we examine a writer's work in terms of the key images he uses, the kind of material he selects for treatment, and the themes that recurrently, sometimes obsessively, engage his attention, we find that he is presenting us with a picture, however implicit, of how men and women relate themselves to the social order, the dialectic in all its modulations of the drama of love, and the struggle that takes place between publicly professed morality, with its support in legal enactments, and the insistent needs of the sexual instinct. The writer deals with conflict-situations in which people are personally involved, their quest for selfhood, love, and sexual fulfillment, their attitude toward Nature, instinct, spirit, God. Each situation he develops in his work is in a sense unique and yet socially representative. Whatever interpretation of love or sex or human nature literature set forth is thus tied up with the ongoing process of social and cultural change. If literature is in large part conditioned by the culture of its time and place, then this helps to explain why nineteenth-century fiction in America carefully observed the existing taboos on the subject of sex. As we have already mentioned, Henry Adams wondered whether any American artist had ever insisted on the power of sex. The only one he could think of in this connection was Walt Whitman. "American art, like the American language and American education, was as far as possible sexless. Society regarded this victory over sex as its greatest triumph...."[1] This judgment may seem unduly harsh but it stands justified. It does apply strikingly to a transition figure like William Dean Howells.

Though as a realist he was willing to include many of the ugly and evil aspects of human nature within the scope of his work, he drew the line sharply at what he considered the unwholesome interest the literary naturalists displayed in the subject of sex. In his essay on "Criticism and Fiction," he affirmed his creed that the practicing novelist finds nothing in life insignificant. Nothing that God created is unworthy of attention. Why then proscribe the frank and full treatment of sexuality in fiction?

Unfortunately Howell's aesthetics of fiction suffered from a number of curious but revealing limitations; he protested austerely against what he felt was an excessive preoccupation with the sexual theme. If Anglo-Saxon fiction, he argued, avoids the distasteful and forbidden matter of physical passion or illicit love, it is because fundamentally it seeks to achieve a greater degree of representativeness in its reading of life. Its truth lies, Howells maintained, precisely in the fact that it concerns itself with chaste love and decent passion in a manner that would not offend the mind of a pure young girl. Howells felt that in the last analysis this controversial issue reduces itself to a question of good taste. Adultery, sexual promiscuity,

---

[1] Henry Adams, *The Education of Henry Adams*. Boston and New York: Houghton Mifflin Company, 1918, p. 385.

rape, abnormality, these are, after all, he declared, the exceptional thing in life. American writers in the twentieth century emphatically did not agree with his conclusions. They strongly believed that it was the duty of the novelist to bring all of life, all of love, the abnormal as well as the normal, within the compass of his vision.

Deeply concerned about the social function and moral effect of the novel, Howells upheld the established canons of decency. According to him, the Anglo-Saxon tradition was in this respect truer to life than the practice honored in French fiction. He did not deny that "vicious" types of love were at work beneath the surface of society. The numerous divorce trials told their own sordid story of marital conflict, sexual incompatibility, and flagrant infidelity, but all this, Howells insisted, was in no way characteristic of American society. A moralist at heart, he contended that the effects derived from the literary exploitation of sex were sensational and cheap. Though the theme of guilty love afforded a sure-fire recipe for success, the serious novelist would not – he really meant should not – thus be willing to soil his artistic conscience. Basically, when the issue came to a showdown, Howells was more interested in preserving the laws of propriety in such matters than in defending the right of the artist to complete freedom of expression. Why should the novelist, in the name of a restrictive morality, be held back from dealing with the theme of "guilty" love? Why should the honest depiction of "the beast-man" – Howells' own epithet – tend to defile and corrupt?

Howells was certainly not ignorant of what actually went on in the America of his day. Why then did he feel that the American people were not faced with more or less the same troublesome sex problems which cropped up frequently in European literature in the work of Flaubert, Tolstoy, Zola, and Hardy? It is this moralistic bias which has done much to obscure his genuine merit as a critic and detract from his importance as a novelist. Though he maintained that it was the duty of a writer to reveal the whole truth about life, in practice his realism, especially in matters relating to love and sex, proved narrowly confining. He would censor the portrayal of passion outside the bounds of wedlock. Firm in his belief that literature was essentially an expression of *moral* truth, he was unable to do full justice to any writer whose work violated the Victorian standard of decency. Too much of the literature of the past, he complained, filled the mind "with filthy images and base thoughts."[2] He looked forward to the time when the beast in man would be tamed and sensual literature would be allowed to

[2] William Dean Howells, *My Literary Passions*. New York and London: Harper & Brothers, 1895, p. 43.

perish. Humane and courageous enough on issues of social justice and economic reform, Howells was arbitrary in his attitude toward the inclusion of sex in literature.

A striking example of his deficiency of psychological insight is the way he handles the vexed problem of divorce in *A Modern Instance*. Though it is written in the realist tradition, Howells is resolved to treat the complex theme of divorce without injecting what he calls the element of shadiness. Published in 1882, the novel concerns itself with the struggle of a wedded but mismatched pair, both of whom are equally to blame for their marital misery. Their marriage is wrecked, but it is the wife, unwavering in her faithfulness even after Bartley's desertion of her, who is accorded a disproportionate share of sympathy, since it is she who is the major sufferer in a masculine-dominated society that conforms to the double standard of morality. Held back by what Edith Wharton assails as his moral timidity, Howells fails to probe the elemental force of sexual passion that played its part in the resolution of the central conflict. Bartley's affair with Hannah Morrison is discreetly glossed over. In the figure of the heroine, Howells draws an absurdly idealized portrait of constancy and devotion in the face of the most outrageous provocation on the part of her errant husband. Unlike Dreiser in *Sister Carrie*, which came eighteen years later, at the turn of the twentieth century, he is decidedly squeamish in his delineation of the vagaries of the sexual impulse.

It is this prudish reticence, this sedulous avoidance of the allegedly debasing theme of sexuality, that brought his work into disfavor with a more enlightened and rebellious generation that espoused the cause of naturalism in fiction. When Victorianism came under attack by the militant exponents of modernism, Howells was singled out as one of the worst offenders and his novels were laughed out of court. One critic, in his defence of Howells, declares: "The worst about Howells and sex was that he was no deviate from the social norm with its taboos on public discussion of the body and its function."[3] Would that he were! It was precisely this glaring sin of omission that the moderns could not forgive: he was guilty of compromising with the repressive sex-ethic of Puritanism. Instead of challenging them forthrightly, he accepted as his own the moral values of his age, an age that drew back with undisguised repugnance from all mention of the sexual instinct. Reference to certain parts of the body and particularly to the sexual act were by common consent to be scrupulously left out. While serving as editor of *The Atlantic Monthly*, Howells carefully respected the moral sen-

[3] Everett Carter, *Howells and the Age of Realism*. Philadelphia and New York, 1954, p. 141.

sibilities of the audience for which the magazine was intended. He advised Mark Twain to eliminate in his work all sexual references which could possibly offend the taste of the public. When compared with novelists like Samuel Butler, Hardy, or Dreiser, he seems needlessly fearful and genteel in all areas that touch on the sexual love of man and woman.

2. The Sexual Morality of the Genteel Tradition

While the Victorians were staunch defenders of intellectual freedom, they were, in matters pertaining to morality, stubbornly conservative. They safeguarded freedom of ideas in religion and politics, but their attitude toward sex remained uncompromisingly strict. Any novel marked by what was then judged as coarseness of tone was instantly condemned; the hostility went so far as to enforce "a spinsterish verbal prudery." [4] Anthony Trollope, in his autobiography, extolled the universal virtues, the established excellencies of the heart and mind, composing novels frankly designed to teach the lesson of virtue rewarded. On the whole, the Victorian writers deliberately excised from their work any explicit reference to the sexual life of man, though even at that the novel was repeatedly brought under attack as a prolific source of evil suggestiveness. The sexual question was outlawed by moralistic fiat. Bowdlerism gained headway. The Society for the Suppression of Vice labored zealously to weed out "pornography" from the garden of literature.

George Moore was the *bête noire* of Victorian England. But despite his addiction to realism and his professed allegiance to Zola, his treatment of sex was pallid compared with the daring sophistication of postwar fiction in the nineteen twenties. To quote one critic of his work:

I doubt that he would have used the cold-blooded word "sex" even if he had known its future implications, but he was prophetic of the "separateness" and "otherness" which D. H. Lawrence so acclaims; he evoked the charm of flowers, silks, scents, and sin. He was modern in his "delighted acceptance of actuality." He was modern in his revolt against convention, restraint, and taboo.[5]

The Victorian code enjoined upon the author the taboo that the male characters and especially the female characters shall stop their love-making at a certain point. If the moral law is transgressed, the transgressor must be fittingly punished.

Nor, as we have already seen in the case of Howells, were conditions at

---

[4] Norman St. John-Stevas, *Obscenity and the Law.* London: Secker & Warburg, 1956, p. 30.
[5] William G. Frierson, "George Moore Compromised with the Victorians," *The Trollopian,* March 1941, Number Four, p. 38.

this time any better in the United States, where genteel writers shared common ground in their glorification of romantic love. This resulted, of course, in a sentimental falsification of the truth of human nature, for love could not be completely divorced from sex nor were women the angels of purity they were represented to be. The idealization of woman as the quintessence of spirit, without any taint of fleshly appetite, produced a tradition that was enormously flattering to the female of the species but definitely harmful to literature.[6] Gentility was in full control. Good inevitably triumphed over evil, and the pure woman was presented as the model of goodness, her mission in life being to inspire the man to noble deeds and to domesticate his physical passions.

Henry James, in *The Bostonians* (1886), had dealt discerningly with the problem of feminism and, by indirection, with the then dangerous issue of sex and homosexuality, but America was not yet ready for his message. Howells was much more to the liking of the reading public, for he cherished and perpetuated the traditional version of pure womanhood. Even a realist like Hamlin Garland declared, in *Crumbling Idols,* his opposition to the unmitigated sexual frankness of the literary naturalists. Like Howells, he deplored this Zolaesque preoccupation with the physical aspects of love.

The reaction was bound to come; writers of integrity could not suffer in silence while Mrs. Grundy dictated the moral laws which literature and art had to obey. Naturalism was on the march. If the scientific interpretation of the universe and the nature of man was valid, then the doctrine of original sin would have to be abandoned. If man is governed by instinct, then the novelist must be prepared to reject or drastically revise the established body of moral values. In full revolt against the cult of sentimentality and romantic idealism, the members of the naturalistic school were resolved to portray man as he is, with all his instincts and aberrant impulses, the product of the twin forces of heredity and environment, without dragging in the irrelevant question of moral judgment.

3. Naturalism on the March

The literary rebels of the twentieth century ceased to look upon man as a responsible agent, ruled by reason, endowed with free will, superior to the animal kingdom. Freudianism exposed the cunning rationalizations to which civilized man resorts in order to justify his irrational and often per-

---

[6] "Womanliness came to mean sexlessness and in the 1840's and later, fiction relied on this conviction wherever it presented an ideal woman." William Wasserstrom, *Heiress of All the Ages.* Minneapolis: The University of Minnesota Press, 1959, p. 24.

verse behavior. The naturalist writers focused their interest on the instinctual life of man. Dreiser, Sherwood Anderson, Eugene O'Neill, Hemingway, and Faulkner depicted human nature without attempting to gloss over the biological facts – and the facts showed plainly that man was at bottom a promiscuous animal, the victim of his sexual compulsions. Hailing sex as the deliverer rather than enslaver, a number of American writers went to great lengths to identify love with sex.

If one humanistic critic called *Manhattan Transfer* an explosion in a cesspool,[7] John Dos Passos could always retort that he was simply painting the truth of life. If life was sordid, cruel, violent, and "immoral," it was not the writer's fault. As an artist whose province was as wide as life itself, he saw no reason why he had to justify his frankness in describing the love life of the human pair. Nothing that was human, however repellent to the moral prejudices of the public, was to be kept out of literature. In one of his essays Arthur Koestler declared that it would take fifty years for fiction to catch up with the discoveries of Freud. He cites a curious example to support his argument. No one, he remarks as if pointing out a serious sin of omission, had ever written a novel about the state of mind of a woman during the nine-month period of gestation. But if everything without exception provides potential material for the writer, it is not, after all, the theme *per se,* be it love or sex or religion or Communism, that counts but what the writer does with it. As dozens of contemporary novels exploiting the sensational pathological features of sex demonstrate, there is no necessary correlation between the choice of an original or forbidden theme and artistic success.

In any event, this excessive interest in sex first came to a head during the twenties when the intellectuals were spiritedly engaged in battling the blight of Puritanism and seeking to end the long reign of Victorian prudery. If the truth, so long crushed to earth, was to rise again, the vicious conspiracy of silence concerning the sexual life of man would have to be abolished. The twentieth-century transvaluation of values in the field of love and sex must be viewed as part of a larger movement that rebelled against the religious absolute and the restrictive humanistic morality of the past. No modern writer could hope to escape the influence of Freud, though it could not always be predicted to what use he would put the science of psychoanalysis. The Surrealists, for all their professed dependence on psychic automatism and the potentialities of the unconscious, preferred to specialize in the erotic

---

[7] *"Manhattan Transfer,* with its unrelated scenes selected to portray the more sordid aspects of New York, and with its spattered filth, might be described in a phrase as an explosion in a cesspool." Paul Elmer More. *The Demon of the Absolute.* Princeton: Princeton University Press, 1928, p. 63.

beauty of the perverse. Reviving the lapsed cult of the satanic,[8] they drew inspiration from the decadent romanticism of the nineteenth century, when sex was "so obviously the mainspring of works of imagination . . . ."[9]

The First World War brought home to the younger generation the bankruptcy of the moral idealism their elders preached. Invoking the sacred name of freedom, they considered it decidedly "modern" to be iconoclastic and nonconformist in matters of sex. Repression – that was the crime of crimes. They eagerly consumed scientific studies of sex, particularly those written by Freud and his disciples. Everyone began to talk and many to write in Freudian terms. Conrad Aiken, for example, after he learned that he was not to be drafted into the War, took up the attempt "to make a modern adaptation, in terms of modern psychology and psychoanalysis (for he was then deep in Freud, Adler, Pfister, Ferenczi, and Rank) of *Punch and Judy* . . . ."[10]

The decade following the First World War was marked by the progressive breakdown of moral barriers. Sexual adjustment – that was the prescribed cure of all mental ills. If one surrendered spontaneously to the power of sex, then happiness would be his as a matter of course. Floyd Dell, the fugleman of the sexual revolution in Greenwich Village during the second and third decade of this century, confesses in his autobiography: "I don't think any of us quite knew what we believed about love and 'freedom.' We were in love with life, and willing to believe almost any modern theory which gave us a chance to live our lives more fully."[11] It took time before the rebels learned to their cost that sex is not to be equated with love. The exciting experiment in sexual freedom during the twenties culminated, in the case of Floyd Dell and a number of other writers, in the reaffirmation of middle-class virtues and in the rediscovery of happiness to be found in a permanent union based on love. The theory of "free love" simply did not work.

Up to this point we have discussed various trends in science, society, psychoanalysis, and religion which accounted for the emergence of new attitudes in the literary treatment of love and sex. Now we shall take up in detail a number of American writers, beginning with Dreiser, and attempt to show how they portray the meaning of love in human affairs.

---

[8] The writer who exerted the most pronounced influence on romantic satanism was the Marquis de Sade, that genius of the psycho-pathological, whom the Surrealists delightedly canonized as their patron saint.

[9] Mario Praz, *The Romantic Agony*. Translated by Angus Davidson. New York: Meridian Books, 1956, p. vii.

[10] Conrad Aiken, *Ushant*. New York and Boston: Duell, Sloan and Pearce, 1952, p. 213.

[11] Floyd Dell, *Homecoming*. New York: Farrar & Rinehart, Inc., 1933, p. 242.

CHAPTER IV

DREISER AND SEXUAL FREEDOM

When the novelist appeals to Nature as the norm, he is in effect trying to lift a heavy burden of guilt ("original sin") from the shoulders of the descendants of Adam. Shaped by heredity, instinct, and the pressure of the social environment, man, as Theodore Dreiser portrays him, is no longer responsible for his actions and therefore the question of innocence or guilt, good or evil, does not arise. Moreover, the naturalistic writer of fiction aims ambitiously to report the whole truth of life, from the lowest reaches to the highest. He seeks to picture conditions as they actually exist and refrains as far as possible from passing moral judgment on human behavior. Though his object is not to shock, unless the truth itself proves shocking, his outspokenness on matters hitherto considered taboo often produces precisely that effect on the reading public. In his efforts to delineate people as they are, not as they ought to be, he directs attention to those biological passions which in many temperaments are the determinants of fate. He is aware that society has the power to punish those who gratify their sexual instinct in ways that are not legally permitted or morally approved – that is, if they are caught. Nevertheless, the negative injunction, "Thou shalt not," is repeatedly violated, regardless of consequences. As Somerset Maugham declares in *The Summing Up,* most men follow the call of desire while keeping a prudent eye open for the policeman around the corner.[1] The conflict between instinct and culture cannot be avoided. Society, concerned solely about the perpetuation of the species, the protection of the family, the safeguarding of the rights of children born into the world, labors, with all the institutional power of enforcement at its disposal, to deflect the mighty energies of the sex instinct into morally sanctioned channels.

[1] Somerset Maugham, like Dreiser, adheres to a physiological conception of love. "However much people may resent the fact and however angrily deny it, there can surely be no doubt that love depends on certain secretions of the sexual glands.... People are very hypocritical in this matter and will not face the truth." W. Somerset Maugham, *The Summing Up.* New York: Penguin Books, Inc., 1946, p. 216.

Despite his iconoclastic contempt for traditional morality, the naturalistic novelist, in his earnest dedication to the truth of life, is giving expression to a moral impulse. It has not been sufficiently recognized to what an extent literary naturalism, in its early development in France, England, and the United States, was animated by a moral motive in its espousal of the cause of "truth." And the truth of human nature was revealed by the findings of biology. Why should society impose an artificial code of moral values and then arbitrarily demand that everyone without exception, regardless of temperament or circumstance, conform to it? The more stringent the ban clamped on the gratification of physical desire, the more impelling – nay, well-nigh irresistible – is the urge to defy it. The novelists of course won their battle in the course of time, the right to deal openly with all aspects of life, including the sexual and even the abnormal. Approximately seventy odd years after the publication of Havelock Ellis' first volume of *Studies in the Psychology of Sex* and the first printing of Freud's *The Interpretation of Dreams* in 1900, a climate of opinion was generated in the United States which made it possible to issue not only such scientific investigations as Kinsey's *Sexual Behavior in the Human Male* and *Sexual Behavior in the Human Female* but also such controversial novels as *The Well of Loneliness, Jurgen, Winesburg, Ohio, Ulysses, Lady Chatterley's Lover, The "Genius", The Memoirs of Hecate County, Tropic of Cancer,* and *Lolita*.

Sister Carrie (1900) led the way. It was a pioneering work in its courageous confrontation of the problem of sexual morality. From the time of its appearance in print, Dreiser, indifferent to abuse and attacks in court, championed the cause of sexual freedom.[2] In 1917, in an essay, "Life, Art and America" (published first in *The Seven Arts* magazine and later included in *Hey Rub-a-Dub-Dub*), he voiced his angry disillusionment with the debased spiritual and creative quality of life in the United States. In particular, what called forth his strongest condemnation was the reactionary way in which the serious treatment in fiction of the theme of sex was persecuted. Victim of a refined eroticism, the American, Dreiser charged, was basically a repressed and hypocritical creature.[3] Because of the deep-seated,

[2] Frank Norris, too, in his novel of naturalistic violence, *McTeague,* was a pioneer in revealing the irrational, compulsive power of sex in life.

[3] As W. A. Swanberg discloses in his massively documented study, *Dreiser* (New York: Charles Scribner's Sons, 1965), Dreiser, whatever inconsistencies appeared in the course of his life, was strikingly consistent in his philosophy of sex. He never abandoned his belief that life was purposeless and meaningless. If he later embraced Socialism as his political faith, it was out of compassion for all the underprivileged, the wretched of the earth. His personal morality, his incessant pursuit of sex, his numerous affairs with women, were all motivated by his conviction that in a universe

life-negating inhibitions that they allowed to govern them, the American people had grown neurotic, as was evidenced by their morbid interest in sex crimes, their patronage of burlesque shows, and their consumption of disguised pornography in fiction. Whereas sexual immorality is fiercely denounced in the press and from the pulpit, it flourishes under cover in all the most puritanical American cities – a point Dreiser later stressed in *An American Tragedy*. For the sex instinct cannot be proscribed by law or moral fiat; if it is blocked in one channel, it will find a way out in another.

But why, Dreiser asks, suppress impulses that are perfectly normal? Why should men and women be kept in infantile ignorance on this subject? Why should this country continue to spread the lying gospel that sexuality is somehow degrading? It is Pauline Christianity, ascetic and life-negating, that Dreiser holds responsible for this conspiracy of silence relating to matters of sex and for spreading the noxious notion that sex is evil. For sex, he argues, means vastly more than is included within the scope of the Christian ethic. The primal source of beauty, the mother of the arts, it provides the vital incentive that makes for progress and achievement. " 'Love' or 'lust' (and the one is but an intellectual sublimation of the other) moves the seeker in every field of effort." [4] Why then must Americans shut off this elemental and inspiring source ef energy and accept neuroticism as the norm? Dreiser characteristically defines sex as "an unregenerate and only partially controlled passion," "a fire, a chemical explosion." [5] Dreiser does not deny that the interest of society calls for the regulation of the sexual instinct, but what he advocates is the establishment of some sort of wholesome balance. "We see," he says, "that in spite of our fixed methods of moral procedure the tragedies continue, the waves and flames of morality and immorality come and go." [6] The high divorce rates, the incidence of crime, the reports of sexual abnormalities – these speak for themselves. The ideal of monogamy is flouted with impunity.

On the basis of his observation of life Dreiser reached the conclusion "that man is not temperamentally or chemically a monogamous animal." [7] The laws of society attempt to make the individual believe that he is and should be strictly monogamous, but Dreiser, the uncompromising realist, discovered that on the whole there was little correlation between a man's

ruled absurdly by King Death, it was better to follow the path of hedonism, and pleasure for him consisted in the possession of young beautiful women.

4 Theodore Dreiser, *Hey Rub-a-Dub-Dub*. New York: Boni and Liveright, 1920, p. 134.
5 *Ibid.*, p. 136.
6 *Ibid.*, p. 136.
7 *Ibid.*, p. 139.

professed moral creed and his sexual behavior. That is why prostitution goes on unchecked, with or without the consent of the government, and why the marriage vows are so frequently broken. Convention, Dreiser remarks, "has not made, and cannot make, any headway against a chemical scheme of life which puts sex desires first and all else as secondary or socially contributory."[8] Though marriage is biologically necessary if the race is to be perpetuated, the social and moral requirement that the couple remain faithful to each other throughout their lifetime causes many cruel hardships and often results in the breakdown of the marriage. The strong, successful man refuses to confine himself to one woman – and this is true of Dreiser's male characters. It is only the weak, the fearful, the economically dependent, who are cowed into conformity. Those who subscribe to the current moral theories of love, sex, and marriage must "perforce accept their chains and slavery, if so they find marriage to be, and make a virtue of their suffering."[9] Many men are clearly unable to adjust to the monogamic ideal. The solution Dreiser proposes for those trapped in an unhappy union is to liberalize the divorce laws; ideals alone will not make a marriage happy or lasting. Nature, in short, is the supreme arbiter of human destiny. "Man does not make or regulate Nature: Nature makes and regulates man . . . ."[10]

One aspect of American life that Dreiser found intolerable was its unfortunate tendency, born of the native tradition of Puritanism, to conceive of woman as an angelic being, not infected with the taint of sexual desire.[11] "Women are now so good," Dreiser declares sardonically, "the sex relationship so vile a thing that to think of the two at once is not to be thought of."[12] Profoundly impressed by the teaching of science, Dreiser became convinced that man is driven ineluctably by two instincts: that of self-preservation and that of the perpetuation of the species. In the early stages of his development as a novelist, he saw life as instinct with cruelty, essentially meaningless, though relieved at times by the illusion of pleasure. But this nihilistic outlook, while it led him to suffer from recurrent moods of metaphysical despair, the syndrome of *Weltschmerz,* did not arrest or curtail his productivity. Beholding the spectacle of eternal energy in action, he found the biological process and the pageantry of life fundamentally fascinating, and his creative passion drove him on to explore reality in all its infinite variety. Man, as he viewed him in the light of his biologically-oriented *Weltanschau-*

[8] *Ibid.,* p. 139.
[9] *Ibid.,* p. 215.
[10] *Ibid.,* p. 218.
[11] See Leo Markun, *Mrs. Grundy.* New York and London: D. Appleton and Company, 1930.
[12] Theodore Dreiser, *Hey Rub-a-Dub-Dub,* p. 266.

ung, was but a cog in the cosmic machine; he was neither endowed with freedom of will nor destined to enjoy an immortal existence in some other world.

While he persisted in his belief that life was essentially meaningless, he was opposed to the suffering principally caused by man, though he found it hard to reconcile this overriding feeling of compassion with his acceptance of Darwinism and the implications to be drawn from it. Not being a formal philosopher but an artist, Dreiser was not too greatly disturbed by these knotted contradictions in the fabric of his thought. At first he argued that social reform would not make any real difference in the final outcome, since the position of man in the universe was hopeless. Later on, however, by the time he came to write *An American Tragedy,* his humane sympathies overrode his deterministic pessimism and focused his work squarely on the social evils of his age. Though he did not abandon the naturalistic method, he essayed to play the role of reformer. These very contradictions in the body of his fiction highlight the complexity of his vision of life, but his attitude toward the moral problem of the place of sex in life underwent no substantial change throughout his career.

His education and all his experiences and observations confirmed his growing conviction that there was no connection between virtue and success. His study of Tyndall, Spencer, and Thomas Henry Huxley deepened his vein of moral skepticism. If all of life was but a series of physico-chemical reactions, then the role of ethics was practically non-existent. *Sister Carrie* voiced his iconoclastic revaluation of the traditional conception of good and evil, his view that life was an impenetrable mystery, and his embattled opposition to those puritanic forces in American society which curbed and frustrated the instinctual needs of man. Like Nietzsche who at one stage in his career influenced him strongly, he contended that the ethical system dominant in America was in conflict with the realities of human nature.[13]

While *Sister Carrie* demonstrates the purposelessness of existence, it also brings out strongly the irony of applying moral standards to the fate that befalls Dreiser's two protagonists, Carrie and Hurstwood. In keeping

---

[13] Nietzsche fought resolutely against the depreciation of the animal heritage in man. Divorcing morality from theology, he showed in *The Genealogy of Morals* that man invented for himself the arbitrary criteria of what constitutes good and evil. The attempt to outlaw sexuality infects the world with a sickly conscience. "The final outcome of this diabolization of Eros is a farce: the 'devil' Eros has gradually become of greater interest to mankind than all the angels and saints, thanks to the mumbo-jumbo and mystification of the Church in all things erotic . . . ." Friedrich Nietzsche, *The Dawn of Day,* quoted in F. A. Lea, *The Tragic Philosopher.* London: Methuen & Co., 1957, p. 144.

with his naturalistic credo, Dreiser carefully refrains from condemning the actions of Carrie Meeber; she may have "fallen," but she is not for that reason to be held unworthy. That is the way things work out. The ways of life are not shaped by predetermined patterns of virtue or poetic justice.[14] Nature is the court of last appeal, but Nature, as Dreiser interprets it, is utterly indifferent to the moral standard society currently imposes. Again and again, Dreiser shows how instinct desregards the negative commands of conscience. Thus a radically new sexual morality emerges in American fiction. Fidelity to the imperatives of Nature is the measure of "good"; whatever is natural is right. It is the hallmark of neuroticism to be obsessed with a sense of sin when one transgresses the moral law clamped as an institutional deterrent on the urgencies of sexual behavior.

Carrie is moved by honorable intentions, but she is not, economically, the mistress of her fate. In the beginning at least, she hopes for nothing better than the married state, even with a flashy salesman like Drouet, the man who had seduced her – if seduction it can be called when the woman willingly gives her consent. But she possesses a temperament, a vital spirit, that is not to be broken on the wheel of life; she keeps striving, through all the vicissitudes that beset her, to fulfill ever higher potentialities of being. Each of her "affairs," which in a conventional novel of that period would have led surely and inevitably to her ruin, serves to facilitate her mental, emotional, and spiritual growth. When she discovers that Hurstwood, who has fallen madly in love with her, is already married, she decides to drop him. He promises to obtain a divorce and marry her as soon as he is free. Thus she drifts into another love relationship that proves of decisive importance in shaping her future. When Hurstwood loses his grip on life and begins to slide downhill, she takes over and becomes the dominant one. Her abounding vitality, her youth and resourcefulness, her eagerness to face up to and experience all that life has to offer, enable her to come out on top. At the end of the novel she is on her way to "success" in the theater, and it was this ending which genteel America could not stomach.

What was shocking to America at the dawn of the twentieth century was Dreiser's deliberate effort to challenge the ruling code of sexual morality. Drouet, for his part, is no slimy sensualist, no designing villain. The diabol-

---

[14] As Charles Child Walcutt says: "Nowhere is there a moral painted. There is no inevitable punishment for transgression, no suggestion that there ought to be." Charles Child Walcutt, "The Three Stages of Dreiser's Naturalism" *Publications of the Modern Language Association.* March 1950, LV, p. 270. According to Maxwell Geismar, the story of *Sister Carrie* "dealt with an immoral woman who was never basically immoral; a heroine who created a storm of sexual controversy but was not directly sexual . . . ." Maxwell Geismar, *Rebels and Ancestors.* Boston: Houghton Mifflin Company, 1953, p. 295.

ically wicked seducer has passed, never to return, out of American fiction. Even when Carrie becomes Hurstwood's mistress, she suffers from no anguished pangs of remorse. Nor is she greatly concerned about the conventions of society according to which "All men should be good, all women virtuous." [15] As Dreiser explicitly points out, the subject of morality is more complicated than many people suspect. Carrie wrestles bravely with the problem of right and wrong, but then she possesses only an average conscience that reflected in a confused way the conditioning of her past and the conventions of her world. She knew, of course, that "the good people" would brand her behavior as flagrantly immoral, but such thoughts troubled her only when she was alone. Besides, Carrie is not a reasoning creature, capable of acting strictly according to the dictates of prudential logic. Passion in her case is stronger than reason, and this holds true of many other Dreiser heroes and heroines. "The majesty of passion," Dreiser says, "is possessed by nearly every man once in his life, but it is usually an attribute of youth and conduces to the first successful mating." [16] It is not the desire to commit evil which directs the steps of the erring, but at bottom the longing for that which is better, the dream of the heart for some finer consummation. "Not evil, but goodness more often allures the feeling mind unused to reason." [17] Dreiser is here upsetting the moral apple cart. The affective mind of the transgressor, a Sister Carrie, may be impelled by a craving for a more satisfying type of goodness. Despite his aesthetic doctrine of uncompromising objectivity, Dreiser is frankly affirming the truth of his underlying thesis that the force of sexual passion cannot be made to obey the repressive laws of social morality.

In *Jennie Gerhardt* (1911), too, we are introduced to a woman who is the victim of circumstance. Dreiser fearlessly examines the moral standards according to which American society is supposed to function and then proceeds to show how artificial and unreal they are. The irony of the story inheres in the fact that Jennie, "a kept woman," is basically a sensitive and blameless character; the persecution to which she is subjected because of her "immorality" serves to point up the cruel irrelevancy of the Christian code of sexual ethics. The novel is intended to drive home the theme that in a world of unpredictable circumstances and chance collisions there is no correspondence between good intentions and the consequences they bring about. In *Jennie Gerhardt* as in *Sister Carrie,* evil – what society judges as evil – is not punished. Why hold people accountable for their actions when

[15] Theodore Dreiser, *Sister Carrie.* New York: The Modern Library, 1917, p. 101.
[16] *Ibid.,* p. 242.
[17] *Ibid.,* p. 556.

in many instances they are pushed into situations beyond their control? Dreiser is seeking to show that the governing morality of American society is not in accord with the fundamental needs of human nature. Like Sister Carrie, Jennie Gerhardt is no sinner. Dreiser portrays her as a good woman at heart, betrayed by the unfortunate circumstances of her poverty. [18]

The *"Genius,"* another vigorous attack on the conventional morality which rules America, was published in 1915. It was suppressed by the New York Society for the Prevention of Vice – an action that brought to a head the struggle against literary censorship in this country. Dreiser by this time was in no mood for shilly-shallying. He had crystallized his thinking on the subject of love – and by "love" he meant "the sex impulse which makes for mate-seeking and union." [19] Glorifying the cult of Eros, The *"Genius"* pictured women as the symbols of power as well as passion. Dreiser tries to deal honestly with the chemistry of sexual desire. He depicts truthfully the rebelliousness of the artistic temperament when caught in the trap of mar-

[18] Considerations of space prohibit an analysis in this context of *Susan Lenox*, by David Graham Phillips, which in some respects is close in outlook to *Sister Carrie*. Women fall into prostitution, Phillips is saying in this novel, through no fault of their own. Talk of morality in this connection is sheer cant. Goodness is not rewarded on earth. Alone, poor, defenceless, the heroine learns to her cost that it does not pay to be honest. Thrust into a man's world, woman must either sell herself into an advantageous marriage or be exploited by employers who pay starvation wages. In "Before the Curtain," dated 1908, Phillips, like Dreiser, points out that the free discussion of the relation of the sexes is not permitted in American fiction. The result of such avoidance is that our native literature becomes discreet, pallid, and dishonest, for no author can "afford to be silent on the subject that underlies all subjects." (David Graham Phillips, *Susan Lenox*. New York and London: D. Appleton and Company, 1931, p. ix.) Phillips declares there are three available means of dealing with human sex relations in literature. The moralistic Anglo-Saxon way of fearful avoidance of the theme is as bad as the continental way of deliberately adding generous doses of spice to sex. The right way is to be candid. Phillips tells us what he means by the standard of "naturalness" that he invokes: "Treat the sex question as you would any other question. Don't treat it reverently; don't treat it rakishly. Treat it naturally. Don't insult your intelligence and lower your moral tone by thinking about either the decency or the indecency of matters that are familiar, undeniable, and unchangeable facts of life. Don't look on woman as mere female, but as human being. Remember that she has a mind and heart as well as a body. In a sentence, don't join in the prurient clamor of "purity" hypocrites and "strong" libertines that exaggerates and distorts the most commonplace, if the most important feature of life. Let us try to be as sensible about sex as we are trying to be about all the other phenomena of the universe in this more enlightened day." (*Ibid.*, pp. x–xii.) What is distinctive about Phillips' approach is that his morality, like that of Dreiser, is grounded in a naturalistic context. Good and evil are relative, not absolute. Like Dreiser, Phillips insists that society with its false conventions and restrictive moral code is guilty of keeping women ignorant and forcing them to play a subservient role in life. It imposes upon them a factitious ideal of "purity" that frustrates their natural needs while the men are at liberty to take full advantage of the double standard.

[19] Theodore Dreiser, *Hey Rub-a-Dub-Dub*, p. 224.

riage but he also traces the steps by which excess of passion leads not only to disenchantment but to the death of passion itself. The gifted protagonist, Eugene Witla, is drawn irresistibly into numerous amours which almost destroy him and prevent the fulfillment of his dream of art.

Whether or not The "Genius" is in large part an autobiographical confession of Dreiser's own ill-fated venture into matrimony, it does express with great imaginative force and a wealth of vividly delineated scenes, the resistance the artist as hero feels when he is tied down by the marriage bond. Eugene, like Sister Carrie, is eager to experience all the joys, especially the joys of love, that life has to offer. As a youth in Chicago just starting out on his career as a painter, he loves women with an indiscriminate sexual appetite. After his first conquest of a woman, he does not feel any sense of shame; the experience heightens his self-esteem and makes him more sure of himself. Then he meets Angela Blue, a school teacher, a thoroughly virtuous girl, who "considered marriage and children the fate and duty of all women." [20] She looks forward to becoming the mistress of an ideal middle-class home. Though temperamentally Eugene and Angela are differently constituted, they are drawn together by the magnetism or (as Dreiser prefers to call it) the chemism of sexual desire. He cares naught for the traditional distinctions between good and evil whereas she clings tenaciously to the conventional notions of right and wrong.

Eugene finally proposes to Angela, who "made him feel the sacredness of love and marriage," [21] and that marks the beginning of his difficulties. For the artist-type, according to Dreiser, is so subtly compounded of various complex emotions that one woman cannot possibly satisfy all sides of his nature. Eugene is primarily interested in furthering his artistic career while Angela cherishes the romantic belief in ideal love and in a marriage that is made to last forever. Eugene, a modern embodiment of Don Juan, is enamored of beauty, in love with love. In brief, "there was no permanent faith in him for anybody – except the impossible she." [22]

Life, he comes to perceive, is somehow bigger and more mysterious than any single theory of moral conduct. Society dictates one pattern of behavior while Nature is instinct with forces that brook no restraint. Though he makes passionate love to Angela, he gives no serious thought to the responsibilities of marriage. He has no craving for parenthood. Angela struggles hard to restrain herself, not to yield to his sensual love-making. If she per-

[20] Theodore Dreiser, The "Genius." Cleveland and New York: The World Publishing Company, 1954, p. 46.
[21] Ibid., p. 81.
[22] Ibid., p. 105.

mitted him liberties reserved for the marriage bed, would she not fall in his estimation? Eugene tries to reassure her. Why should he think any worse of her if she gave herself to him? Her reply is that "good" girls do not engage in such practices. But this, as Eugene is quick to point out, is merely a convention. Moral codes are relative. But Angela is not convinced. She continues to dream of marriage as the one event, divinely sanctioned, which will complete her life.

In New York where he meets other women, Eugene is haunted by the thought of the transiency of youth, the brevity of life. With Christine, who is determined not to spoil her musical career by marriage, he frankly discusses the nature of passion. Both of them reject the notion that "there was any inherent evil in the most intimate relationship." [23] She allows him to possess her with the express understanding that their relationship will not last. Eugene, troubled by the problem of sex, wonders "over and over again what the answer was, and why he could not like other men be faithful to one woman and be happy." [24] In the meantime, remembering the promise he had made, he feels guilty about Angela, his betrothed. Though he visits her parental home, it is passion alone that brings him to her – "in fact he could not see that there was anything much in love outside of passion." [25]

Eugene, who articulates Dreiser's views on the sexual problem, realizes the contradictions present in his own moral code. The world, he knew full well, was built on the foundation of the home, the steadfast affection and loving care of fathers and mothers. Dreiser attempts to resolve the contradiction by arguing that the artist belongs to a special category. Furthermore, why should Eugene be ashamed of passions he had not created? Nature all around him, vigorously blossoming, belied the reality of moral scruples. Unable to resist the call of desire in the night, Angela yields to him "saying she would not yield." [26] When Eugene leaves Angela's home, he is aware that now he must keep his promise of marriage. Otherwise Angela, as she threatened, would destroy herself.

Though Eugene marries Angela, he suspects that he has made a grievous mistake in doing so. It is pity that led him to save her from the fate of spinsterhood. He cannot honestly feel that she represents all of existence for him or that this marriage is meant to last for all his life. "Marriage was a trick of Nature's by which you were compelled to carry out her scheme of race continuance. Love was a lure; desire a scheme of propagation devised by the

[23] *Ibid.,* p. 160.
[24] *Ibid.,* p. 161.
[25] *Ibid.,* p. 173.
[26] *Ibid.,* p. 183.

way."[27] Eugene grows to dislike Angela because she persecutes him with her possessive jealousy. She tries to bind him to her by having a child; he is aghast when he realizes the nature of the biological trap she had sprung for him.

In this novel Dreiser is bent on promulgating his belief that this world is basically an immoral one. What right, then, had a few self-righteous men to interfere on the ground of morality with the work of a writer when Nature offered no justification for their action? Why should ignorant moralists like John S. Sumner, then executive secretary of the New York Society for the Suppression of Vice, be permitted to control the minds of free thinking men by presuming to censor The "Genius"? Dreiser angrily denounced this interference with serious literature as "the worst and most corrupting form of oppression conceivable to the human mind, plumbing as it does the depths of ignorance and intolerance, and checking initiative and inspiration at its source."[28] This brouhaha, the needless controversy over the question of censorship, embittered Dreiser, and only strengthened his conviction that the elemental passion of sex had to be brought into the picture if the novelist wished to depict life truly.

Though Dreiser modified his philosophy of life in several important respects as he grew older, his views on love and sex remained substantially unchanged. In An American Tragedy (1925) he seeks to awaken the reader's sympathy for those who, because of the relentless pressure of their society and the imperiousness of their sex urge, are driven into crime. Yet the novel is thoroughly deterministic in outlook. Dreiser sets out to demonstrate that Clyde, his hero, is a victim of the socioeconomic forces in his environment. The early chapters portray with unflinching but nonetheless compassionate insight the extreme poverty which drives Clyde away from the home of his pious but shiftless parents and plunges him into the maelstrom of life. Clyde is principally concerned with improving his lot in life, but this dynamic ambition is closely linked to his hunger for experience and his ardent craving for love.

Dreiser describes Clyde's initiation into the mysteries of sex when he is first induced to visit a house of prostitution. Despite the rigorous religious training he had received at home, he is irresistibly attracted instead of being repelled by these women whose bodies can be bought for a price. Here at last is his opportunity for him to satisfy "his desire for the more accurate knowledge of the one great fascinating mystery that had for so long con-

[27] Ibid., p. 198.
[28] Robert H. Elias, Theodore Dreiser. New York: Alfred A. Knopf, Inc., 1949, pp. 198–199.

fronted and fascinated and baffled and yet frightened him a little." [29] He is dazzled by this sinful display of fleshly sumptuousness, even though these women for hire possessed dull brains. Thus, despite inward tremors of trepidation and fear of the consequences of his act, he yields to the call of instinct. The ritual of his initiation into the mysteries of sex has begun.

The object of this scene in the house of prostitution is to show that Clyde is not only confused but weak in character. He desires the experience of sex but his religious training holds him back for a while and his aesthetic sensibility makes it seem less than satisfying. He looks upon it as degrading and sinful, but once he has tasted of the forbidden fruit his attitude changes. He is prepared to help his mother who needs money for her pregnant daughter Esta (she has been seduced and then abandoned), but when he must make a choice between duty to his family and pleasure, he decides that his pleasure must come first. This incident leads him to think more deeply about the problem of sex. Though he condemns Esta's lover for deserting her thus ruthlessly, he is wise enough in the ways of the world to perceive that she is not entirely blameless. Had she not gone off with him? He would be the last one to damn the sexual relation as evil in itself. It was not the sexual act which was wrong but the consequences which followed.

A romantic dreamer, a sentimentalist at heart carried away by the promise of sexual pleasure, he refuses to face the truth about himself and his relation to society. When he is given a job in his uncle's shirt factory and is placed in charge of a department where only young girls are at work, he is emotionally disturbed by their presence. "His was a disposition easily and often intensely inflamed by the chemistry of sex and the formula of beauty. He could not easily withstand the appeal, let alone the call, of sex." [30] Then one of the factory girls, Roberta Alden, sensuous, imaginative, warm-blooded, comes into his life, and he dreams of happiness with her but only if he does not have to marry her. For now he aspires to enter the glamorous social world to which his uncle belonged.

The potent chemistry of sex involves Clyde in a relationship with Roberta that proves his undoing. Dreiser underlines the fact that both Roberta and Clyde were ignorant of sex and in their ignorance never attempted anything more "than the simplest, and for the most part unsatisfactory, contraceptive devices." [31] When Roberta discovers she is pregnant, she is terrified, rightly fearful of the disgrace, the censure and condemnation of society.

[29] Theodore Dreiser, *An American Tragedy*. New York: The Modern Library, 1953, p. 72.
[30] *Ibid.*, p. 263.
[31] *Ibid.*, p. 401.

The stigma of unsanctioned concupiscence! The shame of illegitimacy for a child! It was bad enough, as she had always thought, listening to girls and women talk of life and marriage and adultery and the miseries that had befallen girls who had yielded to men and subsequently been deserted, for a woman when she was safely married and sustained by the love and strength of a man....[32]

Clyde cannot possibly abandon Roberta in her plight but because of Sondra, the society girl he loves, he cannot agree to marry her. He journeys to Schenectady to seek out a druggist who will consent, he hopes, to provide him with some effective abortifacient. He is aware that what he is doing is outside the pale of the law. He recalls that Roberta had reminded him of his promise that he would see her through if any such complication arose, but he had not actually meant what he said in the heat of passion. He had never wanted to marry her. In the meantime, though he is fearful of the future, he is willing to wait. He procrastinates. Roberta, who is far more realistic and practical than Clyde, insists that the only feasible solution left is marriage. And why should he not marry her? But Clyde feels no sense of moral obligation towards Roberta. He refuses to give up the glittering world of wealth that Sondra represents and settle down to a life of drab, unrelieved poverty.

Clyde decides that he must get rid of Roberta, since she now stands squarely in the way of his happiness. He must kill her, though never once does he face the thought of committing the murder. When the accident takes place on the lake to which he had brought her and both are thrown into the water, he does not come to her rescue. Had he, in fact, killed her? As he journeys through the dark of night to join Sondra, he realizes that though at the last moment he had experienced a change of heart and would not have gone through with the murder, "yet something had done it for him!"[33] Later, at the trial, the defending lawyer points out that it would be unjust to condemn Clyde for wishing to break off a relationship with a girl he no longer loved, but the plea cannot save Clyde. He was guilty of more than murder; he had violated the moral law by getting this girl pregnant. He must pay the full penalty for his "crime."

From a brief consideration of these four novels alone, apart from his other work, we can see that Dreiser was engaged in a kind of crusade to explode the conventional notion that human nature lacks the sexual element. As Randolph Bourne notes, "he rescues sex for the scheme of personal life."[34] If his fiction teems with sexually active figures, he never indulges in the cheap vice of pornography. Like D. H. Lawrence, he contended

---

[32] *Ibid.*, p. 402.
[33] *Ibid.*, pp. 572–573.
[34] Randolph Bourne, *History of a Literary Radical and Other Literary Essays.* New York: Viking Press, 1920, p. 198.

that the sexual life of man is not a dirty subject to dabble in. Indeed, Bourne maintains that it might have been better if Dreiser rather than Freud had enlightened the sexual imagination of the American intelligentsia, for then they would not have gone to extremes in seizing upon the psychopathology of sex. "Sex," Bourne argues, "has little significance unless it is treated in personally artistic, novelistic terms." [35]

A naturalist who from the opening of the twentieth century dared write what he believed was the truth, however maligned or unacknowledged, about sex, Dreiser led the revolt against the hypocritical moral conventions that were crippling the intellectual and spiritual development of America. The younger generation accepted him as one of their spokesmen. His work, together with that of Sherwood Anderson, Eugene O'Neill, and Ernest Hemingway, was instrumental in effecting a radical change in the love ethic of the lost generation during the roaring twenties. Viewing life through the scientific perspective, Dreiser affirmed that sex was the dominant instinct in man. Society for its protection attempted to enforce a strictly monogamous code of morality, but human beings in America and elsewhere, Dreiser asserted long before Kinsey, were incorrigibly polygamous. Hence the bitter conflict that rages between society and the individual who obeys the voice of his instincts. The law, the courts, the police, the churches, the weight of public opinion, are all arrayed on the side of the social order, and the weak individual is virtually coerced into submission. Dreiser, like Sherwood Anderson, openly champions the cause of the victims of sexual repression: the frustrated, the maladjusted, the neurotic sufferers. He would allow greater room for the play of instinct and give people the opportunity to find some measure of happiness in life.

It is an amusing commentary on the whirligig of moral taste in fiction that some contemporary critics find Dreiser's treatment of the sex problem sentimental rather than daring. Leslie Fiedler dismisses Dreiser's fictional world as

the absolutely sentimental world, in which morality itself has finally been dissolved in pity . . . . No theme but seduction can contain the meanings Dreiser is trying to express, no catastrophe but deflowering starts his heroines on their way toward total alienation. But any allusion to deflowering had become in Dreiser's time tabu . . . . To the anti-bourgeois camp in the literary world of the early 20th century, Dreiser's orthodox sentimental plea for sympathy rather than scorn for the fallen woman seemed, therefore, a revolutionary manifesto, an emancipation proclamation! [36]

[35] *Ibid.,* p. 199.
[36] Leslie A. Fiedler, "Seduction and the Class Struggle," *The New Leader.* February 29, 1960, pp. 22–23.

CHAPTER V

SHERWOOD ANDERSON: THE PHALLIC CHEKHOV

The cause of naturalism finally triumphed. The determined battle in behalf of sexual freedom that Dreiser had fought and won encouraged other writers to explore this hitherto forbidden area of experience. Freudianism prepared the way for the full-bodied emergence of the literary gospel that sex was salvation, and Sherwood Anderson became its anointed prophet. In his autobiography he tells us, like Dreiser in *Dawn*, of his sexual discoveries as a boy. His native town in Ohio afforded ample opportunities for a venturesome lad to gain a variety of sexual experiences, and Anderson is by no means reticent in describing what these were. Later, when he came to Chicago after abandoning his career as a businessman and owner of a factory, he met a band of writers whom he admired, writers who despised worldly success and strove to make an art of life. Writers like Floyd Dell, Ben Hecht, and Maxwell Bodenheim gave him the encouragement he needed to go on with his creative mission. They broadened his intellectual and artistic horizons and enabled him to see more clearly what was wrong with America and with the kind of life he had led in the past. He rejected the example set by the work of W. D. Howells and scornfully repudiated his injunction that the novelist should concern himself only with the cheerful, smiling aspects of life. There was, he charged, no flesh, no vital substance, in Howells' writing. Native writers like Hawthorne, Mark Twain, and Howells, Anderson concluded, were repressed personalities; that is why their recorded vision left out so much of what is fundamental in life. In failing to include the experience of sex within the scope of fiction, they betrayed an unpardonable lack of honesty. "My own experience in living," he remarks, "had already taught me that sex was a tremendous force in life. It twisted people, beat upon them, often distracted and destroyed their lives."[1] These older writers must have known all along the truth about the disturbing

---

[1] *Sherwood Anderson's Memoirs*. New York: Harcourt, Brace and Company, 1942, p. 243.

power of sex, only they were afraid to speak out. He would not be guilty of this cardinal sin of omission. He would paint the whole Adamic man, reveal the truth without internal censorship or evasion about the lives of men and women in America.

Anderson gained recognition as a writer of fiction at a time when Chicago was teeming with geniuses, all eager to cast off the fetters of the past and usher in a new era of creative expression. A group of *avant-garde* writers, who had come under the heady influence of Freudianism, were daring in their revelations. As Anderson says:

Freud had been discovered at the time and all the young intellectuals were busy analyzing each other and everyone they met. Floyd Dell was hot at it . . . . Well, I hadn't read Freud (in fact, I never did read him) and was rather ashamed of my ignorance.[2]

Anderson did not have to read Freud in order to learn what psycho-analysis was all about: the system of repression, the theory of the uncon-scious, the neurotic suffering caused by sexual frustration. He listened to lively discussions of Freudianism. Floyd Dell enjoyed nothing better than analyzing the writers in the group, and the others took up this endlessly fascinating game. They psychoanalyzed Anderson as well. An unregarded remark, a slip of the tongue, a spontaneous gesture, would immediately be interpreted in the light of Freudian symbolism. Anderson listened eagerly to these extraordinary bull sessions which tended to regard all human be-havior from the point of view of the sexual metaphor, and found in them stimulating food for thought. The incidental knowledge of Freudianism that he gleaned gave him a deeper insight into the psychology of inversion. As his stories, "Hands" and "The Man Who Became a Woman," show, he came to sympathize with homosexuals. Indeed, he made the startling dis-covery at the time that *unconsciously* he was one of these people.

The thing was in me too and the fear I had expressed was a sure sign of its presence. On another occasion when I had been walking in the park on a Sun-day afternoon with one of my new acquaintances we sat on a bench, and as we talked of books and life, I leaned over and picked up a twig from the path before us and began to break it between my fingers.[3]

This was sufficient damning evidence for his psychoanalytically-oriented companion, who proceeded to interpret the symbolic significance of this seemingly idle and meaningless act. Obviously "the twig was a phallic sym-bol. I was wanting to destroy the phallic in myself. I had secretly a desire to

---

[2] *Ibid.*, p. 243.
[3] *Ibid.*, pp. 244–245.

be a woman."[4] Outlandish as this episode now appears in retrospect, it affords an amusing illustration of the intellectual temper of the time. It reveals clearly enough the kind of informal education that Anderson, insatiably curious about the hidden secrets of the life of the mind, was receiving from his literary friends.

For these friends talked incessantly, espousing libertarian ideas and unpopular causes. They were specially eloquent when they denounced the plague of sexual repression in puritanical America. Not that they ever advocated "free love." They had not yet reached that extreme point, though Floyd Dell was to preach this cause with ardor when he moved from Chicago to Greenwich Village. As Anderson testifies

I doubt that there was with us any more giving way to the simple urge of sex than among the advertising and businessmen among whom I worked for certain hours each day. Indeed sex was to be given a new dignity and, as for marriage, well, it was obvious that on all sides of us there were men and women living the lives of married men and women without love, without tenderness.[3]

What these emancipated young writers were seeking was, like Dreiser, greater frankness, a more sincere dedication to the spirit of truth. They were not by sex obsessed. At no time, according to Anderson, did they have any intention of exaggerating the importance of sex. They simply wanted to produce fiction that, in defiance of the current taboos, would honestly portray the role that sexuality played in American life. "We wanted the flesh back in our literature, wanted directly in our literature the fact of men and women in bed together, babies being born. We wanted the terrible importance of the flesh in human relations also revealed again."[6]

In opposition to the conspiracy of silence that Puritanism had imposed on all matters relating to the sexual life of man, Anderson endeavored to picture the total personality. He would make no concession to conventional morality or traditional notions of human nature. Whatever lay beneath the surface of consciousness – nameless longings and erotic fantasies and libidinal impulses, however perverse or lawless they turned out to be – would find expression in his work. In probing the subliminal recesses of the self, he revealed what Freud had already discovered in his theory of the neuroses: how thin is the boundary line that divides the so-called normal from the abnormal. In his stories he uncovered the crippling effects of sexual frustration upon emotionally starved and lonely people. In his fiction as in that of Dreiser, the urgent need for love inevitably overrides the voice of reason

---

[4] *Ibid.*, p. 245.
[5] *Ibid.*, p. 245.
[6] *Ibid.*, p. 247.

and the restraints of public morality. When that is not the case, when the individual suppresses his deeper instincts, neurotic suffering and misery is the end result.

It is not surprising that *Winesburg, Ohio,* when it appeared in 1919, was banned in a number of cities. Iconoclastic in content, it exploded like a shell in the face of an outraged public. It stresses the vital, if often concealed, part that sexual repression plays in the life of a group of assorted people in a mid-Western town. If the characters in this collection of stories are "grotesques," that is because of the glaring discrepancy that exists between the moral code of the community to which they are expected to conform and the sexual passions that stir turbulently within them, passions which sometimes break explosively and unpredictably out of control. When the attempt is made to "sublimate" these passions, to tame them by denying their existence, they take on twisted masochistic and aberrant forms. Then, too, if these characters are "grotesques," it is because they cannot or will not adapt themselves to an environment that has become increasingly mechanized – a theme which Anderson developed more fully in *Windy McPherson's Son* (1916) and *Poor White* (1920). Wounded by life, cut off from Nature, the *dramatis personae of Winesburg, Ohio* belong to to the legion of the lonely and unhappy Americans who seek a fulfillment that is cruelly denied them. These "grotesques" were not meant to be taken as studies in psychopathology. These were ordinary people living in a representative mid-Western town, but something in their nature – a dream of desire, a flame of vision, a profound restlessness and hunger of the spirit for love's consummation – drove them into excess and turned them, alas, into "queer" characters, though outwardly in many instances their behavior betrayed no streak of wildness or abnormality. In painting the tragedy of these emotionally starved and sexually frustrated souls, Anderson is saying, in effect, that practically all the men and women in America had become "grotesques."

What, he asks broodingly, happens to people in this land to twist them so hideously out of shape? What poisoned the fountainhead of their dreams, destroyed their spontaneity of spirit, and transformed them into miserably defeated creatures nursing their grievances and their resentment behind closed doors, awaiting bitterly the final reprieve of death? They are so lonely and lost because they have abandoned the dreams of their youth and embraced the mouldy truths of others. By surrendering their ideal under the pressure of social conformity, they could no longer remain open to the regenerative power of love. These "grotesques" are afraid to release the flow of tenderness in their heart; they dare not satisfy their intense inner need for human contact and communion. In the story

"Hands," an imaginative teacher like Wing Biddlebaum feels impelled, when sharing his dreams with the youngsters in his charge, to caress their hair or place a hand lovingly on their shoulder. It is this non-verbal language of abounding love that is viciously misconstrued. When a half-witted boy falsely accuses him of being a pervert, the people of the town immediately believe that he is guilty. He is brutally beaten, almost lynched, and driven out of town. The thought of love is a foul thing in the mind of this community. That explains why, after coming to Winesburg, where he has lived for twenty years, he is fearful of people, terribly afraid to move his hands. But despite the harrowing ordeal through which he has passed, his spirit is not completely crushed. He still believes that one must not pay heed to the anonymous voice of the crowd. Yet the sensitive hands which expressed his love of man have been his undoing.

Anderson introduces us to other strange, lost souls. There is George Willard's mother, a tall, ghostly figure confined to her room, wasting away at forty-five because of some obscure disease. In her youth she had been a confused dreamer, giving vent to her romantic yearning for love by surrendering her body to various men. "It was always the same, beginning with kisses and ending, after strange wild emotions, with peace and then sobbing repentance."[7] What is behind the curse, Anderson asks, that has befallen these men and women? They are accursed because they have denied their instincts and their capacity for love. The theme of alienation from Nature is developed in "Godliness." The growth of industrialism, the spread of the railroads across the country, the building of cities and the extension of towns to outlying farms, all this has wrought a tremendous change for the worse in the character of life in the mid-West.[8] It is this dangerous fever of industrial expansion that has turned the daughter of Jesse Bentley into a neurotic woman. Her uncontrollable hunger for the experience of love tricks her into a loveless marriage.

A much sadder account of sexual frustration is to be found in "Adventure," the story of Alice Hindman, a woman of twenty-seven who works as a clerk in Winney's Dry Goods Store. She had given herself to one man, and

[7] Sherwood Anderson, *Winesburg, Ohio*. New York: Penguin Books, Inc., 1919, p. 20.

[8] See Alex Comfort, *Barbarism and Sexual Freedom: Lectures on the Sociology of Sex from the Standpoint of Anarchism*. London: Freedom Press, 1948. In this book Comfort analyzes the causes and describes the effects of social and sexual maladjustment in our time. He confirms Anderson's point that fundamentally the dysfunction of our society is caused by urbanism, the rapid rise of megalopolitan centers with their hideous congestion and their elimination of communal patterns of life, and the growth of centralization. It is technological society which thrusts upon man the terrible burden of alienation.

after he left her she could not think of marrying anyone else. She does not understand "the growing modern idea of a woman's owning herself and giving and taking for her own ends in life."[9] The privations of loneliness are too great for her to bear. In the privacy of her room she kneels and prays and whispers the intimate things she wanted to say to her lover. She becomes attached to inanimate things and develops a passion for saving money for its own sake. The fields remind her of blossoming, never-ceasing life, the changing of the seasons, the relentless passing of the years. She is afraid of growing old while cheated of her birthright of love. Then, in her twenty-seventh years, a nervous restlessness takes possession of her. At night she cannot sleep but stares fixedly into the darkness, unable to feed any longer on fantasies, demanding some definite answer from life. One night when the house is empty she undresses in the dark and runs out into the rain, driven by a mad desire to rush naked through the streets. She wants to cry out her need, to embrace some man who is, like her, lonely and yearning for love. As a drunken man stumbles homeward she calls to him "Wait!" but then, trembling at the thought of what she had done, she drops to the ground and crawls back to the house on muddy hands and knees. When she gets into bed, she weeps inconsolably.

"What is the matter with me? I will do something dreadful," she thought, and turning her face to the wall, began trying to force herself to face bravely the fact that many people must live and die alone, even in Winesburg.[10]

The tragedy Anderson depicts with such poignant realism in *Winesburg, Ohio* is the characteristic American tragedy of loneliness, spiritual emptiness, disillusionment, and neurotic unfulfillment.[11] These people of Winesburg have been broken on the wheel of life; there is nothing heroic in their existence; they must resign themselves as best they can to their unfortunate lot. So many of them suffer excruciatingly from the failure of their love life. It is impossible to forget a character like Walsh Williams who hates women, all womankind. Something had happened to him, a traumatic experience, which caused him to hate life. The wife whom he loved had betrayed him wantonly with other men. His mother-in-law tries to reconcile the two by bidding him come to her home and sending in his wife, naked, to the room where he sits waiting. Now Walsh is convinced that women were expressly sent to bring about the downfall of man. Sex, he believes, is a dirty trick in Nature. The story is ironically entitled "Respectability."

[9] Sherwood Anderson, *Winesburg, Ohio*, p. 76.
[10] *Ibid.*, p. 80.
[11] For an elaboration of this theme as it appears in *Winesburg, Ohio*, see Edwin T. Bowden, *The Dungeon of the Heart*. New York: The Macmillan Company, 1961, pp. 114–125.

One of the most powerful stories in the collection, "The Strength of God," has a direct bearing on our theme. It deals with the temptations to which the Reverend Curtis Hartman, pastor of the Presbyterian Church, is subjected. A silent, reticent man married to a stout, nervous woman, he conscientiously preaches the gospel of Christ to his congregation. Then he is suddenly – though his whole life of repression in the past accounts for it – beset by carnal temptation. From the room in the bell tower of the church where he prepares his sermons he sees the figure of Kate Swift, the school teacher, lying on her bed. Hitherto he had never permitted himself to think of other women; he wanted to devote all his strength to the service of God. But the temptation to gaze upon the body of this woman proves stronger than all his resolutions. Why, he ponders, must he suffer this thorn in the flesh? Why? Why, after a lifetime of serious study and exemplary living up to the Christian ideal, should he now be led into the insidious ways of sin? But the raging, pent-up desires of his body overpower his reason and override the protests of his moral self.[12] Finally, unable to bear up any longer under this struggle, he declares: "If my nature is such that I cannot resist sin, I shall give myself over to sin."[13] As he waits in the darkness for Kate Swift to appear in the room opposite his window, he thinks of the woman he had married, how she always looked upon passion as shameful and by doing so had defrauded him of the gift of beauty and the sense of joy. Rebelliously he broods:

Man has a right to expect living passion and beauty in a woman. He has no right to forget that he is an animal and in me there is something that is Greek. I will throw off this woman of my bosom and seek other women. I will besiege this school teacher. I will fly in the face of all men and if I am a creature of carnal lusts I will live then for my lusts.[14]

When he beholds the naked body of Kate Swift, he runs through the snow-covered streets to the office of the newspaper and there cries out to George Willard, the central figure in *Winesburg, Ohio,* that God had been revealed to him in the body of a naked woman. This story strikes an authentically new note in American fiction as it portrays with compassionate insight the

---

[12] From the time of Thomas Hardy to the present time, one of the recurrent motifs of fiction is the insistence that reason is not of much help in the conduct of life. Love, as the hero of Maugham's autobiographical novel, *Of Human Bondage,* realizes, is not a matter of rational choice. Maugham writes of his hero's hopeless infatuation for the waitress Mildred: "The power that possessed him seemed to have nothing to do with reason: all that reason did was to point out the methods of obtaining what his whole soul was striving for." W. Somerset Maugham, *Of Human Bondage.* New York: George H. Doran Company, 1915, p. 342.

[13] Sherwood Anderson, *Winesburg, Ohio,* p. 107.

[14] *Ibid.,* p. 108.

struggle of this inhibited minister, lineal descendant of Hawthorne's Arthur Dimmesdale, to face the truth of his carnal nature.

Anderson then describes the torment of unsatisfied desire Kate Swift suffers from. Few people in town suspected the images of passion that rioted in the mind of this schoolteacher. And in "The Untold Lie," Ray, an older man with a family, tries to warn Hal Winter, who has gotten a girl into trouble, against the trap of marriage. To himself he mutters, "Tricked by God, that's what I was, tricked by life and made a fool of." [15]

One theme that repeats itself with obsessive insistence in Anderson's work focuses on the traumatic effect of sexual frustration on the individual, the spiritual tragedy caused by the culturally imposed necessity for the repression of instinct. If people in this country are afraid of sex because they are ashamed of their body and its needs, their lives will be joyless and they will never know the beauty of fulfillment in love. Like Dreiser, Anderson is levelling the charge that Americans, infected by the Puritan tradition, accept the myth that sex is dirty and sinful, that the body is to be used exclusively as an instrument for procreation, that it is downright immoral to exploit sex for the purpose of pleasure.

Many Marriages (1923) is Anderson's fictional version of the tragedy of sex-starved America. In his Freudianized novel Anderson is saying in shrill tones of indignation that in the United States of the early twenties anyone who has the moral courage to advance directly toward the goal of love will be considered insane. He presents the case of John Webster, a prosperous manufacturer of washing machines in a small town in Wisconsin, and describes the sensual awakening of his body, his determined search for love. He has discovered that in the past he was ashamed of passion and frightened by sex; that is how, he realizes, he gradually destroyed in himself the spontaneity of the sex experience; that is why he engaged in furtive erotic affairs in other cities. Then he finds the true meaning of love and he is at last able to perceive that a man may have many marriages and that life in all its challenging freshness and variety must be faced.

And why, Anderson asks pointedly, should this liberating experience not happen to all those locked up in stuffy houses, the victims of loveless marriages, shut up like prisoners within themselves, afraid to venture forth and start anew, terrified by the specter of freedom, terribly afraid of what life will do to them. Sex is not to be condemned or feared, for sex is more than the coupling of two bodies, the spurting out of seed from the loins of the male into the womb of the female. John Webster, the protagonist who voices the Andersonian message of sex emancipation, hopes that a time will come

[15] *Ibid.*, p. 150.

when love like a flame will sweep through the cities and towns of America. This is the new gospel of redemption through love Anderson is preaching to the inhibited and unhappy husbands of the land. There is no earthly reason why marriage must become the graveyard of passion. Two people sacramentally joined together for life frequently discover, alas, that they were never really married. John Webster's wife, for example, seeks to conduct her life according to a conventional system of moral purity, but that system is a sickly lie, a rank perversion of the holy truth of the body. To check the flow of the libido is to hold back the divine source of energy. The grievance that Webster bears against his wife is that long ago, when their love-making was at its height, she had made him feel unclean. He had then acquiesced in this betrayal of instinct, pretending that the body was shameful, that marriage, sanctified by the spirit, could transcend the cravings of the flesh. It was the internal corruption wrought by this lie that had wrecked their marriage – the lie "that spiritual love was stronger and purer than physical love, that they were two different and distinct things."[16] Now he is free of his bondage; he has gained the salvationary insight that he must respond to the call of the flesh.

Perhaps what had saved him, Webster points out, but had destroyed his wife, was that he ran away at times and committed "the sin" of sex, while she, by clinging to dream of purity, her genteel goodness, until she had aged and withered and died within. For this national conspiracy of silence about sex, this widespread repression of instinct, what was it but a kind of death. One was faced with the choice of either worshiping life (and that meant embracing love) or accepting death-in-life (and that meant a denial of love.) Most Americans gave themselves to the God of Death, thereby stunting their growth and losing their self-respect. This is the way in which Anderson celebrates the Dionysian life of instinct:

> There was a deep well within every man and woman and when Life came in at the door of the house, that was the body, it reached down and tore the heavy lid off the well. Dark hidden things, festering in the well, came out and found expression for themselves, and the miracle was that, expressed, they became very beautiful. There was a cleansing, a strange sort of renewal within the house of the man or woman when the god Life had come in.[17]

This is the primitivistic cult of the unconscious as a creative power countering the malignant agency of death. Sherwood Anderson announces the tiding that the door of one's being must be kept open to all the winds of

---

[16] Sherwood Anderson, *Many Marriages*. New York: B. W. Huebsch, Inc., 1923, p. 189.
[17] *Ibid.*, p. 217.

experience: sun and air, freedom and fantasy, dream and desire, the body and all its animal appetites.

A thesis-ridden novel replete with Freudian symbols of sexual death and resurrection, *Many Marriages* does give expression, however perfervid in tone, to Anderson's underlying philosophy of love. He has disposed of the dualism of good and evil. The imagination requires no such artificial distinctions. The imaginative artist is not concerned with questions of morality. In the world of the imagination there is only the ugly and the beautiful, the quick and the dead. All morality, then, "becomes a purely aesthetic matter. What is beautiful must bring aesthetic joy; what is ugly must bring aesthetic sadness and suffering." [18]

It must be noted, however, that in vigorously denouncing what is wrong with the love life of his countrymen, Anderson is not writing in a purely aesthetic spirit – at least, not in *Many Marriages*. He is, through the persona of John Webster, preaching an urgently needed moral lesson. He is roundly condemning the American people for their irrational fear of the flesh, their peculiar conviction that the body is evil. He blames industrialism for crushing the spirit of man and frustrating his instincts so that he becomes neurotic or impotent. Having lost his capacity for love, the American male cannot give himself to woman or to work. Anderson sought to lift the curse of the machine from the lives of these trapped Americans, to cure them of their impotence and so free them to enjoy to the full the art of loving. He wanted love to be accepted as a natural, joyous experience. He could not understand why his writing was attacked so viciously (even his friend, the critic Paul Rosenfeld, had called him, though in no derogatory sense, the phallic Chekhov) when all he tried to do was to tell the truth about life as he had known it.

But the "truths" he enunciated did not go deep enough or far enough. Possessed of a lyrical, intuitive mind, he lacked sufficient awareness of the inextricable complexity of the issues he dealt with and was often naive in his approach to the problem of sex in modern life. As one sympathetic critic justly points out, his theme in *Winesburg, Ohio, Many Marriages,* and *Dark Laughter* is "the repression of sex, not its liberation." [19]

Anderson's was but a single if loudly raised voice in the blasphemous chorale during the twenties that decried and derided the reign of Victorian morality. *Jurgen,* by James Branch Cabell, was censored when it was pub-

---

[18] Sherwood Anderson, *A Story Teller's Story.* New York: B. W. Huebsch, Inc., 1924, p. 78.

[19] James Schevill, *Sherwood Anderson.* Denver: The University of Denver Press, 1951, p. 210.

lished in 1919 and became a *cause célèbre,* a novel to be bought *sub rosa* and read secretly. Jurgen, the twentieth-century quixotic Don Juan, debunked the conventional notions of the sanctity of marriage. The sexual symbolism of this novel, now largely forgotten, titillated the imagination of the intelligentsia.[20] But it was *This Side of Paradise,* not *Jurgen,* that became the Bible of flaming youth during the jazz age.

---

[20] "Cabell's contribution to early American sex literature lay not merely in his extraordinary frankness; he treated sexual diversion not as being necessarily reprehensible or admirable, but as being merely natural .... And over the philanderings of Jurgen Cabell cast a radiance of poetry, wit, and what the young critics called 'civilized sophistication' which did a good deal to justify the conduct in parked cars and on country club lawns of young men who felt the same yearnings which Jurgen experienced when he beheld Dorothy and Helen and Anaïtis." Irene and Allen Cleaton, *Books & Battles: American Literature, 1920–1930.* Boston: Houghton Mifflin Company, 1937, pp. 18–19.

CHAPTER VI

FITZGERALD AND THE JAZZ AGE

Unlike Dreiser or Sherwood Anderson, Fitzgerald was no crusader in the cause of sexual freedom. He is nonetheless important for our purpose in that he became the chief spokesman of the jazz age. He was the coryphaeus of its orgiastic dance, the articulate symbol of its heady aspirations, and, later, after the spree was over, the disillusioned recorder of the reasons for the collapse of its wildly romantic hopes. If he was inferior to Lawrence in prophetic passion and to Hemingway in the sense of disciplined devotion to his art, he was surely equal to both in the strict imaginative fidelity with which he delineated the life of his time. He was more than a naturalistic novelist whose work mirrored the mad, foolish excesses and irresponsibilities of a "lost generation;" he was also its conscience and its judge. A subtle and sensitive artist, he was the moral critic of the movement of revolt which he represented and which, indeed, he led. Until his breakdown and his despairing retreat into alcoholism, he lived with giddy abandon the life of his time, but he came soon enough to know the experience of horror and unavailing regret that the sense of waste and failure produces. If *This Side of Paradise* (1920) was the manifesto of the postwar generation, *The Crack-Up*, a series of magazine articles published posthumously in book form in 1945, was its pathetic epitaph.

During the twenties the young came exuberantly into their own; they ushered in a ten-year period of irreverence, iconoclasticism, and boundless insurgency. Youth was not only its own excuse for being but also a warrant for reckless, uninhibited behavior. It was as if the young of the time had taken for their motto Blake's proverb: *"Damn braces. Bless relaxes."* They eagerly absorbed the ideas preached by such men as Havelock Ellis and Sigmund Freud, who warned them of the dangers they ran if they failed to satisfy their sexual needs – or so many of them interpreted their teaching. They were bent on testing the limits of sexual morality. Extra-marital affairs were the mark of a free spirit. Fidelity in marriage they considered a doubtful bourgeois virtue. Avidly interested in the problem of sex, they were resolved to bring what was hidden frankly to light. The decline of religion, the aftermath of the First World War, the militant rise of feminism, the effects of prohibition, the popularization of psychoanalytic doctrine, these combined influences led them to throw off the restraining traditions of the past and invoke a new moral order. In Greenwich Village Floyd Dell proclaimed the gospel of "free" love, which the young intellectuals found eminently to their liking. They wanted to pour out their energies tumultuously, to burn with a hard, gemlike flame, to live dangerously, to fulfill themselves in love and art, not to stifle the voice of spontaneous desire.

Fitzgerald shared many of these libertarian beliefs, but even as a lapsed Catholic he was still inwardly affected by the dogmas of the Church he had renounced. He suffered from a divided nature: he was the successful novelist who was at the same time a wretched outsider. The young romantic who went to extremes in almost everything he did was also a Catholic whose conscience passed severe judgment on the outbreak of "immorality" in his time. One part of his being plunged eagerly, all too eagerly, into the flowing stream of experience and consequently became somewhat corrupt, but the other part remained innocent and unsoiled. As Andrew Turnbull sums him up in this respect:

He was normally but not overly sexual. Perhaps one could say that with him a strong sex drive had been geared to beauty and creation, while the destructive side of his nature found an outlet in drink. For someone who had been instrumental in relaxing censorship his writing was remarkably chaste.[1]

His fiction was born of this tug-of-war between these opposed impulses: the hedonistic and the ascetic, the desire to soak up experience to the limit and even beyond and the need to be morally disciplined. A creature of intense but shifting moods, driven by his daimon, he spent himself so prodigally, without counting the cost, that he learned to fear the fate which finally overtook him – that of emotional bankruptcy. After the publication of *This Side of Paradise,* he married Zelda Sayre, a Southern belle as impulsive and unpredictable in her behavior as he was. She wished to be a law unto herself, to do as she pleased, and to the devil with the requirements of middle-class respectability. Like Fitzgerald, she paid the full price for her excesses. After her nervous breakdown and confinement in a mental institution, Fitzgerald's alcoholism increased. The spirit of hope died in him. He drank compulsively in order to drown the tormenting memories of the

---

[1] Andrew Turnbull, *Scott Fitzgerald.* New York: Charles Scribner's Sons, 1962, p. 262.

past and to forget that he was, judged by his own exacting standards, a failure.

This Side of Paradise, which voiced the masculine protest of the jazz age, was read at the time of its appearance as if it were a rousing call to revolt. The girls who walk through the pages of this novel kiss with impetuous ardor and make love with untroubled promiscuity. "The sofa was the *mise-en-scène* of the post-war decade, and the kiss was réveille for a generation that watched twilight fall over cocktails at the Biltmore, and dawn strike the windows of Childs' Fifty-Ninth Street."[2] The novel caught the temper of the twenties, its feverish promise, its persistent nostalgia, melancholy, and even occasional moods of painful disenchantment. On the whole, though, it pictured an age of license, an exhilarating inebriated period that was distracted by few, if any, social or political concerns, an orgiastic party that it seemed would never break up.

Yet beneath the glittering portrait Fitzgerald paints of the bacchantic devotees of the jazz age we discern the traces of emotional tension, the incipient fissures of neurosis, the distinct symptoms of the despair that would attend the inevitable hangover. For the Fitzgerald hero, even as he pursues the primrose path of pleasure, gets drunk, and makes love, is tormented by a sense of sin and filled with an obscure hunger for redemption. *This Side of Paradise* gives expression to the spiritual distress of a young generation headed for a war which would not only kill off the best among them but also shatter the faith in Western civilization of those who survived. Now that the cultural ideals of the past, especially the American past, were discredited, love seemed to provide a sovereign cure for all that ailed the young. Girls now gaily engaged in amorous adventures that had only a few years back been considered downright immoral. Fitzgerald's novel vividly describes the moral letdown of a whole generation: the new cult of love-making that was established by flappers bent on doing precisely what was forbidden. They have been aptly called "undergraduate Madame Bovarys."[3]

This Side of Paradise presents an authentic picture of college life at Princeton. Fitzgerald shows how Amory Blaine, the egotist, grows into a serious-minded young man. He has read Keats and Swinburne, Shaw and Chesterton, Barrie and Yeats. He enjoys the new American practice of petting and heartily approves of the new freedom of the young female. Apparently, if some novelistic accounts are to be trusted, the morality of

[2] Maxwell Geismar, *The Last of the Provincials.* Boston: Houghton Mifflin Company, 1947, p. 289.
[3] *Ibid.,* p. 294.

college youth in this country after the Second World War has not greatly improved. For example, in *The Groves of Academe* (1951), Mary McCarthy furnishes a sardonic version of undergraduate life in a progressive college – the dancing, the drinking of spiked punch, the necking, the occasional smoking of marijuana. Every year, we are told, "there were rumors of seduction, homosexuality, abortion, lesbian attachments, and what shocked the students about these stories, some of them very circumstantial, was the fact that they appeared to take place in a moral vacuum . . . ."[4] The girls wanted a good time and were not inclined to be too choosy. They talked about Freud and Jung and – a new intellectual sensation – the orgonomy of Wilhelm Reich. Mary McCarthy describes the enthusiastic necking that went on nightly in the social rooms. Ideals were badly worn down; "students of both sexes had the wary disillusionment and aimlessness of battle-hardened Marines. After six months at Jocelyn, they felt that they had 'seen through' life, through all attempts to educate and improve them, through love, poetry, philosophy, fame . . . ."[5] But the undergraduates of Fitzgerald's time were making these discoveries on their own for the first time.

When the United States declares war, Amory Blaine realizes that his generation is breaking away decisively from the moorings of the past. After he goes off to war, the novel recounts his love affairs, his restlessness, his state of disillusionment, and his search for meaning. What troubles him profoundly is the problem of working out a sex ethic that he can live by. "What am I for?" he asks himself. "According to the American novels we are led to believe that the 'healthy American boy' from nineteen to twenty-five is an entirely sexless animal."[6] This belief, he perceives, is based on a lie. The myth of purity in love is exploded. One girl with whom Amory Blaine has fallen in love declares: "Oh, just one person in fifty has any glimmer of what sex is. I'm hipped on Freud and all that, but it's rotten that every bit of *real* love in the world is ninety-nine per cent passion and one little soupçon of jealousy."[7]

Fitzgerald's hero tries to be honest with himself. He discovers that women will marry for security rather than romance. He understands what is wrong with his generation, which is rebelling against a materialistic civilization in which love is bought and sold like a commodity in the marketplace. He is

[4] Mary McCarthy, *The Groves of Academe*. New York: Harcourt, Brace and Company, 1951, p. 25.
[5] *Ibid.*, p. 64.
[6] F. Scott Fitzgerald, *This Side of Paradise*. New York: Charles Scribner's Sons, 1920, p. 231.
[7] *Ibid.*, p. 255.

resolved to fight against cant and hypocrisy and throw off the shackles of a false and effete tradition. He does not despair of life. He sees a new generation springing up, a new generation "grown up to find all Gods dead, all wars fought, all faiths in man shaken . . . ." [8] Fitzgerald is portraying a restive younger generation in search of a happiness that their elders, victims of a crippling set of puritanic inhibitions, had completely missed. Freeing themselves from the clutch of all spurious ideals, they would put a new sexual morality into practice. Desire, they became convinced, was the soul of duty. Down with the Ten Commandments!

In *The Beautiful and the Damned*, the hero marries a woman who is incapable of passion, not fitted to give love. A child of the jazz age, she is cold, interested solely in the ritual of self-gratification. Fitzgerald sensitively depicts the excesses of Flaming Youth. He shows that these were born of the adolescent's fear of growing up. Dreading the onset of old age and the inexorable march of time that leads to the grave, the romantic adolescent uses up all his energies in the quest for immediate pleasure and the fullness of sexual experience. But he cannot remain obsessed by sex without later having to face the horror of an empty, wasted existence.

The Beautiful and the Damned (1922) contains some revealing passages of dialogue on the meaning of life. If the world is meaningless, why should one devote himself to writing? The very attempt to give life purpose is purposeless. Fitzgerald is expressing here the nihilistic *leitmotif* of the twenties, the conviction that life is meaningless and purposeless. It was this despairing metaphysical insight which led the younger generation to experiment recklessly with the new ethic of sexual freedom. Like Hemingway's protagonists, Fitzgerald's beautiful and damned souls are haunted by the thought that life is short. One should therefore live fully in the present, they conclude, and that meant abandoning all illusions about the problematical future. Hence the girl who pets would, according to Fitzgerald, turn out to be a better wife in the end, for she would be free of the romantic illusions of love and less likely to be promiscuous.

This was the moral attitude, romantic in its vehement repudiation of romanticism, that dominated the literature of the twenties. The clarion call to freedom was generally interpreted as implying that one should seize the day and take as much as one can out of life. Both Fitzgerald and his wife tried to keep faith with this absurd and ruinous doctrine. Inhibition was looked upon as a curse, repression a vice. Gradually this doctrine degenerated into a hedonistic policy of following the caprice or impulse of the moment, without any concern for future consequences. Confused in their

8 *Ibid.,* p. 304.

striving for absolute sincerity of expression, Fitzgerald and Zelda ended up by destroying themselves and their future. Fitzgerald felt responsible for his wife's mental deterioration. Had they not led dissipated, undisciplined lives? He suspected, and not without reason, that his drinking had contributed to her outbreak of mental illness.

The Great Gatsby (1925), too, offers us a brilliant study of the intensely alive but confused twenties, a decade in which the moral fiber of many people was put severely to the test. Most of the characters in this consummately wrought novel are spoiled, self-engrossed, jaded, corrupt. From the start, Daisy Buchanan's remark that she is paralyzed with happiness takes on a different meaning when interpreted within its ironic context. She is bored, forever craving excitement, driven by the chronic need to escape from boredom. She confides to Nick, through whose eyes the story is told, that she is pretty cynical about everything. "I've been everywhere and seen everything and done everything."[9] This strikes the familiar note of the twenties, with its insatiable craving for experience, its "knowingness," its air of worldly sophistication, but also its inner feeling of weary cynicism. We behold what goes on at Gatsby's parties. In a number of incisively etched scenes, Fitzgerald pictures the men and women of the twenties off on a glorious spree, drinking themselves into insensibility, indifferent to the morrow, doing the most insane things.

Elements of irony are woven deftly into the fabric of the tightly constructed plot. When Tom Buchanan sees his mistress, a lusty, sumptuously fleshed, but shallow and vulgar creature, slipping away from him and his wife Daisy breaking out of his control, he makes himself decidedly unpleasant. He waxes indignantly moral. "Nowadays people begin by sneering at family life and family institutions, and next day they'll throw everything overboard and have intermarriage between black and white."[10] He refuses to take seriously this trumped-up business of love between Daisy and Gatsby. Though he admits that he goes off on a spree once in a while and makes a fool of himself running after other women, he declares that he really loves Daisy – in his own way.

Jay Gatsby, the romantic dreamer, is defeated by those who are less decent, less scrupulous in their behavior. A moralist at heart, he had possessed Daisy in the past, but he was convinced he had no right to be near her; after all, he is a nobody, with no family, no wealth, no social status.

---

[9] F. Scott Fitzgerald, *The Great Gatsby*. New York: Charles Scribner's Sons, 1925, p. 15.
[10] *Ibid.*, p. 99.

But once he has "taken her," he feels married to her.[11] He will make himself worthy of her by amassing a fortune, by whatever available means, legal or illegal, and then come back to claim her love. He is the idealist who cherishes the purity of his dream, but Daisy, for whom life was a perpetual whirl of gayety, cannot afford to wait. "She wanted her life shaped now, immediately – and the decision must be made by some force – of love, of money, of unquestionable practicality – that was close at hand."[12] She married Tom, the promiscuous brute, and the two of them are the careless creatures who, protected by their wealth, smashed up things while the others are left to clean up the mess they had made.

    Tender Is the Night (1934), which also covers the period of the twenties, forms a fitting successor to *This Side of Paradise, The Beautiful and the Damned,* and *The Great Gatsby.* But there is a pronounced difference in tone and attitude. Fitzgerald is now presenting the other side of the picture; he is bringing into focus the doubts that afflicted the gay young blades of the jazz age, the existential dread that motivated their efforts to defeat the mighty adversary Time, the final disillusionment they suffered in their quest for happiness. We watch a motley group of characters in action in a colony on the Riviera, people who are strenuously engaged in the game of amusing themselves; they are killing time, attempting to run away from the fate of boredom and to anesthetize the oppressive sense of futility. Abe North, the fictional persona of Ring Lardner, gets drunk persistently. When his wife says, "I used to think until you're eighteen nothing matters," he replies, "That's right. And afterward it's the same."[13] He has given up the struggle. He is tired of the world, of friends, and his only aim in life is to destroy himself. His will to live has turned into a fixed will to die.

    One of the important themes in this complexly structured and superbly written novel is designed to show how the power of money can poison human relationships. Toward the end Dick Diver realizes that his marriage to Nicole is doomed. His wife, who has resumed her relationship with Tommy Barban, is a bit shocked at first as she contemplates the idea of committing adultery, but then she asks herself why not. Other women have lovers. Why not she? This is the kind of feminine logic she uses to justify her infidelity. Now she looks forward eagerly to the affair and fights Dick with her

---

[11] Lionel Trilling makes the observation that "no one, I think, has remarked how innocent of mere "sex," how charged with sentiment is Fitzgerald's description of love in the jazz age . . . ." Lionel Trilling, "F. Scott Fitzgerald," in Frederick J. Hoffman (ed.), *The Great Gatsby: A Study.* New York: Charles Scribner's Sons, 1962, p. 235.

[12] F. Scott Fitzgerald, *The Great Gatsby,* p. 115.

[13] F. Scott Fitzgerald, *Tender Is the Night.* New York: Charles Scribner's Sons, 1934, p. 122.

money, her beauty, "her unscrupulousness as against his moralities."[14] Dick Diver, like the author who tells his story, is broken in spirit.

But Fitzgerald lived on to write the epilogue to the twenties. In "Echoes of the Jazz Age," an essay published in 1931 while he was at work on *Tender Is the Night,* we get his bitter retrospective evaluation of the immoralities of the twenties. The jazz age began about the time of the May Day riots in 1919 and ended suddenly and spectacularly in October 1929. Though the essay repeats the same themes developed in his fiction, the emphasis is now differently distributed; the tone has changed; it has become accusatory and penitential, though the underlying refrain of *mea culpa* is kept under control. He makes a determined effort to understand what happened to the members of his generation. Having lived through the inferno of the First World War, the young men were tired of Great Causes, the mendacious rhetoric of idealism and moral righteousness. As Fitzgerald phrases it: "The events of 1919 left us cynical rather than revolutionary . . . ."[15] The jazz age, largely indifferent to the drama of politics, was an age of creativity, an age of introspection, satire, and revolt. The automobile afforded young people the privacy that made courtship an enjoyable experience, free from the supervision of parents. "At first petting was a desperate adventure even under such favorable conditions, but presently confidences were exchanged and the old commandments broke down."[16] To be sure, class distinctions affected the behavior of the young. Only the upper or wealthier classes could indulge in these audacities of petting. Among other young people the older moral code still held sway and a kiss meant a proposal was expected. In 1920, when the jazz age was ushered in, the wildest of all generations danced into the limelight. Here were daring flappers and earnest immoralists determined to enjoy life to the limit. Here were the young men and women who, though feeling "lost," overreached themselves in their lust for life, "less through lack of morals than through lack of taste."[17] Ironically enough, they succeeded in corrupting their elders.

Liquor flowed freely during this period of Prohibition. The term "jazz," as it rose to respectability, ceased to mean sex and referred to dancing and then to music. It was associated with "a state of nervous stimulation . . . ."[18]

[14] *Ibid.,* p. 320.
[15] F. Scott Fitzgerald, *The Crack-Up.* Edited by Edmund Wilson. New York: New Directions, 1945, p. 14.
[16] *Ibid.,* p. 15.
[17] *Ibid.,* p. 15.
[18] *Ibid.,* p. 16.

Young girls read such forbidden fare as *Lady Chatterley's Lover, Winesburg, Ohio, Jurgen, Ulysses,* and *This Side of Paradise.* The realistic or ironic treatment of the sexual theme appealed strongly to the then contemporary audience of intelligentsia. By 1926, however, as Fitzgerald points out, "the universal preoccupation with sex had become a nuisance. (I remember a perfectly mated, contented young mother asking my wife's advice about 'having an affair right away,' though she had no one especially in mind, 'because don't you think it's sort of undignified when you get much over thirty?')."[19] Erotic plays, plays harping on the harmful effects of suppressed desire, appeared on the stage. By 1927 the symptoms of a widespread neurosis made themselves felt. People broke down, cracked up, committed suicide.

When the financial crash came, the most expensive orgy in American history was brought to an inglorious end. The artificial palace of pleasure came tumbling down; the jazz age became a dim memory of a discredited "lost generation." Now the reaction set in, the period of sober stock-taking. Looking back, Fitzgerald spells out the tragic waste and horror of an intemperate age when people drank themselves into a stupor "and every day in every way was growing better and better, and there was a first abortive shortening of skirts . . . ."[20] New York had led the bacchanalian rout, but though morals were slipping there was no inner peace, no attainment of happiness.

Fitzgerald had of course himself participated in these Dionysian revels, playing the role of high priest, dissipating his energies riotously, spending his money extravagantly; then came the inevitable recoil, the crack-up, the terrors of insomnia that no sleeping pills could assuage. He kept on drinking and when he did not drink the anticipation of the sleepless night he faced would torment him long before bedtime. In the night he felt lost, damned. The excitability of his nervous system conjured up nightmarish visions of the real horror taking place over the rooftops: the horror and waste, "what I might have been and done that is lost, spent, gone, dissipated, unrecapturable."[21] Fitzgerald is sitting in harsh judgment on the kind of life he had lived. He is, like Floyd Dell, judging not only himself but the age of which he was a part.[22] But though Fitzgerald repented of his "sins," there were

---

[19] *Ibid.,* p. 18.
[20] *Ibid.,* p. 22.
[21] *Ibid.,* p. 67.
[22] Particularly telling in this connection is Floyd Dell's denunciation in 1930 of the curious perversion of the twenties, which looked upon sex as a form of amusement. "Sexual intercourse eviscerated of its deepest emotional meanings, divorced from

other literary leaders of the moral revolution in the twenties, writers like Eugene O'Neill and Ernest Hemingway, who never repudiated their espousal of freedom in love and sex.

reality, robbed of hope, is flung to the boys and girls as a toy to amuse themselves with." (Floyd Dell, *Love in the Machine Age*. New York: Farrar and Rinehart, Inc., 1930, p. 173). But that, declares Dell discarding his former views, is to debase sex, to degrade human beings, to encourage an attitude of frivolous irresponsibility. There is no romance, no adventure, no beauty, no true satisfaction to be found in such unchartered sexual freedom.

CHAPTER VII

EUGENE O'NEILL:
THE TRAGEDY OF LOVE WITHOUT GOD

Eugene O'Neill started his career as a playwright during a period of bold experimentation and fervent hope for the future greatness of American literature. His reading of Nietzsche, particularly of *The Birth of Tragedy*, filled him with the ambition of bringing Dionysus back to the theater. He was influenced, too, in his expressionistic sorties, by such European iconoclasts as Strindberg and Wedekind. He began composing plays at a time when new and disturbing ideas were in the air. As we have already noted, psychoanalysis was then attracting public attention. The discovery of the unconscious, the growing interest in the peculiar logic of dream-imagery, the increasing knowledge of the damaging effects caused by sexual repression, the dynamic insight that only a thin partition divided the normal from the abnormal personality, led writers to abandon the practice of personifying the character of evil. A more permissive sex-ethic emerged. What was evil but an upsurge of libidinal energy, an explosion of the primordial, amoral id. Flaming youth, as we remarked in our analysis of Fitzgerald's work, was now affirming its inalienable right to release its instincts, to obey the "natural" law of desire. The passion of sex was no longer to be fearfully denied or furtively indulged. The theology of original sin was debunked. In matters of sex, the younger generation undertook to free itself from the incubus of guilt. Semantically and psychologically, the opposite of suppression was taken to mean uninhibited sex expression.

The contributions of psychoanalytic theory left their impress on all branches of American literature at the time O'Neill was first launching forth on his career – on biography and literary criticism as well as poetry, the drama, and fiction. What was originally a therapeutic method became a literary cult, *a Weltanschauung,* a salvationary faith, a surrogate for the lost God. Here was a *science,* of profound interest to the dramatist and novelist, that purported to reveal the deepest recesses of the human psyche and portrayed the nature of man as governed primarily by his instincts. Then, too, as we observed in our discussion of Sherwood Anderson, psychoanalytic jargon was fast becoming a part of the American language. People talked glibly about complexes, suppressed desire, the oedipal conflict, and those who could afford it were undergoing analysis. An increasing number of writers became convinced that here was a vast storehouse of original material that could be put to fruitful literary use. Here was a new, challenging way of interpreting the human tragicomedy that the *avant-garde* playwrights could not afford to ignore. In an age dominated by the figure of Freud, few American dramatists remained unaffected by the psychoanalytic movement. They were interested chiefly not in its scientific doctrine but in its aesthetic implications: its exploration of dream symbolism, its disclosure of the irrational control exercised by the unconscious, its interpretation of the complex manifestations of the sex instinct, its study of neuroses and the etiology of madness, its potentialities for adding new ironic tensions and new sources of insight to the drama.[1]

All this helped to undermine the sexual morality of the time. We have already seen how, at the turn of the twentieth century, moral values were still supposed to conform to the Victorian system of ethical norms. Men judged women rigorously in the light of the double standard: she was pure or fallen, a Madonna or a harlot. The tradition of mistrust of and antagonism toward the female of the species still persists and results in a male conspiracy of hypocritical pretence. The double standard, though vigorously attacked in many intellectual circles and no longer defended publicly with conviction, is nevertheless still adhered to.[2] The passionless mother of children, the Victorian woman was not expected to feel the stirring of sexual desire. Brought, however, under the relentless probing of the psychoanalytic method, the character of man – and woman as well – was seen to be driven by powerful instinctual impulses that the Victorian code of respectability had stubbornly refused to acknowledge. Freudianism revealed what had long been suspected, that few men and women actually lived up to – or could afford to live up to without developing some form of neurosis – the artificial and repressive ideal of conduct established by public morality.

Eugene O'Neill was caught up on the tide of these exciting revolutionary ideas, but his was too skeptical a temperament to become the slave of any

[1] See W. David Sievers, *Freud on Broadway*. New York: Hermitage House, 1955.
[2] In his brilliant study of misogynist sentiment in the history of Western culture, H. R. Hays defines the double standard as follows: "In actual practice the double standard means that sexual experimentation before marriage and rejection of ironclad monogamy is permitted to the male while the female is allowed the same privileges only secretly and if she is not stigmatized by unlegal pregnancy." H. R. Hays, *The Dangerous Sex*. New York: G. P. Putnam's Sons, 1964, p. 289.

system of thought. He possessed a mind that was too creative, too original, to regard Freudianism as providing an open sesame to the playwright. He was understandably annoyed by those critics who interpreted his plays as case histories derived from the major texts of Freudian psychology. After all, he protested, that is not how the creative mind operates. Though he had read some books by Freud, he was actually more impressed by the work of Jung. In reply to a direct question on this moot matter of "influences," this is what he had to say:

There is no conscious use of psychoanalytical material in any of my plays. All of them could easily have been written by a dramatist who had never heard of the Freudian theory and was simply guided by an intuitive psychological insight into human beings and their life impulses that is as old as Greek drama. It is true that I am enough of a student of modern psychology to be fairly familiar with the Freudian implications inherent in the actions of some of my characters while I was portraying them; but this was always an afterthought and never consciously was I for a moment influenced to shape my material along the lines of any psychological theory. It was my dramatic instinct and my personal experiences with human life that alone guided me.[3]

O'Neill is perfectly right. No genuine artist mechanically borrows the theories of science, nor is his vision of life summed up by any abstract doctrine, be it metaphysical, religious, or psychological. It is out of his own experiences that he draws the material of human conflict which he incorporates and imaginatively transmutes in his work. O'Neill's early plays highlight the contradiction between truth and dreams, reality and illusion, desire and frustration. In those of his plays that deal with the subject of love, what he inveighs against is the sickly lie of romantic love, especially when coupled with the disingenuous and forbidding ideal of premarital purity. *Diff'rent* is a study of mental aberration, a grim story of a woman who out of a compulsive sense of purity rejects the man who loves her and wishes to marry her, because he was guilty of sexual "infidelity" while away on a cruise, and remains a spinster. She will not marry a man who is thus defiled. She can forgive the sin itself but she cannot go through with the marriage, for she had all along cherished the belief that he was "different." It is not so much her Puritanism as her temperamental perversity, her stubborn pride, that makes her reject her suitor; the rest of her seafaring family laugh at these peccadillos of the flesh. She is simply the victim of an irrational, repressive ideal. But time inexorably exacts its revenge; she must pay dearly for this neurotic denial of her deepest life instinct. As she grows older, she becomes obsessed with sex. The play ends tragically with the suicide of both

---

[3] W. David Sievers, *Freud on Broadway*, p. 98.

her and her long faithful lover. The table of values has been turned: the price of sexual repression is neurosis – and death.

In *Welded* we behold O'Neill deploying a stark Strindbergian-Laurentian mood. The husband in the play, himself a playwright, wants to possess the soul as well as body of his wife, an actress. Michael Cape, the romantic perfectionist, demands nothing less than the fusion of their two bodies, their two souls, their two lives, into one, but the ineffable nature of love baffles his efforts at communication since it cannot be captured in words. The truth is that men and women, try as hard as they will, can never achieve this perfect union. Eleanor is compelled to resist this force which would take possession not only of her body but her very soul. It is because she loves him that she must struggle jealously to retain her identity. "If I am destroyed," she cries, "what is there left to love, what is left for you to love?"[4] She must remain essentially herself if she is to have a self capable of loving and a self worthy of being loved. Michael reminds her, strangely enough, that when they contemplated marriage they had both agreed "that unfaithfulness would be the unpardonable sin – not because we regarded it as a crime in itself but because it was a symbol of our separate weak attitudes toward love in the past...."[5]

Their quarrel rises to a climax of vindictive fury. Michael rushes out determined to revenge himself; he will drag their love in the mire. He picks up a woman of the streets. When he tells her that hell is now his home, the prostitute asks him whether he believes in God. "I believe in the devil!" he answers.[6] When she finally realizes what is wrong with him, she assures him that it is possible to get used to any suffering life imposes on us. And Michael in his anguish agrees: "But it's true – it's the insult we all swallow as the price of life."[7] O'Neill here describes the ambivalent, strife-torn nature of love as he pictures the difficult attempt at reconciliation between husband and wife. Eleanor informs Michael that if she came back to their home, it is not to him that she returned. Love conquered, not his possessive ego. It is she who proclaims the meaning of the truth of love: "There is only one way we can give life to each other. We must redeem our love from ourselves."[8] Love is shown to be no condition of lasting peace, no state of exclusive possession. It is a source of torment as well as ecstasy. In their moment of achieved truth, stripped of the attitudes which make up the

[4] Eugene O' Neill, *All God's Chillun Got Wings* and *Welded*. New York: Boni and Liveright, 1924, p. 107.
[5] *Ibid.*, p. 116.
[6] *Ibid.*, p. 142.
[7] *Ibid.*, p. 148.
[8] *Ibid.*, p. 165.

vanity of personality, they are able at last to communicate with each other from within. Michael confesses how often he wakes up in the night, terrified by the cosmic darkness,

alone in time – a hundred million years of darkness. I feel like crying out to God for mercy because life lives! Then instinctively I seek you – my hand touches you! You are there – beside me – alive – with you I become a whole, a truth! Life guides me back through the hundred million years to you. It reveals a beginning in unity that I may have faith in the unity of the end![9]

A lapsed Catholic like Fitzgerald, O'Neill is always aware of the transcendental element in love, the dimension of the mystical, the ineffable, the numinous that includes and yet transcends the plane of physical passion – the power of love, in the fleeting fraction of time that measures out a life span, to hold at bay the forces of darkness and the ever-present threat of death.

Just as they are about to be sacramentally united in body and soul, as Eleanor stands on the stairway bidding Michael come to her, she moves her arms back until they are stretched out to left and right, forming a cross. When Michael asks her why she is standing in that position, she replies, her eyes closed: "Perhaps I'm praying. I don't know. I love."[10] That is how O'Neill attempts to create a symbolic identification of love with prayer, love with God. When Michael, deeply moved, says "I love you!" it is his wife who utters the response of love liberated from the trammels of selfhood: "We love!" As he moves closer to her and their hands touch, they form one cross. Despite their torturous conflict of wills, they are welded together. In this somewhat overwrought play O'Neill presents his favorite theme of love-hate, his conception of love as a crucifixion as well as a communion of flesh and spirit.

In *Anna Christie,* we are introduced to Johnny-the-Priest's waterfront saloon, where O'Neill had lived as a young man and where he had once tried to commit suicide. In this play as in *The Iceman Cometh,* he shows how the characters are ineluctably shaped by the forces of their environment and the pressure of their conditioning in the past. An old, gay sea-dog like Chris had shuffled off his family responsibilities and gone aroving, getting drunk each time he reached the end of a voyage, never content to settle down. He utterly neglects the care and welfare of his daughter. She is cruelly exploited by the family of relatives in Minnesota to whom he had sent her. Seduced by one of the sons, she is finally driven into prostitution. She hates men for

---

9 *Ibid.,* pp. 168–169.
10 *Ibid.,* p. 170.

all that they have done to her. Matt Burke, a stoker, an Irishman with a
golden tongue, falls in love with her, but he cannot forgive her when she
confesses to him the truth about her sinful past. He loves her madly, but
how can he, a devout and superstitious Catholic, marry a former prostitute?
This cannot be. It runs counter to his fixed idea of marriage as a sacrament
in which he (never mind his own unsanctified past) is joined to a virgin. As
far as he is concerned, women fall into two separate and opposed classes:
the whores whose bodies can be bought in every port of call and those unsullied souls who become wives and the mothers of families. O'Neill de-
vises a way out of the tragic impasse by having Matt, after he gets roaring
drunk, come back and forgive Anna; he decides magnanimously to marry
her after all, though he has already signed up, together with Chris, for a
voyage to South Africa. In an original version, O'Neill resolves the conflict
by having Anna commit suicide, which is surely the more logical ending.
But O'Neill, even in his revised draft, has scored his point. Anna is bitter,
hardened, without hope for the future. Life has taught her to fend for herself
and not to trust the base sensual motives of men. They are all alike in their
sexual craving. When Matt had brusquely rejected her, she was not surprised. She had expected that reaction on his part, though, as she points out,
his morals had been no better than hers.

With uncompromising realism O'Neill paints men and women as they
are. Many playwrights from Ibsen on have attacked the romantic ideal but
none more savagely than O'Neill. What lends ironic tension to his work is
that he himself, as was evident in *Welded*, suffered from the romantic
malady. In one sense, his plays represent a determined and persistent effort
to cure himself of this tendency. In love as in life, he felt that man must
learn to face the bitter truth of reality. Illusions must be abandoned, though
he knew full well how desperately men clung to them in their hours of dere-
liction and despair. Like Dreiser, he insisted that the world is utterly indifferent to human aspirations and desires. There is, however, a mystical
streak, a touch of the frustrated poet and idealist *manqué,* which makes him
unreconciled to such a nihilistic stance. An incurable outsider, he cannot
come to terms with life. In *Long Day's Journey into Night,* Edmund (who
represents O'Neill himself) describes his years of wandering and his moments of mystical illumination when, drunk with the beauty of the sea, he
became one with the pulsing rhythm of the universe, merged in something
greater than himself. Then he makes this confession:

It was a great mistake, my being born a man. I would have been much more
successful as a sea gull or a fish. As it is, I will always be a stranger who never

feels at home, who does not really want and is not really wanted, who can never belong, who must always be a little in love with death![11]

Therein lies the secret of his extraordinary power as a dramatist, in this irreconcilable conflict between Nature and spirit, the crushing truth of life and the vain longing of the heart for the Absolute. Though he frequently gave in to black moods of despair, he would not nourish the seeds of illusion. He rejected not only the romantic ideal but also the Puritanism which was endemic in America. Puritanism was to be fought because it denied the possibility of joy in life; it placed an abnormal stress on the renunciation of instinct. It is the essentially evil force of repression which O'Neill, like Dreiser and Sherwood Anderson, sought to combat. In *Dynamo,* Reuben Light repudiates his father's dogmatic religion, but he cannot rid himself of the old God. He remains a Puritan at heart, believing that all of life, including sex, is evil. In O'Neill's imaginative world, the Christian synthesis not only blocks but perverts the human quest for happiness on earth. Abjuring all absolutes, O'Neill, like Hemingway, embraces a naturalistic outlook and a relativistic code of ethics. His protagonists, however heavily burdened with religious scruples, are not inclined to be straitlaced, ascetic, strictly monogamous. O'Neill preaches no evangel, but there is one theme that informs much of his work: it is incumbent on man not to conform to creeds that negate life but to reach out for whatever measure of happiness he can hope to attain.

In *Strange Interlude,* O'Neill delineates the character of a complex, passionate woman who is in full revolt against her father and all he stands for: the cultured New England environment in which he brought her up, his stern ethic of restraint, the repressions he had forced upon her. It is the father, a professor of the classics living in a remote, rarefied world of books, who had been instrumental in preventing Gordon, the man Nina Leeds loved, from marrying her before he went off to the war in which he was killed. When she first appears on the stage at the beginning of the play, she has made up her mind to leave her father's home. She plans to complete her training as a nurse and work self-sacrificingly at a sanitarium for crippled soldiers. She has suffered a nervous breakdown and is not yet completely recovered from the shock of Gordon's death in the First World War. Out of a neurotic guilt compulsion to make atonement for the happiness she denied Gordon, she feels she must give herself physically to those who had been wounded in the war. Perhaps in this way she can make up for what she considers her cowardly treachery to Gordon. For Gordon had wanted

[11] Eugene O'Neill, *Long Day's Journey into Night,* New Haven: Yale University Press, 1956, pp. 153-154.

to possess her the night before he sailed. Why did she hold back and forever forfeit her happiness?

A year later her father dies, and she comes back, cynical, spent, devoid of feeling, to the house of death. She is befriended by Dr. Edmund Darrell, who knows something of her sick condition, her morbid longing for martyrdom, her desire to expiate her festering sense of guilt by pretending to "love" the men in her care, though she fails to fool them. There can be no faking in the act of love. The body betrays the unacknowledged emotion. Each time she gives herself to a wounded soldier her conscience is lacerated, but this only spurs her on to further ordeals of self-punishment. Dr. Darrell, a neurologist who feels he has conquered the weakness of love because he understands so well its sexual origin, recommends that the best solution for Nina is to get her to marry Sam Evans. Marriage, by affording her an opportunity to bear children, would provide a normal outlet for her masochistic craving for martyrdom.

Nina laughs at Darrell's inhuman devotion to the objective truths of science. When she was upstairs gazing at the dead body of her father, she tried to pray

to the modern science God. I thought of a million light years to a spiral nebula – one other universe among innumerable others. But how could that God care about our trifling misery of death-born-of-birth? I couldn't believe in Him, and I wouldn't if I could! I'd rather imitate His indifference and prove I had that one trait at least in common.! [12]

Though this utterance speaks for Nina who is at this moment in a highly distraught and neurotic state, it voices a recurrent theme in O'Neill's dramatic work: the struggle between the absolutism of religion and the absolutism of science, the conflict between the God on the Cross (in *Days Without End*) and the God of electricity (in *Dynamo*). O'Neill is convinced that this conflict inevitably affects the character of modern love. Nina had wanted to believe in God at any cost, but like Catherine Barkley in *A Farewell to Arms* she cannot achieve the miracle of faith. Why, she cries out in protest, was God created in the image of man? Why was God not shaped in the image of a woman? God has always been male, authoritarian, and it is this that makes life on earth so perverted and death so unnatural. "We should have imagined life as created in the birth-pain of God the Mother." [13] Her outcry is an expression of her desperate need to believe. She wants to regain her religious faith so she can recover her power to feel. She is sick

---

[12] Eugene O'Neill, *Nine Plays*. New York: The Modern Library, 1952, p. 523.
[13] *Ibid.*, p. 524.

of sickness and desires no more tragic complications in her life. She wants to bear children.

After six months of marriage to Sam Evans, she finds herself happily pregnant; she is soon to experience fulfillment in motherhood; but then tragic complications again enter into her life. Her mother-in-law, in a scene reminiscent of Ibsen's *Ghosts,* reveals to her the dreadful secret that there is a taint of insanity in the Evans family. Mrs. Evans tells Nina how, when she was bearing Sam, she

> used to wish I'd gone out deliberate in our first year, without my husband know-ing, and picked a man, a healthy male to breed by, same's we do with stock, to give the man I loved a healthy child. And if I didn't love the other man nor him me where would be the harm? Then God would whisper: "It'd be a sin, adultery, the worst sin!" But after He'd gone I'd argue back again to myself, then we'd have a healthy child, I needn't be afraid . . . . But I was too afraid of God then to have ever done it! [14]

But for Nina, who does not believe in God the Father, the act would not be difficult. Mrs Evans has herself ceased to believe in God, purged of her faith by long suffering. Living "with poor folks that was being punished for no sins of their own, and me being punished with them for no sin but loving much," [15] she has stopped worrying about what God demanded of her. Though belonging to an older generation, she sums up with painfully earned common sense the naturalistic morality that governed the mind of the twenties, the hedonistic rule of conduct that is also expressed in *The Sun Also Rises* and *A Farewell to Arms.* "Being happy," she says, "that's the nearest we can ever come to knowing what's good! Being happy, that's good! The rest is just talk!" [16] In her considered judgment, it is Nina's plain duty to make Sam happy. Whatever she does, let the world call it by what-ever bad name it will, which contributes to that end is "good."

When Darrell arrives, she tells him the whole case history of the Evans family and how she had the child she was bearing aborted. She points out that he was partly responsible, like God the Father, in making this mess. Then comes her plea for another child, eugenically conceived. She appeals to him to give her the courage to go ahead with her plan. What she has in mind is to select "a healthy male about whom she cared nothing" and have a child by him "that Sam would believe was his child . . . ." [17] Confronted with this plea, Darrell finds that his scientific intellect refuses to function.

[14] *Ibid.,* p. 545.
[15] *Ibid.,* p. 546.
[16] *Ibid.,* p. 546.
[17] *Ibid.,* p. 567.

Through the use of the interior monologue, O'Neill discloses the hidden tangle of impulses motivating both Nina and Ned Darrell. Why, the latter asks himself, can he not view the whole affair as simply an experiment? Why can he not offer himself as a guinea pig and still remain the disinterested and uninvolved neurological observer? In a professional tone, though his pulse beats fast and he is filled with feverish desire, he recommends that it is her duty to find a healthy father for Sam's child. It would be insanely cruel and stupid, beside, to let Sam know the truth, for then all possibility of making him happy would be destroyed. Her duty toward her husband in this case is clear. Nina, who has already resolved inwardly to snatch at happiness regardless of moral considerations, says: "It's adultery. It's wrong."[18] He finally perceives that she has chosen him as the ideal guinea pig. When she tells him that she would be humbly grateful for this service, Ned Darrell, the dedicated scientist, is carried away by his irrational craving for happiness. Falling on his knees (a symbolic act of surrender and an acknowledgment of her power over him), he takes her hand in both of his and kisses it with a sob. That is how this eugenic covenant is sealed. He must be her good friend, but he must not fall in love with her.

The experiment proves biologically successful but, alas, it does not work out according to scientific expectations. Nina is transfigured by this experience of love's fulfillment. Now that she feels Ned's child stirring in her womb, the world seems perfect; she knows the blessedness of consummation and the peace that passeth understanding. She wishes to get a divorce from Sam, but Ned at this point is determined not to be diverted from his medical career; his love for her must not stand in the way of his professional advancement. He wants to remain objective, to live up to the agreement they had made, which, of course, ruled out the madness of love. Darrell declares: "Romantic imagination! It has ruined more lives than all the diseases! Other diseases, I should say! It's a form of insanity!"[19] The profound physical attraction he feels for her, he argues, as if reason had a say in the matter, is not love. Refusing to sacrifice his career as a scientist, he flees for safety to Europe.

Once her child is born, Nina is calm and contented. She now respects her husband, who has become an aggressive and successful businessman, and can give herself to him without revulsion. How queerly things work out, she thinks to herself, all for the best. She does not feel in the least wicked because of what she has done in deceiving her husband. In the meantime, Darrell, who cannot efface the memory of Nina in the arms of other men

[18] *Ibid.*, p. 569.
[19] *Ibid.*, p. 584.

abroad and who no longer cares about promoting his career, comes back and demands that Nina go off with him. The tables are neatly turned. But there is Sam to be considered – and the baby, whose happiness comes first with her. When Darrell angrily asks why Sam should get everything while he gets nothing, Nina reminds him that he possesses her love. He can become her lover again. "Sam will never know . . . . And as long as we can love each other without danger to him, I feel that he owes that to us for all we've done for him."[20]

The experiment in eugenics that was supposed to exclude the irrational element of love leads to an ironic aftermath. Ned is forced to accept Nina's terms; he cannot help himself. Nina is the new woman, no longer held back by social conventions or moral scruples, concerned solely with her quest for happiness. She watches the three men sitting in her home, Sam, her husband, Ned, her lover, and Charles Marsden, a father-figure who is strongly attached to his mother and who fears the contaminating power of sex. In an interior monologue that marks one of the high points of the play, she reveals her thoughts:

My three men! . . . I feel their desires converge in me! . . . to form one complete beautiful male desire which I absorb . . . and am whole . . . they dissolve in me, their life is my life . . . I am pregnant with the three! . . . husband! . . . lover! . . . father! . . . and the fourth man! . . . little man! . . . little Gordon! . . . he is mine too! . . . that makes it perfect! . . .[21]

Nina at thirty-five has reached the full bloom of her womanhood, but she has now come to a point where she is tired of this endless feverish struggle to achieve happiness. She feels the dread approach of middle age; the age of forty is a time when "a woman has finished living."[22] The violent passion of her love for Darrell has subsided. Lacking the courage to demand that she give him all, he had bitterly resigned himself to sharing her, and the compromise resulted in corrupting his character. But why, Nina reflects, is it her fault that he has lost his grip on life! No woman "can make a man happy who has no purpose in life!"[23] Only Charles Marsden does not suffer from the debilitating fevers of the flesh, and Nina recognizes that he would make a perfect lover for her old age when she was past all passion. Ten years later, we see a Nina who is battling to stave off the ravages of time. She endeavors to enlist Ned's aid in her plot to break up her son's marriage but he refuses to do her bidding. He has learned his lesson. She must not

---

[20] *Ibid.*, p. 612–613.
[21] *Ibid.*, p. 616.
[22] *Ibid.*, p. 619.
[23] *Ibid.*, p. 620.

interfere in the lives of others as if she were God. Life is not governed by reason. Life, declares Darrell, "is something in one cell that doesn't need to think!" [24]

Foiled in her attempt to keep possession of her son, Nina turns to Marsden for comfort. After Sam dies and her son leaves her, she decides to go back to her father's home and, with Charlie for companionship, revert to the peace of childhood. Darrell returns to the study of unicellular life that floats in the sea and is not afflicted with the all-too-human but disastrous hunger for happiness. Laughing up at the sky, he cries out: "Oh, God, so deaf and dumb and blind! . . . teach me to be resigned to be an atom!" [25]

If *Strange Interlude* is shot through with intimations of Freudian complexes, as is true to an even greater degree of *Mourning Becomes Electra,* a modern version of the Oedipus-Electra theme, the portrayal of Nina Leeds is invested with universal appeal. In this play O'Neill shows how the moral certitudes of the old faith have been overthrown and how the various characters react, each in his own way, to the inexorable pressure of instinct. When man was originally close to Nature, able freely to statisfy his instinctual needs, he suffered from no neurotic disorders (a point that Malinowski confirms in his anthropological study of the Melanesian Islanders), but once civilization supervened he became the victim of repression. Like Ibsen in *The Wild Duck,* O' Neill is convinced that it is dangerous, since man is not God, to interfere in human lives. Though O'Neill valued the light of understanding psychoanalysis shed on the irrational nature of man, he was not as a playwright bound by the canons of Freudian orthodoxy. Much as he respected the contributions made by science, he felt that science was of limited efficacy in dealing with the aspirations of the human soul and its pursuit of the will-o'-the-wisp of happiness. Though he diagnosed the neurotic sickness of our time and warned against the danger of yielding to the insidious romantic myth of love, he nevertheless made it clear that the scientific outlook is no safeguard against "the disease" of romantic love.

In that strangely haunting play, *The Great God Brown,* which was brought out on the stage in 1925, before *Strange Interlude* was written and produced, O'Neill offers another complex interpretation of the erotic nature of man. Each of us, he seems to believe, is a bundle of conflicting impulses and appetencies, good and evil, noble and base, cynical and spiritually exalted. That is the conflict which rages in the heart of Dion Anthony (a combination of Dionysus, the God of intoxication and instinctual abandon, and St. Anthony, the archetype of ascetic denial). His efforts to paint having

24 *Ibid.,* p. 680.
25 *Ibid.,* p. 680.

come to naught, he proceeds deliberately to wreck his life. Dissolute, reckless, he neglects his wife and children and consorts with a prostitute. Spiritually he feels homeless, alienated, despairing, lost. The woman he married is the incarnation of the dutiful but commonplace wife and devoted mother, who has no great capacity for passion, no awareness of his real, yearning, agonized self. Unbroken in spirit, driven by a demon of self-destructive fury, Dion seeks the nepenthe of forgetfulness in the arms of Cybel, in whose presence he can remove his social mask and be his "natural" self.

O'Neill makes his creative intention clear in his description of each of the characters. Whereas Brown, the embodiment of the conventional, is practical, conformist, unimaginative, Dion is nervous, tense, divided within himself, wearing the mask of a defiant and sensual Pan. He represents the artist in American society who is persecuted because of his rebellious genius. He is the sensitive, suffering pilgrim whose quest for spontaneity and genuineness in love is thwarted. He loves love but is afraid to love. Though people mouth the words of love they are worn and shabby commonplaces, emptied of content, for in reality love is done to death in this hypocritical world and people, whatever they may pretend to the contrary, walk alone in darkness, unable to communicate with each other. Since his wife cannot love or even get to know the real Dion Anthony, he resolves never to let her see his "true self." He will love her, as it were, by proxy. His mask becomes more mocking and defiant, its Pan quality turning Mephistophelean. Here are two strangers yoked together in marriage, indulging in an elaborate charade, a game of make-believe.

At the home of Cybel he finds forgetfulness, understanding, compassion. Cybel, who wears the mask of a heavily rouged, professional prostitute, is a simple, genuine person at heart. She is like "an unmoved idol of Mother Earth,"[26] calm, profound, forgiving. When Dion, whose mask now wears an expression of diabolical cruelty, hears that Brown has started to "keep" Cybel, he betrays his jealousy, but Cybel tells him: "What makes you pretend you think love is so important, anyway? It's just one of a lot of things you do to keep life living."[27] It takes all kinds of love to make a world. Life is not important. "There's millions of it born every second. Life can cost too much even for a sucker to afford it – like everything else. And it's not sacred – only the you inside is. The rest is earth."[28] She bids him not to be afraid: life is only a game. After he leaves, Cybel cries out piercingly: "What's the use of bearing children? What's the use of giving birth to

[26] *Ibid.*, p. 335.
[27] *Ibid.*, p. 336.
[28] *Ibid.*, p. 337.

death?"[29] The motifs of love and death are fused in her anguished outburst of affirmation at the end: "Always spring comes again bearing life! Always again! Always, always forever again!"[30]

Convinced that it was impossible for modern man to find a faith that would satisfy the demands of the rational mind, O'Neill labored to produce a form of the tragic vision that would not be rooted in a God-centered universe. He exalted the realistic, tough-minded, truth-seeking spirit, though fully aware of man's inescapable limitations of knowledge, his inability to grasp the absolute truth. The solution lies not in apotheosizing the mystery that defies the best efforts of the Promethean intellect but in abandoning the illusion of the supernatural. Like Hardy and Dreiser, O'Neill pictures the universe as basically amoral. God is an efflux of energy that is infinite but, from the human point of view, meaningless. In such a godless universe, love is stripped of the aura of the sacred. O'Neill's naturalistic nihilism conditions his depiction of the dialectic of love and sex. The heart of his message as a playwright emerges in *Welded,* when Michael Cape voices his realization: "To love the truth of life – to accept it and be exalted – that's the one faith left to us!"[31]

It is also the one faith left to Hemingway, whose fiction faithfully represents the excesses and upheavals in the sexual morality of a given historical period. His postwar heroes must live dangerously and strive for immediate fulfillment in sexual love as the only meaningful reality in a world that has gone berserk with the lust to kill and destroy.

---

[29] *Ibid.,* p. 339.
[30] *Ibid.,* p. 375.
[31] Eugene O'Neill, *All God's Chillun Got Wings* and *Welded,* p. 151.

CHAPTER VIII

THE HEMINGWAY CULT OF LOVE

The Hemingway hero, though he is sensitive and feels deeply the pains and penalties of life, is resolved not to give in to his feelings. He holds himself under tight control. He has worked out a code of behavior of his own, a "grace under pressure," which enables him to bear up with honor in a situation of danger. *The Sun Also Rises,* with its striking epigraph, "You are all a lost generation," a remark made by Gertrude Stein, the high priestess of the expatriates in Paris during the twenties, presents one version of the Hemingway hero. The incapacitating wound Jake has received in the genitals is intended to symbolize how a whole generation of the young have been emasculated and crippled by the war. Jake, like his boon companions, is in revolt against the mores of middle-class society, but it is a revolt that is despairing in its negativity. The novel exemplifies the theme of futility, the mood of reckless nihilism that infected the lost generation. Jake is the victim of a hopeless love for Brett, a love that cannot in the nature of things be consummated. In the wasteland of the twenties both the life of the spirit and that of the senses have been perverted. As in the fictive world of the jazz age that Fitzgerald so luminously portrayed, the old distinctions between good and evil have broken down. The horror of war strips the experience of sexual love of the need for moral sanctions; the belief in the sanctity of life has been destroyed. The Hemingway protagonist may regret committing a given act because it brought about a series of unfortunate consequences but not because he has violated some moral principles. He is not deceived or held back by the socially established categories of good and evil, and yet he abides by a moral code of his own.

Daring for its time in its attack on the sexual morality of the past, *The Sun Also Rises* sums up the bitter disillusionment of the postwar younger generation. Despite their hard-boiled talk, their alcoholism and carefree promiscuity, the chief characters in this novel suffer from all sorts of mental torment and fears. Brett, who sleeps with a number of different men, has her moments of wretched disgust with the kind of loose, aimless life she is leading. In her sane moments of reflection she realizes that sex is not everything. She knows, too, that one must pay in the end for all the things one does. Jake is fully aware of her promiscuous nature, but there is nothing he can do about it. He tries to treat his infirmity as a joke. If he had not met Brett, he could have borne his misfortune with some measure of fortitude; life would not have been so bad for him. As he broods at night about his wound and his love for Brett and the Catholic Church, misery overcomes him and he starts to cry. "It is awfully easy to be hard-boiled about everything in the daytime, but at night it is another thing." [1]

When Jake wonders whether, despite his disabling wound, they could not live together, Brett decides firmly against it, for she knows that she would deceive him with everybody in sight and that he could not bear it. That is the way she is constituted. They love each other, true, but what is the use of bucking an impossible state of affairs. Then comes the scene of the riotous fiesta in Spain. Brett, though she is heartily ashamed of herself, falls passionately in love with Romero, the young bull-fighter. She cannot overcome her passion for him. She is honest enough to confess all this to Jake. She is not trying to justify her behavior; inside of her she feels like a bitch but she must go ahead just the same – and she does. Like a twentieth-century Hedda Gabler but without her romantic illusions, she has always done what she wanted. Though the affair with Romero brings her some happiness, she finally decides to leave him – for his sake. This self-sacrificing gesture makes her feel good. "You know," she says, "it makes one feel rather good deciding not to be a bitch." [2] When Jake agrees, she adds: "It's sort of what we have instead of God." [3]

Thus *The Sun Also Rises* portrays characters of the lost generation who work out their own moral code. They are willing to accept stoically whatever is coming to them; if they give up something then they get something else in return. Jake meditates: "You paid some way for everything that was any good." [4] What he craves is not knowledge but some means of mastering the terribly complex art of living in the world. If the Hemingway hero seems to be irresponsible when judged by conventional standards of good and evil, he is, for all his rebelliousness, endeavoring to define and abide by his own moral values. Jake reflects: "That was morality; things that made you dis-

---

[1] Ernest Hemingway, *The Sun Also Rises*. New York: The Modern Library, 1926, p. 35.
[2] *Ibid.*, p. 256.
[3] *Ibid.*, p. 257.
[4] *Ibid.*, p. 153.

gusted afterward. No, that must be immorality."[5] The sense of spiritual lostness that dominates the twenties serves to account for the sexual be- havior of Lady Brett Ashley, who can forget the crushing burden of time only by heavy drinking and fornication. She is among the first of American fictional heroines who is promiscuous without any feeling of wrong-doing or remorse.

Hemingway, like D. H. Lawrence, hates the destructive type of woman who seeks to dominate the male. Though he never descends to the extreme of misogynistic vilification to be found in Strindberg's plays and novels, he detests in his own way the kind of woman, especially the American pos- sessive female, who seeks to subjugate the spirit of the lordly male. He sees her as the modern Delilah, the castrating demon. Women of this description are notoriously unable to love, and man must protect himself against their cunning destructiveness. By way of contrast, Hemingway admires and ideal- izes the type of woman who surrenders her individuality, who gives her all, to the man she loves. A character like Catherine Barkley, in *A Farewell to Arms*, embodies this romantic cult of feminine devotion and self-abnega- tion.

What starts out as a casual erotic affair turns into genuine love. At the be- ginning of the novel we see the hero, an American attached to the ambulance force on the Italian front, sitting with his friends in a bawdy house. Sex and drink, drink and sex, these are the major absorbing interests of the officers with whom he associates. When he is given his leave, he visits many Italian cities and spends his time chiefly with prostitutes. He tries to explain to the Italian priest at the base why he did not visit Abruzzi while he was on leave. "We did not do the things we wanted to do," he says; "we never did such things."[6] Instead of going to the high places in the mountains where there was snow, he went to large cities where there were cafés and hotel rooms; he regularly got drunk and woke up the next morning with a strange woman lying beside him. Drunkenness and sex were the only things that could make him temporarily forget the ongoing horror of war. His main object in life at this time is not to think, not to care, not to become emotionally involved. Sex – that was the only drug powerful enough to narcotize his memory of the senseless inferno of death and destruction in which he was caught up. The orgasm is his affirmation of the will to live. Only the nights of love-making are real.

Then he meets Catherine Barkley and feels the disturbing, at first unwel-

[5] *Ibid.,* p. 153.
[6] Ernest Hemingway, *A Farewell to Arms.* New York: The Modern Library, 1929, p. 13.

come, but irresistible awakening of the binding emotion of love. From her he learns that the man she had loved and planned to marry was killed in the war. Like Nina Leeds in *Strange Interlude*, she bitterly regrets not having married him or at least given herself to him physically. Had she known it would turn out this way, nothing would have held her back. The war has transformed her whole outlook on life. When her lover was blown to bits, that, for her, was the end of everything – the end of hope, the end of faith, the end of her dream of happiness to come in the future. Now she wants desperately to be loved, to be told that she is loved. Frederick makes the response she craves, though he thinks she is a little crazy.

It was all right if she was. I did not care what I was getting into. This was better than going every evening to the house for officers where the girls climbed all over you and put your cap on backward as a sign of affection between their trips upstairs with brother officers. I knew I did not love Catherine Barkley nor had any idea of loving her. This was a game, like bridge, in which you said things instead of playing cards.[7]

He will play the game of love according to the rules of romantic rhetoric.

Catherine, however, is basically too honest a person to allow the game of make-believe to go on. She tells him that he does not have to pretend that he loves her. Why lie? She has satisfied her intense emotional need, and that is that. In the meantime, the war goes on. Frederick is sent to the front. A shell strikes his dugout and he is wounded. Rinaldi comes to visit him at the hospital, complaining that there are no new girls in the bawdy house. He teases Frederick about Catherine Barkley, the English goddess, who is fit only for worship. A doctor, a cynical sensualist, he harbors no illusions about women. They are all alike. "There is only one difference between taking a girl who has always been good and a woman. With a girl it is painful."[8] That is how he disposes of the romantic nonsense of idealized love. Love is but a contrived euphemism for the physiology of sex. Though Frederick, too, has few or no illusions left, he cannot share this crude, debunking version of love. He cannot believe in God, though he confesses that sometimes he is afraid of Him in the long stretches of the night. His fundamental trouble is that he cannot love and he cannot believe. It is not made clear whether he cannot love because he cannot believe or cannot believe because he cannot love.

Then Catherine arrives in the hospital where he is a patient and she gives herself to him freely. When it is over she asks, "Now do you believe I love

[7] *Ibid.,* pp. 31–32.
[8] *Ibid.,* p. 71.

you?"[9] Hemingway realistically analyzes the inner motives of Frederick, his reaction of dismay to this overwhelming experience of love. "God knows I had not wanted to fall in love with her. I had not wanted to fall in love with anyone."[10] He had made the effort to safeguard himself against this treacherous invasion of feeling, this painful disease of love, but his heart, now "love's feverish citadel," as Keats calls it, has at last been stormed and captured.

Ironically enough, the room in the hospital is their secret bridal chamber where they enjoy their unconsecrated honeymoon. They talk about the fine children they will have. Catherine, who longs to feel that Frederick belongs entirely to her, is curious about the other women he has "loved," the girls he has slept with. Do the girls who are paid for the use of their body, she wants to know, mention the price? Do they say they love the man? In order to spare her feelings, Frederick lies to her. The girls, he informs her, say and do what the man asks them to.

Catherine represents the Hemingway woman, the mistress who is prepared to yield everything, including her sense of selfhood, for the sake of her lover. She is all sacrifice and devotion. "I want what you want," she declares. "There isn't any me any more. Just what you want."[11] This total capitulation of the heroine seems to meet with Hemingway's hearty approval. He fails to realize that the mutuality of love is dependent on the enhancement not only of the male but also of the female self, but he does show the degree to which this essentially romantic conception of love is conditioned by the apocalyptic background of war and the demoralizing fear of sudden death.

Ferguson, also a nurse and a friend of Catherine, foreshadows the tragic ending of the novel. Catherine and Frederick, she is convinced, will never get married; they will either quarrel or die. "Fight or die. That's what people do. They don't marry."[12] This is her bitter cry. She is morally outraged by this violation, caused by the war, of the normal course of love's fulfillment. She begs Frederick not to get Catherine into trouble, saddled with a war baby. But they are too deliriously happy to heed her warning. To be physically close together – that was enough to make them happy. Their interlude of tender, rapturous love-making offers them a temporary relief from the thought of war – the screaming shells, the muddy trenches, the carnage. No question of sin or guilt arises to mar their idyllic union. They felt married

[9] *Ibid.*, p. 99.
[10] *Ibid.*, p. 100.
[11] *Ibid.*, p. 113.
[12] *Ibid.*, p. 115.

that first day when she had arrived. Frederick wanted to marry her but she feared that, because of legal complications, they would be separated, and under no circumstances would she let that happen. Frederick thinks: "I wanted us to be married really because I worried about having a child if I thought about it, but we pretended to ourselves we were married and did not worry much and I suppose I enjoyed not being married, really." [13] Even though he is deeply in love with her, he is reluctant to give up his freedom.

But Catherine, for her part, is wholly dedicated to the ideal of love, without regard for moral or religious sanctions. She remarks: "There isn't any me. I'm you. Don't make up a separate me." [14] That is one facet of the theme of love stressed in the novel: she feels married, married to Frederick, and she is trying hard to make him a good wife. After that first shattering experience with the young man she had loved, she is determined henceforth to take no chances with life. She will clutch at happiness now, in the living present, while it is still there to be enjoyed. When Frederick protests that he wishes to make sure of her future if anything happened to him in the war or if she became pregnant, she has her answer ready: "There's no way to be married except by church or state. We are married privately. You see, darling, it would mean everything to me if I had any religion. But I haven't any religion." [15] As in the case of Nina Leeds, the utter loss of faith in God justifies the abandonment of the old moral covenants and restraints.

There we have it: Hemingway underlines the cruel necessity that compels men and women in wartime to reach out desperately for fulfillment in love while they still have the opportunity, lest they be destroyed and left with nothing at the end. The emergency conditions of war, the saturnalia of slaughter, the dreaded imminence of death, and their consciousness of the absence of God, all this makes the legal or clerical stamp of approval on their relationship seem utterly irrelevant to the young couple. The fact that they are in love is enough to hallow their union. The only thing they fear is deprivation of love, the trauma of being separated; the only true happiness lies in being together. As Catherine phrases it, without sacrilegious intention: "You're my religion," she tells Frederick. "You're all I've got." [16] Why must he make an honest woman of her? She feels no sense of shame or wrong-doing. "You can't be ashamed of something if you're only happy and proud of it." [17] This is the moral code that Catherine lives up to. Whatever may happen to them, she has plighted troth and will never leave him.

[13] *Ibid.*, p. 122.
[14] *Ibid.*, p. 122.
[15] *Ibid.*, p. 123.
[16] *Ibid.*, p. 123.
[17] *Ibid.*, p. 123.

In this time of war-madness, it is essential for them to snatch at happiness before it is smashed to pieces by the hand of death.

During his period of recuperation, Frederick spends his leisure hours at the café, waiting for the night of love with Catherine at the hospital. The war continues; perhaps it will go on forever. At one point Catherine confesses fearfully: "I'm afraid of the rain because sometimes I see me dead in it."[18] The rain (the novel is saturated with the misery of rainfall as if all of Nature wept for all the lives to be lost in battle) casts a shadow on the radiance of their love. Summer passes. Frederick is to be called back. When Catherine hears the bad news, she is prepared to go away with him during his short leave. Life, she says, is not hard to manage "when you've nothing to lose."[19]

It is then she lets him know that she is three months pregnant. She strives to behave strictly according to the code they believe in – to be courageous and controlled, not messy and soft. She asks him if he is angry or feels trapped, and he replies:

"Maybe a little. But not by you."
"I didn't mean by me. You mustn't be stupid. I mean trapped at all."
"You always feel trapped biologically."[20]

Catherine reminds him how bravely she has tried to be the way he wants her to be. They must not quarrel and lose what they have. "Because there's only us two and in the world there's all the rest of them. If anything comes between us we're gone and then they have us."[21] In this time of tragic trouble, they have formed an alliance against a hostile world. Love, and love alone, can enable them to hold out against the enmity of the world, the concentrated malice of life.

But the menace represented by the world in Catherine's remark is not to be foiled or outwitted. Frederick is scheduled to return to the fighting front. In Milan on the night when he is about to leave, the fog turns to rain. When they decide to go to a hotel near the railroad station, Catherine tells him she feels like a whore, but a bit later the mood passes and she says: "I wish we could do something really sinful . . . . Everything we do seems so innocent and simple. I can't believe we do anything wrong."[22] This is the private "morality" that sustains their love. Experience has not corrupted their innocence or at least Catherine's innocence; they feel happy being "married" to each other. The rhythm of love is speeded up by the relentless pressure of time,

[18] *Ibid.*, p. 135.
[19] *Ibid.*, p. 146.
[20] *Ibid.*, p. 148.
[21] *Ibid.*, p. 149.
[22] *Ibid.*, p. 164.

by the sound of "Time's winged chariot hurrying near." Life hurries along at an absurdly fast, hectic pace.

When Frederick gets back to the front, he meets the irrepressible Rinaldi, who proceeds to bait him in friendly fashion about such exalted matters as love and conscience and virtue. Rinaldi's earthy cynicism has not undergone any change. A confirmed materialist, he believes frankly in living for the pleasures of the moment. Apart from his professional work as a surgeon, there are only two things he likes: drink and sex. When Frederick assures him he will find other things, he replies: "No. We never get anything. We are born with all we have and we never learn."[23] He reviles Saint Paul for leading a lustly life of the senses and then suddenly repenting and drawing up austere rules against all those who follow the promptings of instinctual desire.

Then comes a vivid description of battle. When Frederick hears Gino declare that there must be no talk of losing the war, that "What has been done this summer cannot have been done in vain," he indulges in a passage of introspection that brilliantly highlights the debased meaning of love and idealism in a time of war.

I was always embarrassed by the words sacred, glorious, and sacrifice and the expression in vain. We had heard them, sometimes standing in the rain, almost out of earshot, so that only the shouted words came through, and had read them, on proclamations that were slapped up by billposters over other procla- mations, now for a long time, and I had seen nothing sacred, and the things that were glorious had no glory and the sacrifices were like the stockyards at Chi- cago if nothing was done with the meat except to bury it. There were many words that you could not stand to hear and finally only the names of places had dignity . . . . Abstract words such as glory, honor, courage, or hallow were ob- scene beside the concrete names of villages, the numbers of roads, the names of rivers, the numbers of regiments and the dates.[24]

Again the rain starts falling heavily. During the panicky retreat of the Italian troops Frederick reaches the river where the carabanieri are posted, selecting victims, chiefly officers, who are shot after a brief inquiry. Fre- derick has no intention of becoming another victim. He ducks, dives into the river, and the current carries him away. He has cast off his social moorings. Now he is alone against the world. The horror of war, his military obligations, his anger and frustrations are all washed away by this plunge – a baptism of rebirth – into the river. "I was not against them. I was through."[25] It was no longer his concern. That part of his life was over. He

23 *Ibid.*, p. 181.
24 *Ibid.*, p. 196.
25 *Ibid.*, p. 248.

would have to stop thinking. "I was not made to think. I was made to eat. My God, yes. Eat and drink and sleep with Catherine."[26]

Once he finds Catherine he is no longer alone. Now he can bear the difficult ordeal of the night, the night which "can be a dreadful time for lonely people once their loneliness has started."[27] He has only Catherine to depend on; she makes up his world, his life. He does not believe in the war and he cannot believe in religion, though Hemingway seems to intimate that love is in itself a kind of substitute for religion. Frederick and Catherine escape to Switzerland and there wait for the birth of their child. They are still in no hurry to get married. It would not do at present. Once the child is born they will sign the nuptial bond, but there is no urgency in the matter. The war stands in the way. Frederick feels happy being with Catherine and not seeing other people. Without her he is lost. When she is finally brought to the hospital, Frederick waits in the hall and, unbeliever though he is, prays for her. She is having a hard time of it in the delivery room. When he sees her lying in the grip of pain he thinks:

And this was the price you paid for sleeping together. This was the end of the trap. This was what people got for loving each other . . . . So now they got her in the end. You never get away with anything. Get away hell! It would have been the same if we had been married fifty times.[28]

The moral implications are clearly underscored: this is not a punishment visited upon Catherine because of her sinfulness. Her condition has nothing to do with morality or the sacrament of marriage. It is life that cunningly prepares and springs the trap, and sooner or later everyone is caught in it. No one ever gets away with anything.

After the Caesarian operation (the child is stillborn), Catherine dies. Her death makes Frederick realize the sinister and implacable hostility of the powers leagued against him. He broods:

You die. You did not know what it was about. You never had time to learn. They threw you in and told you the rules and the first time they caught you off base they killed you. Or they killed you gratuitously like Aymo. Or gave you the syphilis like Rinaldi. But they killed you in the end. You could count on that. Stay around and they would kill you.[29]

What does the pronoun "they" stand for? The forces of Nature, the irrational rules of life, the brutal and stupid oppression of the world? A clue is provided by Frederick's recollection of what he had once observed: men are

[26] *Ibid.*, p. 249.
[27] *Ibid.*, pp. 266–267.
[28] *Ibid.*, pp. 341–342.
[29] *Ibid.*, p. 350.

like the ants he had seen scurrying on a log placed on top of a fire. He watched their frantic but futile efforts to escape; a few managed to get away from the incinerating flames but most of them did not know where they were going and fell off plump into the fire. Life is like that ,and love ,too – a trap, a blind, feverish rushing hither and thither, only to drop finally into the immolating fire. Catherine, as she lies dying, says, "It's just a dirty trick." [30]

In *A Farewell to Arms* Hemingway painted a world that is caught in the fiery vortex of war, a world instinct with hostility, violence, and destructiveness. His leading characters, beset by danger on all sides, may be killed at any moment. Courageous despite the fear that grips them, they are compelled to grasp their pleasures hastily while they can. Forced to live in the cataclysmic climate of war, they adopt an *ad hoc* morality suited to the circumstances of the time and their immediate pressing needs. Since life is a series of battles in a war that never ends and that can never be won, one must summon forth the courage to endure and the courage to love.

The literary importance of *A Farewell to Arms* does not derive from the fact that it deals with an "immoral" love situation. After all, this is not a casual wartime amour. Hemingway deliberately stresses the point that the catastrophe which befalls Catherine has nothing to do with her unmarried state. There is no connection between the pleasures of love-making in Milan and the narrow pelvis that kills the unwed mother in the pains of child-birth. Hemingway, like Dreiser, contends that there is no moral law at work punishing the sinful and rewarding the virtuous. But all Hemingway's "immoral" heroines, whether demonic like Brett Ashley or devoted and self-effacing like Catherine, live under unusual or emergency conditions. Even in *For Whom the Bell Tolls,* written at a time when Hemingway's social and political values had undergone a marked change, he presents a hero who is obsessed by the thought of death and who is keenly attached to the pleasures of the body. Maria in the novel belongs to the type of heroine Hemingway describes in lyrical, eulogistic terms. Etherealized to the point of fantasy and yet capable of responding sexually, she is without a personality of her own, merely a submissive shadow of the man she loves. The victim of Fascist bestiality, she symbolizes the ideal of loves in an age of fraticidal horror.

Hemingway's conception of love and its relation to sex remained fairly consistent throughout his writing career. *Across the River and into the Trees* (1950) reads like an ingenious parody of *A Farewell to Arms.* There are the same interlinked motifs of love and death; the horror of warfare is again contrasted with the only happiness man can possess on earth, the love of a

[30] *Ibid.,* p. 354.

beautiful woman. One recognizes, too, the familiar picture of the Hemingway hero, only now he is fifty-one years old, tough, hardened, tight-lipped, courageous in the face of suffering and the knowledge of his imminent death. He realizes that the young Italian girl of nineteen who loves him devotedly is his last love. He has fought in two wars and been, like Hemingway, wounded in many parts of his body, but he still keeps faith with "the code." Pain is to be borne with fortitude, love is not to be intellectually analyzed. Love can only be expressed by the simple phrase "I love you" and by the language of the body.

The weakness of the novel is that, unlike *A Farewell to Arms,* it lacks a dramatically integrated body of action. The tone is reminiscent and nostalgic. The Colonel maintains his nihilistic stance with a show of serenity. It would be good to believe in the doctrine of the resurrection of the body and the idea of immortality, but there is no point in it since there is nothing after death. There is only the good earth on which to exercise the virtue of courage and enjoy the blessedness of love. Apart from the brief attempts at philosophizing, there is no story, no conflict, to speak of: the aging Colonel visits his beloved, this beautiful young girl Renata in Venice, before he goes off on a week-end of shooting ducks. On the way back after the good hunting, the heart attack he knew would come finally strikes him and he meets the enemy in good order.

Having resigned himself to death, aware that the time left to him is very short, the Colonel treasures the things that are good: the art of drinking, the art of being friends with simple, trustworthy men, and the art of love. He would rather not give in to love, not surrender to this emotional weakness, but inwardly he knows that there is no happiness when there is no love. He considers himself fortunate in being able to enjoy this love of Renata, who conforms to the Hemingway image of the ideal woman. Like the lovers in *A Farewell to Arms,* they discuss the idea of getting married, but this is out of the question. They have no choice open to them except to enjoy themselves in their "one and only life," as the Colonel puts it with cheerful finality.[31] He calls her "daughter," even though this makes their relationship sound like incest, but the thought of sin does not frighten them in the least in the midst of this wicked city. When Renata insists on giving him her painting and he insists that it is not honorable for her to do so, she proceeds to define the code of honor in a manner that is characteristic of the admirable Hemingway heroine: "What you do to give pleasure to another whom you

---

[31] Ernest Hemingway, *Across the River and into the Trees.* New York: Charles Scribner's Sons, 1950, p. 94.

love is most honorable." [32] That is how the question of morality is handled. The high point in the novel is the scene of passionate and despairing love-making in the gondola. The woman declares that he is the discoverer and she is only "the unknown country." It is the woman who wishes to be taken, who is eager to be "possessed."

Hemingway in his fiction exalts "the natural" man. It is the animal in man that is holy. Nature is not a moral teacher but it will not betray the heart that loves her truly. Viewed from this perspective, Hemingway appears as the spokesman of a romantic naturalism that effects a transvaluation of the conventional notions of good and evil. The characters he presents are intensely concerned about their instinctual urges. The myth of romantic love as passion spiritualized, is debunked. The natural man has come into his own and is not to be cheated of his erotic happiness by moral taboos. Complete fulfillment in sexual love is what counts; the rest is the product of illusion and neurotic evasion.

It is not at all surprising that the Dionysian celebration of carnal love is coupled with the metaphysics of despair. If many members of the lost generation were sexual libertarians it was because they felt that life was meaningless. In a world given over periodically to the destructive madness of war, what was there to believe in? The only abiding reality was the life of the senses. Why credit the sickly lie of Agape? Sex was at least quiveringly alive and pleasurable and therefore good. Suffering from the crippling effects of the war, the Hemingway heroes and heroines are devotees of an Eros who rejects the traditional categories of good and evil. [33] Convinced that meaninglessness is ultimately the whole of the human story, they glory in their nihilism but do not, except in a few cases, give in to suicidal despair. Somehow they derive some measure of vitality and even exhilaration from this very feeling of spiritual lostness. They talk spiritedly of doomsday but they do not actually believe it will come; they continue to live with wild feverishness and élan. What remains consistent in their rebellious attitude is their faith in the primacy of biological as opposed to spiritual values. The clarion call of patriotism, the philosophy of idealism, the teachings of the Christian gospel, the demand for moral responsibility and restraint, all this they condemned as a patent fraud, a monstrous betrayal. The main thing was to strive for happiness on earth, and happiness meant sexual freedom.

[32] *Ibid.,* p. 104.
[33] "In one way or another, the tragic fact of war or the after-effects of social disruption tend to inhibit and betray the normal course of love, not only in *The Sun Also Rises* but also in *A Farewell to Arms, To Have and Have Not, The Fifth Column, For Whom the Bell Tolls,* and *Across the River* and *into the Trees.*" Carlos Baker, *Ernest Hemingway.* Princeton: Princeton University Press, 1956, p. 92.

Hence they angrily repudiated what Ezra Pound called, in "Hugh Selwyn Mauberly," "a botched civilization," "an old bitch gone in the teeth," and concerned themselves with the good of the personal life. Pagan enjoyment, without painful scruples of conscience, is the aim and end of life, the alpha and omega of Hemingway's naturalistic morality. As Hemingway states in *The Sun Also Rises* and *Death in the Afternoon,* what is moral is what causes one to feel good afterwards. It is as simple and uncomplicated as all that.

Yet how does "the code" work out in Hemingway's fiction when applied specifically to matters affecting sexual morality? His protagonists are shown to have reached a point in their development where promiscuous sexual indulgence induces in them no sense of guilt. Nature is the goddess presiding over these rites of love and pleasure is the burden of her enticing song. Love is the supreme, if irrational passion, but it exacts a price that Hemingway's heroes are reluctant to pay; it imposes an irksome limitation on their sense of freedom. Though visiting a whorehouse is in many ways more desirable than the troublesome experience of falling in love, the love of woman remains an exalted value, but it is love that is reduced to the lowest common denominator, the physical.

It is nevertheless unfair to maintain that Hemingway's characters make no distinction between sex and love.[34] They often pretend or assert that no such distinction exists, but love, despite their psychic resistance, overcomes them just the same.[35] It happens to Frederick Henry and it happens to Robert Jordan who, in *For Whom the Bell Tolls,* realizes that there is all the difference in the world between a casual sexual encounter and a genuine

[34] John Killinger argues "that Hemingway's love, even at its most idealistic, is almost always related to sexual intercourse. That is only natural for a Nietzschean apostle who believes not in eternity but in loving the earth; to rob man of God is to make him revert to a kind of animalism, albeit a special kind, and love and copulation are difficult to distinguish from one another on that level. Probably the closest Hemingway's men ever come to a real acceptance of the two-in-one motif is during the act of intercourse." John Killinger, *Hemingway and the Dead Gods.* Lexington: University of Kentucky Press, 1960, p. 95.

[35] One recent study attempts to show how Hemingway's idea of love underwent a series of significant changes in the course of his career. "First he writes in reaction to romantic love without quite accepting his own rejection of it (*The Sun Also Rises* and *A Farewell to Arms*). He accepts eros at all points, in all his works, but eventually he supplements it with agape and finally sees agape as 'the way out.'" (Robert W. Lewis, Jr., *Hemingway on Love.* Austin & London: University of Texas Press, 1965, p. 6.) Even this qualified statement puts the case too strongly. Agape never wins out. Hemingway never abandoned his belief in physical union as the basis of love. When his protagonists are caught in the toils of love, they come to it first through the experience of sex. It is only through the senses that the spirit knows the bliss and the bondage of love.

love relationship, like his feeling for Maria. But though the transfiguration of love does take place, it does not eliminate the fixation on sex. The difference is that between enjoying sex for its own sake and enjoying sex that is accompanied by the feeling of love. Robert Jordan, like Frederick, fights against the lure of love, his mind warning him that this is only a biological trap, but he cannot honestly deny the reality of the love that he feels for Maria.

Actually Hemingway, as we have said, romanticizes the act of love. He clearly demands a great deal of the love relationship, especially on the part of the woman, who, in giving of herself completely, must sacrifice her identity. He emphasizes the precariousness and fatality of love in a world at war. Living in an age of crisis, his characters turn to sexual love for salvation. The old morality is of no account in the final reckoning. Sexual fulfillment in love – that is the sole meaningful reality.

CHAPTER IX

FAULKNER'S WORLD OF LOVE AND SEX

Faulkner expresses his own code of values; there are a number of such old-fashioned virtues as honor, courage, generosity of spirit, and compassion that he admires; but he is too complex a novelist to impose this code on his characters. Intensely curious about people of all sorts, the evil as well as the good, the degenerate as well as the so-called normal, he portrays them with a genuine effort at imaginative understanding of what basically motivates their lives. Even his worst villains, a Popeye, a Flem Snopes, a Jason Compson, is endowed with some redeeming human trait. Even a collection of stories like *Go Down, Moses* bears out the impression of Faulkner's universality of vision. He is aware of the continuing power of the past on the lives of the present generation and its shaping influence on the future. His sense of cultural continuity, his reverent but not uncritical evaluation of the Southern historical past, his respect for the deeply-rooted myths and mores of the folk in Yoknapatawpha, clearly link him in part with the conservative outlook.[1]

The world of the South that Faulkner describes is a white man's world, a virtual feudal order in which the white man is free to sleep with black women, despite the murderous hatred this calls forth on the part of the Negroes. The story of the Negroes is the story of their struggle not only for survival but also for self-respect; they are shown as truly capable of love and sacrifice and devotion as any of the white characters. They are imbued with one quality Faulkner admires: the capacity to suffer and endure. He also admires a man like Isaac McCaslin, "Uncle Ike," the patriarch of the woods, who owns nothing but what he can carry in his pockets and the material he needs for camping out when hunting deer or bear or going

---

[1] "It may well be that Faulkner is closer to Conservatism than to any other paradigm of social organization, but the case will have to be made with account taken of the Faustian drive of his Sutpens and his Snopeses." Allen Guttman, *The Conservative Tradition in America*. New York: Oxford University Press, 1967, p. 74.

fishing. Here is Nature's philosopher, wise in his native simplicity and goodness of heart, owning no property and never coveting possessions, "since
the earth was no man's but all men's, as light and air and weather were."[2]
He voices one ot the major themes in *Go Down, Moses* when he tells the
boy:

Think of all that has happened here, on this earth. All the blood hot and strong
for living, pleasuring, that has soaked back into it. For grieving and suffering
too, of course, but still getting something out of it for all that, because after all
you dont have to continue to bear what you believe is suffering; you can always
choose to stop that, to put an end to that. And even suffering and grieving is
better than nothing; there is only one thing worse than not being alive, and
that's shame. But you cant be alive forever, and you always wear out life long
before you have exhausted the possibilities of living.[3]

In the light of such an all-encompassing tragic vision, sex can be accorded
no exclusive position; it is one of the passions that govern the young, and
frequently the old too, but it is not elevated to the proportions of a special
mystique in the sense that the world is well lost for love, though Faulkner is
able to do justice, as in *Wild Palms*, to that theme of doomed romantic
passion.

But unlike many of the important writers of the lost generation or the
sex-obsessed American novelists who have sprung up in the fifties and
sixties, Faulkner promulgates no mystique of sex. He propounds no thesis
and points no moral. A naturalist in his attempt to depict the human condition in all its fascinating diversity, he does not pass moral judgment on his
characters, however criminal or depraved they may be; they pass judgment,
as it were, on themselves; their fate provides its own tragic commentary. He
is moved by no impelling desire to improve mankind or reform the world.
Like Chekhov, he tries to be "objective," to picture man as he is, regardless
of how he ought to be. Hence he preaches no message of salvation. As he
says: "Maybe the writer has no concept of morality at all, only an integrity
to hold always to what he believes to be the facts and truths of human behavior, not moral standards at all."[4] This does not mean that the novelist
omits the moral dimension entirely. No such thing. In picturing the truth
of human nature as he sees it, in relying solely on the integrity of his imaginative insight, he reveals the consequences of choices and commitments
that are evil. For example, he shows that the instinctual nature of man can-

2 William Faulkner, *Go Home, Moses*. New York: The Modern Library, 1942, p. 3.
3 *Ibid.*, p. 186.
4 Frederick L. Gwynn and Joseph L. Blotner (eds.), *Faulkner in the University*.
Charlottesville: The University of Virginia Press, 1959, p. 267.

not be repressed with impunity, just as he shows that it cannot be indulged with unbridled excess.

Faulkner depicts the horror as well as irrationality of life in the South, the savagery of lust that flows like molten lava beneath the surface of easy-going gentility, the tragic conflicts generated by the forces of Puritan repression. Present in practically all his fiction is the theme of Negro blood as an ancestral and inescapable curse, a source of defilement and guilt. This obsession with the motif of blood, the biological antipathy and yet also fatal attraction between white and black blood, exists not only in the horror-haunted mind of Faulkner but in the collective psyche of the South. In his treatment of love and sex Faulkner, as a naturalist, is sometimes carried away by an overweening faith in the determinism of blood. Love, man's attempt to sublimate the primordial energy of the libido, is foredoomed to failure, for it is based fundamentally on illusion, but it is a noble and precious illusion for all that. In the lurid, surrealist landscape that Faulkner paints with such hallucinatory vividness, sex with its attendant perversions is an oppressive but never dominant reality; it is a compulsion against which conscience and morality struggle in vain.

Faulkner's presentation of love and sex cannot be torn from its organic context of form and treated in isolation as attitudes or abstractions. He is not a novelist of ideas like Sartre. Nor is he to be identified, especially in his major novels, with the utterances or the actions of his characters. They live out their "passion" of which he is the privileged but uninvolved recorder. But a number of traditional motifs appear in his work from the beginning of his career as a writer. In *Soldier's Pay* he links sex with death. Then, too, Faulkner, with an irony that is never free from compassion, focuses like Hemingway on the precariousness of love in the world. Nothing lasts, no human attachment can withstand the assaults of time, and grief is soon forgotten. The steadfast devotion of which lovers are capable is betrayed and undone by the hand of death. Thus the complex of love is rendered by Faulkner with compelling honesty and breadth of vision.

The authentic Faulkner, both in thematic substance and style, is prefigured in *Soldier's Pay,* his first novel: his literary mannerisms, his metaphysical questioning, his ironic insights, his bitterness and his compassion. Here, in his first venture into fiction, we behold Faulkner introducing a number of *personae*: the poet, the satirist, the prosecuting attorney condemning the ways of God, the all-seeing eye that is not in the least surprised by the cruel vagaries of fate or the strange malformations of character in man. This postwar novel, whose basic themes are those of sex and death, communicates the senseless horror of war, the monstrous waste of life, the hideous aberrations of reason, the upsurge of sadism, that war calls forth. The reader is never allowed to forget the sight of the young lieutenant's dreadfully disfigured face. What good are this man's ribbons and medals on his military uniform now that his face is too horribly mutilated to look upon and his mind has lost its reason. One chapter begins as follows:

> Sex and death: the front door and the back door of the world. How indissolubly are they associated in us! In youth they lift us out of the flesh, in old age they reduce again to the flesh; one to fatten us, the other to flay us, for the worm. When are sexual compulsions more readily answered than in war or famine or flood or fire? [5]

What seems at first glance only a contrapuntal device, a subtle resource of irony, turns out to be an integral part of Faulkner's metaphysical vision. Love and death, sex and death, as in *The Great God Brown,* are indisseverably conjoined. It is this existential contradiction that looms large in the Faulknerian cosmos.

If Faulkner is interested in examining the anomalies of sexual behavior, it is not because they provide him with a rich mine of sensational material. Faulkner never panders to the public. Though his fiction includes scenes of seduction, adultery, rape, incest, and sodomy, these are never brought in for their own sake but form part of a larger plan. They are designed principally to reveal the potentiality for evil present in each human being. Depth psychology led in the twenties to the eager exploration of the subliminal reaches of the self, the unconscious and therefore unacknowledged springs of motivation. Faulkner is aware of the profoundly irrational character of much of human behavior and of the extent to which the biological will rather than abstract reason or ethical principles are in control. Faulkner had some knowledge of Freudianism and, like O'Neill, he took from the science of psychoanalysis what he could put to creative use: namely, those insights that confirmed his own observations and experiences. If Faulkner is drawn to the study of characters who betray some psychological abnormality, it is because he "apparently believes that one shows human character more illuminatingly by putting it in an abnormal sex situation." [6] This is certainly true of *Sanctuary.*

Sanctuary is not, despite its manifest content, a sensational sex-thriller. It embodies Faulkner's reading of life, his conception of evil, but his vision of despair is so unmitigated that the novel has often been called "sensation-

---

[5] William Faulkner, *Soldier's Pay.* New York: Liveright, 1926, p. 295.
[6] Harry Modean Campbell and Ruel E. Foster, *William Faulkner.* Norman: University of Oklahoma Press, 1951, p. 45.

al."[7] Evil is represented by the baleful and pathetic character of Popeye, a degenerate gangster who has been mentally retarded since birth. He is impotent and sadistic, but is there, Faulkner seems to ask, much to choose between this grotesque psychopath and Temple Drake, daughter of a Judge, brought up in a fine home with a long tradition behind it of gallantry and gracious living? She is herself the incarnation of evil. She could have escaped if she had wanted to but she perversely seeks out the evil. The irony of the situation is compounded by the fact that Temple Drake has been brought up in a Southern community which fiercely persecutes those "caught in sin," though it is perfectly willing to shut its eyes to sexual transgressions if the decencies are outwardly observed. But in a girl like Temple Drake, her attraction to evil violates the fundamental morality of the South.

Here, then, is the force of evil rampant in each of us that is hard to sublimate or control. When Temple Drake is put to the test, the flaw in her nature inevitably betrays her. By a calculated stroke of irony, Ruby, the woman who had worked as a prostitute in order to earn enough money to win the release of Goodwin from prison, is shown as more honorable, more loyal, more admirable in every respect than the Temple Drakes of the South. When Horace Benbow, the narrator through whose eyes we view the course of action, tries to help her, she assumes that he wants to possess her body by way of payment. It is incomprehensible to her that men should be actuated by other than carnal or self-seeking motives. Then there is the shuffling, slimy Clarence Snopes, one of the most repulsive characters in the novel, who frankly accepts the double standard of morality that most men subscribe to. Though a husband owes something to his wife, he feels that what she does not know cannot possibly hurt her.[8]

In *Sanctuary,* Faulkner holds up for our contemplation the power of evil over which reason and morality and the injunctions of the law have little or no control. He builds up the central situation with fullness of insight but without passing moral sentence on his obsessed *dramatis personae.* It

---

[7] "If life itself is the outrage it seems in *Sanctuary,* if the will is always impotent and the intelligence baffled, if all our values must in the end lie 'prone and vanquished in the embrace of the season of rain and death,' then to call the novel sensational in such a tone as to imply a dismissal of it is surely to reveal the tameness and timidity of our own vision of life." Hyatt Howe Waggoner, *William Faulkner.* Lexington: University of Kentucky Press, 1959, p. 89.

[8] Malcolm Cowley regards *Sanctuary* as "an example of the Freudian method turned backward, being full of sexual nightmares that are in reality social symbols. It is somehow connected in the author's mind with what he regards as the rape and corruption of the South." *The Portable Faulkner.* Edited by Malcolm Cowley. New York: The Viking Press, 1946, p. 15.

is the mark of his mastery as an artist that Popeye's rape of Temple Drake with a corn-cob pipe, though sufficiently horrifying in itself, is not exploited but is brought in to underline the basic theme, the pervasiveness of evil in the world. Temple Drake has been brutally defiled, the sanctuary of love violated, but there are men in the underworld for whom nothing is sacred. But even more appalling is the disclosure that Temple Drake develops a liking for evil. She is not really ashamed of what had happened to her; secretly she is proud of it. Faulkner relentlessly reveals how the forces of goodness are defeated. Horace Benbow finds that the world is not as he had hoped or thought it would be. It is he who reflects: "Dammit, say what you want to, but there's a corruption about even looking upon evil, even by accident; you cannot haggle, traffic, with putrefaction." [9]

Faulkner continues the story of Temple Drake in *Requiem for a Nun*. She is now Mrs. Gowan Stevens, the mother of a child. Gowan, the feckless young man who originally got her involved in the tragic series of events recounted in *Sanctuary,* has married her out of a sense of honor and duty, but he does not allow her to forget her guilty past. The novel, constructed like a play, is divided into three acts. In the beginning of the first act we get a long historical disquisition on the birth of a courthouse and the growth of a city in the South – a magnificent mythic account of the development of this section of the country, the heroic legend of America's past. Faulkner, like Ibsen, stresses the theme that the past never dies. Gowan remembers the night when he got drunk and Temple was raped and then placed in a Memphis house of prostitution. He cannot shut out the knowledge that Temple seemed to have enjoyed her stay there. Nor can Temple forget the night of the accident in the car, the rape, her experience in the whorehouse. Looking deep into her own self as she reviews those nightmarish events of her past, she catches a frightening glimpse of the nature of evil. It is not enough to avoid looking at evil, for often that cannot be helped, nor is it enough to know that evil must be resisted. At this moment of spiritual crisis she perceives that the fight against evil must start long before that. "You've got to be already prepared to resist it, long before you see it; you must have already said no to it long before you even know what it is." [10]

If Temple succumbed to temptation in the past and again after her marriage, it was because at heart she was drawn to evil. Her marriage cannot wipe out the traumatic impact of the past. What made her marriage a living hell was the expression of gratitude Gowan was constantly demanding of her for his act of forgiveness. When the child is born, she realized that she

9 William Faulkner, *Sanctuary*. New York: Penguin Books, Inc., 1947, p. 74.
10 William Faulkner, *Requiem for a Nun*. New York: Random House, 1951, p. 134.

could not escape from her marriage nor from the consequences of her past. If *Sanctuary* dwells on the reality of evil, the degree to which evil is ingrained in the very texture of existence, it is Nancy Manningoe who, before going to her death, charged with the killing of Temple's child, articulates the counterpointed theme that the salvation of the world is to be found in suffering. When Temple protests against such a conception of God, Nancy, who had been a drunkard and casual prostitute, patiently explains that God cannot help himself. Temple at last sees that it was she, not Nancy, who had murdered the baby; the murder began five years ago when she went off with Gowan and was "raped" by Popeye.

The Sound and the Fury is another study in violence, this time about a neurotic, tragically doomed family. Quentin Compson, tormented by the thought that his sister, Caddy, had coupled with others, is himself troubled by a sense of guilt, for he is incestuously in love with her. For him the odor of honeysuckle is closely associated with his shocking discovery that Caddy had been sexually intimate with Dalton Ames. The memory of honeysuckle is thus symbolically bound up with the profane mystery of sex, the sexual promiscuity of his sister, the possession of whose body he would fain reserve for himself and safeguard against the lustful desires of other men. Roses, too, are coupled in his mind with images of sex and the scene of Caddy's wedding.[11] He is haunted by the revolting picture of her lying in the arms of another man, reenacting the primal drama of the beast with two backs. Before he commits suicide he recalls that "In the South you are ashamed of being a virgin. Boys. Men. They lie about it. Because it means less to women, Father said. They said it was men invented virginity not women."[12]

Faulkner describes the different varieties of love in *The Sound and the Fury:* the instinctive love of Benjy, the idiot, for Caddy; the self-centered, conventional love of the mother, Mrs. Compson, that is no love at all; the promiscuity of Caddy and her daughter; the neurotic attachment Quentin feels for his sister; and last, Jason's diseased love of money and power and his incapacity for the surrender of self that genuine love demands. Though Quentin talks of incest, he lacks the courage to commit it; he is afraid of asking Caddy for fear that she will accede to his wishes. But self-destructive as this abnormal passion proves, he is better off than Jason, an inferior version of the type represented by the Snopeses, the man who hates every-

[11] "Roses are Caddy's sex, her promiscuity and her 'sin' made socially respectable." Olga N. Vickery, *The Novels of William Faulkner.* Baton Rouge: Louisiana State University Press, 1959, p. 41.

[12] William Faulkner, *The Sound and the Fury.* New York: The Modern Library, 1946, p. 97.

one and bears a paranoiac grudge against the world. If he goes to a woman it will be to a prostitute whose services he can purchase for a stipulated price; sex, as far as he is concerned, is a commodity to be bought without any taint of emotional involvement. But Quentin is differently constituted. Neurotically obsessed by the idea of sin, he is caught between two conflicting forces: nostalgia for the past with its religious absolute and high ideals of honor and bitter hatred of the godless, nihilistic present. He broods painfully over the loss of Caddy's honor and grieves even more because there is nothing he can do about it. An idealist thrust into an amoral world, he sees no way out for him except suicide. He is distressed by the utter collapse of the traditional moral values and particularly by the manner in which the shining ideal of purity in woman is foully dragged in the mud.

Caddy, a wanton from her early youth, is not portrayed as wicked. She cannot help herself. From the moment she fell into the branch and wet her drawers – a neat bit of symbolic foreshadowing – her "fall" into promiscuity was inevitable. Like Temple Drake, she is biologically driven, and her wild behavior breaks her mother's heart. For Mrs. Compson had been taught the rigid moral code of the South, "that there is no halfway ground that a woman is either a lady or not but I never dreamed when I held her in my arms that any daughter of mine could let herself . . . ."[13] And Caddy's daughter, named Quentin, is promiscuous like her mother, but she lacks the latter's capacity for love. Having never known love, she is incapable of giving love.

Light in August is shot through with variegated symbols of sexual passion. It contains scenes of terrifying violence. It opens with the picture of a pregnant girl wandering the roads from Alabama to Jefferson, Mississipi, in search of the man, Lucas Burch, a precious rascal, who had gotten her with child. Unlike Lucas, Byron Bunch is a gentle, decent, good-hearted person who acts as Lena Grove's protector. He is friendly with Hightower, the preacher who was driven from his pulpit because his wife was discovered in a hotel room in another town with a stranger. Even after her suicide, the malicious rumors do not stop, the gossips whispering that Hightower was a monster of perversion. This provides the general background of the novel, but the heart of the story is connected with the tragic fate of Joe Christmas.

McEachern, the righteous Puritanic sadist who had adopted Joe Christmas, the alienated "hero" of the novel, feels thoroughly justified in his personal war against lechery, his crusade against harlotry and the vicious sinfulness of his "son." With vengeful fury he tries to redeem brutish men from their carnal abominations, to make them fully aware of the retribution

13 *Ibid.,* p. 121.

of hellish torture waiting for them on Judgment Day. Singlehandedly he wrestles with Satan, for he knows him well; the excesses of sensuality he inveighs against so frenziedly are the same ones that tempt and torment his body. When Joe kills McEachern, his flight from self begins, his wandering through endless streets of strange cities, sleeping with white women and paying them and, when penniless, brazening it out by announcing that he is a Negro. He makes the shocking discovery that some white women did not mind cohabiting with Negroes. He is torn between the two poles of his being, the black and the white.

> He lived with Negroes, shunning white people. He ate with them, slept with them, belligerent, unpredictable, uncommunicative. He now lived as man and wife with a woman who resembled an ebony carving. At night he would lie and bed beside her, sleepless, beginning to breathe deep and hard. He would do it deliberately, feeling, even watching, his white chest arch deeper and deeper within his ribcage, trying to breathe into himself the dark odor, the dark and inscrutable thinking and being of Negroes, with each suspiration trying to expel from himself the white blood and the white thinking and being. And all the while his nostrils at the odors which he was trying to make his own would whiten and tauten, his whole being writhe and strain with physical outrage and spiritual denial.[14]

This is the biological and spiritual conflict Joe Christmas must wage. It is this self-destructive battle, fought within the fastness of his mind and heart, that constitutes the major recurrent motif in the novel: the incomprehensible and fatal dualism of black blood and white blood, Negro thinking and white thinking, as if an unbridgeable gulf separated the two races, as if they moved to an ineradicably different, primordially opposed rhythm, one blood-centered, instinctual, and earth-rooted, the other analytical and introspective. Though *Light in August* seems to present Joe Christmas as possessing Negro or mixed blood, this is only a supposition. The context, however, appears to bear it out, but Faulkner offers no positive proof on this score. As Cleanth Brooks says: "At any rate, we are never given any firm proof that Joe Christmas possesses Negro blood . . . ."[15] But the fact that he has no identity, racial or social, that he is caught in the no-man's land between the whites and the colored folk, not accepted by or at home in either group, does not make the biological issue, as Cleanth Brooks argues, quite irrelevant – not in the eyes of the community nor in Joe's own reactions.

The portrait of Joanna Burden well illustrates the complexity of Faulk-

[14] William Faulkner, *Light in August*. New York: The Modern Library, 1950, p. 197.
[15] Cleanth Brooks, *William Faulkner*. New Haven and London: Yale University Press, 1963, p. 50.

ner's treatment of the close relationship between sexual frustration and the compensatory need for martyrdom. In dedicating herself austerely to the cause of uplifting the Negro in the South, she has repressed her natural instincts. One part of her being is identified wholly with the role of moralist and reformer, the fanatical abolitionist who is carrying on a sacred family tradition, but her womanly self cries out in protest, demands the experience of love and sexual fulfillment. Joanna is a repressed creature, a Puritan from the North whose sexual desires are aroused by Joe. Internally ridden by Calvinistic conflicts, she approaches "the sin" of sexuality with a strange mixture of intense longing and loathing. She cannot give herself freely and spontaneously in the act of love. Through uninhibited sex she seeks to find a way to express her essential being, but since she cannot help regarding sex as fundamentally evil her relationship to Joe becomes neurotically compulsive and perverse. Joe Christmas, the black demon lover, must pursue her, he must seduce her, he must take her with violence.

After Joe breaks through the defences this elderly Yankee woman had set up, she tells him the story of her life, how her family, coming to this land as "foreigners," had been accused of stirring up Negroes to commit rape and thus threatening the rule of white supremacy. After hearing her father's prophetic words that Negroes were "doomed and cursed to be forever and ever a part of the white race's doom and curse for its sin,"[16] she ceased to see Negroes as part of the landscape and beheld them for the first time not as people but as "a shadow" in which all white people moved. What is more, she seemed to behold this black shadow in the shape of a cross. She has come to feel that the black race is God's curse. "But the curse of the white race is the black man who will be forever God's chosen own because He once cursed him."[17] She is the true believer, the fanatic who devotes herself heart and soul to the enlightenment and redemption of the Negro people.

Light in August brilliantly demonstrates the way in which Faulkner combines the study of sexual frustration with the pervasive motif of Negro blood. When the moral scruples of Joanna, this gray-haired spinster, are overcome, she turns into a nymphomaniac, as if bent on making up for all her long years of ascetic denial. It is the strain of Puritanism in her blood, the inner conviction that damnation will inevitably overtake her, which leads her to drain the last drop of passion from her sex-starved body. Faulkner describes how she writhes in this hell of lubricity, striving to distill from each physical sensation its "filthiest" poignancy. She revels in filth at the

---

[16] William Faulkner, *Light in August*, p. 221.
[17] *Ibid.*, p. 222.

same time that she acknowledges the enormity of her sin. She is damned
and she knows it.

She had an avidity for the forbidden wordsymbols; an insatiable appetite for
the sound of them on his tongue and her own. She revealed the terrible and
impersonal curiosity of a child about forbidden subjects and objects; that rapt
and tireless and detached interest of a surgeon in the physical body and its
possibilities.[18]

She insisted on secrecy and concealment in order thereby to heighten the
sense of sin and depravation and enhance her feeling of pleasure. He would
have to seek her out in the dark house

until he found her, hidden, in closets, in empty rooms, waiting, panting, her
eyes in the dark glinting like the eyes of cats. Now and then she appointed trysts
beneath certain shrubs about the grounds, where he would find her naked, or
with her clothing half torn to ribbons upon her, in the wild throes of nymphomania, her body gleaming in the slow shifting from one to another of such
formally erotic attitudes as a Beardsley of the time of Petronius might have
drawn. She would be wild then, in the close, breathing halfdark without walls,
with her wild hair, each strand of which would seem to come alive like octopus
tentacles, and her wild hands and her breathing: "Negro! Negro! Negro!" [19]

Her corruption is complete, without help from Joe, for he is at heart conventional in his very sexual promiscuity, accepting "sin" as the normal state
of a healthy, virile male, untroubled, in fact, by any notion of sin. It is she
who is corrupting him, making him afraid. She is the divided being, at one
moment inaccessible, ringed around with impregnable barriers of virtue,
and at another aflame with shameless, uncontrollable desire. But she cannot
hold out too long against the stern voice of her Puritan conscience, which
condemns sex as vile and sinful. She must make her peace with God. She
reverts to her Calvinist faith. She resolves to save this black sinner from the
pit of damnation, to remake him in her own image of the redeemed Negro,
and thus save her own soul. The crisis in their relationship is reached when
her neurotically tortured self repudiates the horrible sin of sex and she tries
to save Joe Christmas, who has no wish to be saved. And that is when he
murders her.

Immediately, once the sensational news spreads, the region is in an up-
roar, farmers and townsfolk arriving from all parts, far and near, to view
with morbid interest the almost decapitated body of the New England
spinster. Among them, says Faulkner with pointed irony, the casual Yankee
and the poor whites and even those Southerners who had lived for a time in
the North "believed aloud that it was an anonymous negro crime committed

---

[18] *Ibid.*, p. 226.
[19] *Ibid.*, p. 227.

not by negro but Negro and who knew, believed, and hoped that she had been ravished too: at least once before her throat was cut and at least once afterward." [20]

The later somewhat melodramatic unfoldment of the plot represents the typical Faulknerian denouement, but it contains a number of scenes that have a direct bearing on the intertwined themes of blood and sex. *Light in August* draws to an apocalyptic close. After escaping from his captors, Joe Christmas flees in a manner that reveals his tragically split nature. First he runs to a Negro cabin, his black blood guiding his footsteps. Then in revulsion he flees to the house of Hightower, where he thinks he will find sanctuary. At the end he is shot by Percy Grimm, who then castrates him. As Gavin Stevens declares:

It was the black blood which swept him by his own desire beyond the aid of any man, swept him up into that ecstasy out of a black jungle where life has already ceased before the heart stops and death is desire and fulfillment. And then the black blood failed him again, as it must have in crises all his life. [21]

The Wild Palms sets forth the tragic consequences that follow from the attempt in our civilization to make love the sole basis of and justification for existence. It is a bitter fictional critique of the myth of romantic love, the myth which believes that the world is well lost for love. As in *A Farewell to Arms,* love is exalted as the supreme virtue, the *summum bonum,* the height and crown of earthly felicity. [22] Faulkner depicts the fascination the experience of illicit love exerts on those romantic souls who cannot resist its lure. Charlotte Rittenmeyer, the married woman with whom the young doctor runs off, is a priestess of the cult of love, fanatical in her demand for perpetual ecstasy. She will allow nothing, neither duty nor shame, to stand in her way. The arch-romantic devotee of the religion of love, she will not compromise with the ethic of respectability. Though she is the mother of children, she wishes to live wholly for love, refusing to surrender her romantic ideal or her individuality to her maternal instinct.

In *The Wild Palms* the scene of action is laid in New Orleans, Chicago, Utah, and the Gulf Coast, not Faulkner's native region: Yoknapatawpha County. Here are the star-crossed lovers defying social, legal, moral, and religious conventions in the name of love. Harry gives up his internship

---

[20] *Ibid.,* p. 251.

[21] *Ibid.,* p. 393.

[22] Waggoner lodges a cogent protest agains the naturalistic tendency in literature to reduce life to a biological version of love. He argues that "the explaining away of love in biological or other terms the 'reductionism' of those who, especially in the twenties and thirties, could believe that 'love' was real only insofar as they could identify it with a glandular secretion, a chemical, is one of our ways of denying love." Hyatt Howe Waggoner, *William Faulkner,* p. 134.

in order to go off with Charlotte, who without hesitation abandons her home, her husband, and her two children. For the first time she believes she knows what love is; it is one with suffering; "the value of love is the sum of what you have to pay for it and any time you get it cheap you have cheated yourself." [23] If Joanna Burden is at first willing to be damned for her sin of sex, Charlotte is thoroughly convinced that the religion of love justifies whatever suffering its devotees are made to endure. And she is able to convert Harry Winterbourne, her lover, so that he espouses her romantic faith. What they are doing, he contends, is not a sin; their crime lies in getting out of rhythm with the anonymous lockstep of their generation. Society with its formal regulations and restraints is the implacable enemy of love. In this modern acquisitive world it is impossible to live for love alone. "There is no place for it in the world today, not even in Utah." [24] One must conform or perish. Society is leagued against them, and that is why they and their love are doomed. With its imagery of fate relentlessly hounding the two lovers, *The Wild Palms* constitutes a Shelleyan hymn in defiance of the cruelly repressive social order, but Faulkner keeps the balance even by showing the disastrous outcome of this mystique of love. In one passage descriptive of the orgasm, Faulkner, like D. H. Lawrence, lifts the sexual experience to the cosmic plane:

You are one single abnegant affirmation, one single fluxive Yes out of the terror in which you surrender volition, hope, all – the darkness, the falling, the thunder of solitude, the shock, the death, the moment when, stopped physically by the ponderable clay, you yet feel all your life rush out of you into the pervading immemorial blind receptive matrix, the hot fluid blind foundation – grave-womb or womb-grave, it's all one. [25]

But it is not society alone that dooms these lovers. As in *A Farewell to Arms,* they are the victims of a biological accident. She becomes pregnant. The performance of the abortion Charlotte insists upon results in her death. They have engaged with whole-hearted passion in the romantic quest as if they were in pursuit of the Absolute, they have sought to live for the sake of unalloyed intensity of experience, without taking on the burden of responsibility of the practical social world. It cannot be done. Nature as well as society is against them. They are trapped in a meaningless universe, in a Nature that is blankly neutral and indifferent, in a society that is immoral and harshly oppressive.

---

[23] William Faulkner, *The Wild Palms.* New York: Penguin Books, Inc., 1939, pp. 28–29.

[24] *Ibid.,* p. 80.

[25] *Ibid.,* p. 82.

Absalom, Absalom! is a highly complex novel in structure and in the integrated body of its meaning. Though Sutpen, who may be regarded as the protagonist, is a man with as single-minded and obsessive a purpose as that of Flem Snopes in the trilogy (*The Hamlet, The Town,* and *The Mansion*) which we shall discuss later on, he is not so cold-bloodedly calculating. The chosen instrument of an ambitious plan, he is determined to carry it out regardless of cost. He is sustained by his own moral values, his own sense of justice, but where his life-plan is at stake no moral principle can act as a deterrent. The details of the story are cunningly relayed to the reader bit by bit so that he catches brief tantalizing glimpses of the ugly family secret, the fact of miscegenation, which, combined with the theme of incest, forms an integral part of the plot. Here again, as in *Light in August,* we can trace the working of lawless passion, the frustrations and the fatality that are rooted in the blood. We are told the story of Sutpen and the huge stately mansion he built, and how he married Ellen Coldfield, who bore his two children, Judith and Henry. There is a close relationship between brother and sister, a kind of emotional incest. Charles Bon (that is how Sutpen names his illegitimate son), a college mate of Henry, courts Judith. Though Faulkner offers little concrete evidence to support the theory of Bon's Negro blood, it plays a crucial part in the story as it is reconstructed by Quentin (the one who appeared in *The Sound and the Fury*) for the benefit of his Canadian friend, Shreve. Then comes the discovery that Charles is already married, according to Creole convention, and has a son. In seeking the acknowledgement of his sonship, he is prepared to give up his octoroon mistress. Through the period of the Civil War, each of the two men, Henry and Charles, fights to win the soul of the other. Charles, worldly and sardonic, hopes to break through the ice of Henry's Puritanic armored character while Henry strives to make Bon renounce his "marriage" and come to his sister unfettered and unsullied.

Essentially what Henry balks at is the marriage contract, not the Creole mistress and child. For in the South the second sex is divided into three categories: ladies, women, and females: "the virgins whom gentlemen some-day married, the courtesans to whom they went while on sabbaticals to the cities, the slave girls and women upon whom that first caste rested and to whom in certain cases it doubtless owed the very fact of its virginity . . . ."[26] In New Orleans, Charles introduces Henry to the world in which colored women are bred for the special delectation of men, those women who embodied the eternal feminine, devoted exclusively to catering to men's plea-

[26] William Faulkner, *Absalom, Absalom!* New York: The Modern Library, 1951, p. 109.

sure and entertainment. Were it not for this institution of honorable con-
cubinage, these Negro women would be slaves in the field, toiling like beasts
of burden. A lapsed Catholic, Charles insists that God is old enough and
wise enough to understand the wisdom of such an arrangement. Indeed,
why should God be particularly concerned about the way in which men
yield to the solicitations of the flesh. And how, after all, did these exquisite
creatures of beauty and pleasure come into being? White men gave them
the shape and pigment of what is called beauty. They are neither whores nor
courtesans.[27]

This is sufficient to indicate what Faulkner is seeking to convey in this
intricately constructed novel: the element of horror that is characteristic of
the romantic past in the South. Few novelists in the South possess Faulkner's extraordinary ability to evoke the spirit of its historic, guilt-laden past.
This is a land of saints and sinners, lecherous by instinct and inclination yet
fiercely moral in their defence of the purity of Southern ladies and the
sanctity of marriage, a caste-ridden land in which the gentry live off the

---

[27] Faulkner has been criticized on the ground that his women characters are one-
dimensional, never rendered in all their emotional and spiritual complexity. "Consequently his fiction suffers in part from his inability to portray women as both physical
and spiritual." (Irving Malin, *William Faulkner*. Stanford: Stanford University Press,
1957, p. 46.) And Cleanth Brooks defines Faulkner's view of women as "radically
old-fashioned – even medieval. Woman is the source and sustainer of virtue and also
a prime source of evil. She can be either, because she is, as man is not, always a little
beyond good and evil. With her powerful natural drives and her instinct for the concrete and personal, she does not need to agonize over her decision." (Cleanth Brooks,
The Hidden God. New Haven and London: Yale University Press, 1963, p. 27.) Again,
he declares that in nearly all of Faulkner's fiction, "the male's discovery of evil and
reality is bound up with his discovery of the true nature of woman. Men idealize and
romanticize women, but the cream of the jest is that women have a secret rapport with
evil which men do not have . . . . Women are the objects of idealism, but are not in the
least idealistic." (Cleanth Brooks, *William Faulkner*, pp. 127–128.) While these gener-
alized conclusions can be defended by references to numerous passages in Faulkner's
novels, it must be pointed out that Faulkner is not to be identified with the expressed
views of any of his characters; he is drawing what he considers a faithful picture of
the moral physiognomy of the South. If woman is a prolific source of contradictions,
these contradictions, as Faulkner shows, appear most strikingly in the attitude of the
male. If Faulkner on occasion voices the typical American hostility toward "the
weaker" sex, as Leslie Fiedler charges in *Love and Death in the American Novel,* there
is no basis for assuming that he shares or approves of the hostility. He is presenting
the ambivalence in the Southerner's conception of woman. She is serpent and seraph,
nymphomaniac (Joanna Burden) and fertility symbol (Lena Grove), Delilah and saint,
prostitute and mother figure. Hence the multiple role woman must play as virgin,
mistress, harlot, wife, and mother. As Simone de Beauvoir says: "She is an idol, a
servant, the source of life, a power of darkness . . . she is man's prey, his downfall,
she is everything that he is not and that he longs for, his negation and his *raison d'être*."
Simone de Beauvoir, *The Second Sex*. Translated by H. H. Parshley. New York: Alfred
A. Knopf, 1953, p. 143.

sweated toil of ignorant Negroes and poor whites. The final twist to this tale of horror in *Absalom, Absalom!* is given when we learn what happens to Charles Bon's son, brought from New Orleans to live with Judith after the death of his mother. Silent, impassive, inarticulate, he rebels against his fate by casting in his lot with Negroes, refusing, despite all that Judith does to change his mind, to be white, marrying a hideously black Negro woman. What profound changes are wrought in him by his discovery that he is a "nigger," he who had been affectionately brought up in luxury and seclusion in a New Orleans milieu where differences of color played no part! Finally he proceeds to destroy himself with wilful fatalism, vicious in his sudden, inexplicable attacks on Negroes with whom he has been gambling and drinking, though refusing in court to explain what motivated his violently irrational behavior. After marrying this black woman, he gets periodically drunk and hunts out situations

in order to flaunt and fling the ape-like body of his charcoal companion in the faces of all and any who would retaliate: the negro stevedores and deckhands on steamboats or in city honky-tonks who thought he was a white man and believed it only the more strongly when he denied it; the white men who, when he said he was a negro, believed that he lied in order to save his skin, or worse: from sheer besotment of sexual perversion; in either case the result the same....[28]

He fought with the fury of despair against all those who would oppose him, not caring about the injuries they inflicted on him, continuing to deny his white blood and stubbornly exaggerating his Negro blood.

The secret that is finally disclosed in *Absalom, Absalom!*, the secret on which the resolution of the plot hinges, is that Charles Bon, who has Negro blood in his veins, is the son of Colonel Sutpen. Sternly faithful to the code of the South, the father refuses to acknowledge or even notice this product of miscegenation. Since Bon is partly Negro, Judith, though she is ready to marry him despite her father's opposition to the match, is thereby condemned to spinsterhood. The race problem – that is the cross the South must bear. In the novel it is the miscegenation, the taint of Negro blood, not the incest, which sets up an insuperable barrier.

Needless to say, Faulkner's picture of life in the South includes vastly more in its sweep than the fevers and frailties of the flesh or the accursed heritage of the race problem. If, in *The Hamlet,* he depicts the lechery the human animal is capable of and his acquisitive itch for land, money, and power, he also delineates the saving virtues of honor, loyalty, courage, and decency that hold a community together. If there is the rampant force of evil present in some men, as embodied in the Snopes family, it is countered by

[28] William Faulkner, *Absalom, Absalom!*, p. 206.

the goodness and kindliness of many others, and this goodness, this kindliness, is not monopolized by the whites; it is evident in equal measure
among the Negroes in the South. Sex, in Faulkner's fiction, is not exalted
to the status of a mystique; it is simply one of the passions that drive men
to folly. Eula, in *The Hamlet,* is a kind of personified Eros, endowed
with the power, merely by her presence, of arousing the sex-consciousness
of all the men who behold her. But it is important to note that in portraying his characters and the vagaries of love and lust to which they are
addicted, Faulkner sides with no one point of view; he is not censorious or
hortatory; he probably sympathizes most with Ratliff's genially detached
vision of the follies of human nature. Faulkner, like Ratliff, is filled with
wonder at the deversity of human beings, the complex and contradictory
nature of man.

Eula, Varner's young daughter, is the incarnation of sensuality. Even
though she was not yet thirteen, Faulkner tells us,

she was already bigger than most grown women and even her breasts were no
longer the little, hard, fiercely-pointed cones of puberty or even maidenhood. On
the contrary, her entire appearance suggested some symbology out of the old
Dionysic times – honey in sunlight and bursting grapes, the writhen bleeding
of the crushed fecundated vine beneath the hard rapacious trampling goat-hoof.[29]

She is all body, a potent aphrodisiac, a flaunting if unconscious provocation,
intuitively possessed of the wisdom of her femininity, an instinctive erotic
force that she wielded without having to become aware of it, for her body
seemed entirely separated from her mind. Small wonder that Labove, the
student who is fighting against the worst odds of poverty in order to attend
college and become a lawyer, is magnetically drawn to this seductive vessel
of flesh. A virgin, a fanatic, he has lived ascetically, disciplining his will,
burning up his excess energy in work and football, eating frugally in order
to save his money. Then one morning, in the schoolroom where he is temporarily employed as a teacher, he sees Eula, who brought with her "a moist
blast of spring's liquorish corruption, a pagan triumphal prostration before
the supreme primal uterus."[30] Wherever she walked or sat or rode horseback, there the goddess presided, and all the young scholars in the class,
some of them nineteen and twenty years old, felt the sexual challenge of her
presence.

Faulkner describes this irrational, compulsive power of sex, as well as
other varieties of love, without a touch of condemnation. Like drunkenness,
like the mad erotic passion of Ike Snopes, the idiot, for the cow, like Flem

[29] William Faulkner, *The Hamlet.* New York: The Modern Library, 1940, p. 95.
[30] *Ibid.,* p. 114.

Snopes' abnormal lust for money and possessions, sex is but another manifestation of the strange behavior of the human animal. Faulkner neither
glorifies it nor despises it. He makes no fetish of it. His task, as he sees it, is
to reveal as honestly and objectively as he can the workings of the dynamism of passion. If Ike's sodomy with the cow calls forth a reaction of horror,
Faulkner makes us feel the greater horror of Flem Snopes' disease, his
mania for owning things, the "perversion" that is probably responsible for
his impotence, his inability to love. Faulkner's "grotesques," like those of
Sherwood Anderson in *Winesburg, Ohio,* are intended to present the image
of human nature in all its astonishing variety.

   Here is the young schoolmaster, who had gladly sacrificed everything for
the sake of gaining a college education, subjugated by the witchery of this
mindless girl. He knows full well what he wants. The thought of waiting till
Eula grows up and then asking for her hand is out of the question. He did
not want to be burdened with a wife nor did he desire her as a wife, but he
cannot cure himself of this singular obsession. He realizes she is incapable
of love, and yet he worships her. He cannot curb his mounting passion for
her. He was mad and he knew it. "There would be times now when he did
not even want to make love to her but wanted to hurt her . . . ." [31] Frustrated
love turns into sadism, a love-hate polarity. He cannot hold out much longer
against this madness that had taken hold of him. He is afraid of what he
might do in some reckless moment, though he realized beforehand that, do
what he will, he would be vanquished. For she was in possession of a knowledge that lay beyond him, not to be grasped by the effort of his intellect. She
was invulnerable. He attempts to rape her but she throws him off, withering
in her display of contempt for him. He is not even important enough in her
life to report the incident to her brother.

   The other youths court her ardently, wistful and desperate in their balked
plans of seduction. They pursue her in the "leashed turmoil of lust like
so many lowering dogs after a scarce-fledged and apparently unawares
bitch . . . ." [32] Eula is unique. She is not interested in men, though McCarron
does finally arouse her to a furious pitch of passion. She gives herself to him.
When he learns she is pregnant, he leaves the region. The community, by
means of grapevine rumors, hears that she is in trouble. The last one to
know of it is her father, Will Varner, "the man who cheerfully and robustly
and undeviatingly declined to accept any such theory as female chastity
other than as a myth to hoodwink young husbands with . . . ." [33] With a real-

31 *Ibid.,* p. 120.
32 *Ibid.,* p. 131.
33 *Ibid.,* pp. 141–142.

ism that is unfaltering and ironic, Faulkner exposes the sex mores of the region. Will Varner, a prosperous man and a leading citizen, is no saint. At the time of Eula's "trouble," he was

engaged in a liaison with the middle-fortyish wife of one of his own tenants. He was too old, he told her baldly and plainly, to be tomcatting around at night, about his own house or any other man's. So she would meet him in the afternoons, on pretence of hunting hen-nests, in a thicket beside the creek near her house, in which sylvan Pan-hallowed retreat, the fourteen-year-old boy whose habit it was to spy on them told, Varner would not even remove his hat.[34]

But Eula is pregnant and something must be done about it at once. And so the father marries her off to Flem Snopes, who is emerging as a growing power in the community.

Written seventeen years after *The Hamlet, The Town* records the fortunes of the Snopes clan, the Varner family, and a number of other characters, as viewed through the eyes of Charles Mallison, Gavin Stevens, and Ratliff. Faulkner advances no thesis and elaborates no doctrinaire psychology or sociology of sex. He is saved from the danger of philosophizing by his inveterate curiosity about the inner being of people, what makes them behave as they do, and his curiosity in this behavioral field is boundless. He is concerned to reveal the truth about the assorted characters he introduces, and the truth he reveals is never simple. His fictional device of relating the story through shifting and diverse points of view makes it possible for him to achieve a genuinely detached and yet intensely humanized objectivity, since the truth of any experience is ambiguous and multifaceted, as seen, felt, and experienced by a given spectrum of subjectivity. And there are almost as many points of view as there are characters in the novel. The way in which Gavin Stevens sizes up a situation is not the way, say, Eula or Flem Snopes or Mrs. Mallison, Gavin's sister, would look at it. The universality of vision Faulkner struggles to create in this trilogy is such that it is impossible to single out one theme or one aspect of life, be it love or sex, as representative of the whole. Faulkner is as much interested in the peculiarities of the Snopes tribe as he is in the idealized love Gavin feels for Eula and then her daughter, Linda.

The story of *The Town* carries on where it left off in *The Hamlet,* though there is much recapitulation of material. The Snopes clan had settled in the area from the time Flem became a clerk in Varner's store; more members of the prolific Snopes family continue to arrive until there are as many Snopeses in Frenchman's Bend as there are Varners; more in fact. Flem moves to Jefferson. He is now married to Eula and the child is legally his,

[34] *Ibid.,* p. 142.

though fathered by another man. Eula is still the goddess of love, a female who even in her adolescence was richly endowed with all the physical attributes of her sex, gifted with a magical, irresistible power of attracting the susceptible male.

De Spain, who represents the liberal, reformist element in the town, is elected Mayor of Jefferson. He is a bachelor who, as everyone in town knows and either approves or condemns, is Eula's lover. Most of those who worshipped Eula from afar, grateful for the privilege of beholding her beauty, were on his side. "We were his allies, his confederates; our whole town was accessory to that cuckolding." [35] The people of the town supported him not because they were opposed to Flem Snopes; they had not yet learned how formidable and sinister a danger he represented. Nor did they defend De Spain because they were secretly in favor of adultery; "we were simply in favor of De Spain and Eula Snopes, for what Uncle Gavin called the divinity of simple unadulterated uninhibited immortal lust which they represented . . . ." [36] That was an enviable achievement in itself.

Though the townspeople relish the affair between Eula and her lover, they are aware of and insist on maintaining the distinction between good and evil. The moral law is not to be flouted with impunity. It is a Puritanic town. This community, consisting of Baptists and Methodists, believed that sin was punished, that sin punished itself, that divine justice always triumphed in the end. According to Charles Mallison, the town was split into two camps of thought:

the women who hated Mrs Snopes for having grabbed Mr De Spain first or hated Mr De Spain for having preferred Mrs Snopes to them, and the men who were jealous of De Spain because they were not him or hated him for being younger than they or braver than they (they called it luckier of course); and those of both sexes – no: the same genderless sex – who hated them both for having found or made together something which they themselves had failed to make, whatever the reason . . . . [37]

Even the romantic Stevens knows what enormous power the community wields and the severe punishment it metes out to those transgressors who are unlucky enough to be caught. The adultery could not be condoned, not when the matter came to a public showdown. So long as the husband said nothing and did nothing the adultery could be decently covered up, but once it became public knowledge then the sinners must be brought to justice.

The youthful Gavin, who is in love with Eula, defends her against attack

---

[35] William Faulkner, The Town. New York: Random House, 1957, p. 15.
[36] Ibid., p. 15.
[37] Ibid., p. 308.

when Mr. Mallison, his brother-in-law, refers to her notorious liaison with Manfred. His sister establishes peace between them and then tells them what is wrong with both of them: they do not know women, they misjudge their character and motives, they idealize them. She declares:

Women are not interested in morals. They aren't even interested in unmorals. The ladies of Jefferson dont care what she does. What they will never forgive is the way she looks. No: the way the Jefferson gentlemen look at her.[38]

This appears, at first glance, to be Faulkner's conception of the female of the species: sagacious, practical, down-to-earth, not interested in morals or ideals, but Mrs. Mallison embodies only one point of view. Faulkner is not unfair in his portrayal of women. He does not hate them at bottom, as some critics have argued: he is simply unmasking the illusion of love from which men suffer.[39]

If Gavin, the peerless knight, wants to save Eula, why, Mrs. Mallison asks, must he take up arms in her behalf? He refuses to believe that Eula is carrying on an affair with Manfred de Spain. At the Cotillion Club dance he deliberately provokes Manfred, who is dancing with Eula, and is badly beaten up for his pains. He is defending the principle of virtue in women, even though they possess it not. And his sister calls him a downright fool. "You fool! They don't deserve you! They aren't good enough for you! None of them are, no matter how much they look and act like a – like a – like a god damn whorehouse!"[40]

Eula comes to Gavin's office and offers herself to him. She assumes that this is what he wants. Otherwise why did he get involved in a fight with her lover? An idealist as far as women are concerned, he is shocked by her proposal. He tries hard to understand the true meaning of her sacrificial gesture. "Not just to prove to me that having what I want wont make me happy, but to show me that what I thought I wanted is not even worth being unhappy over."[41] But Eula is not one given to such refined analysis. He expects too much. She reveals the guiding motive behind her offer when she says bluntly: "You just are, and you need, and you must, and so you do."[42] He cannot take her on these terms. When she realizes that he is rejecting the

---

[38] *Ibid.*, p. 48.
[39] "In his novels Faulkner has found his special interest in the failures of love – love violated, or love betrayed, or love perverted, but he knows the fact of love fulfilled, and the failures of love as he treats them actually point by implication to the positive case." Cleanth Brooks, *William Faulkner*, p. 207.
[40] William Faulkner, *The Town*, p. 77.
[41] *Ibid.*, p. 94.
[42] *Ibid.*, p. 94.

proffered gift of her body, she remarks that he behaves this way because he is a gentleman "and I never knew one before."[43]

Gavin becomes interested in Linda Snopes, who does not look like her mother, but he is still bewitched by the image of Eula. He is still tormented by a number of questions: had Manfred de Spain seduced a chaste creature or had he stumbled upon a "rotating nympholept?"[44] He prefers to think of her as chaste, a faithful wife. He has no peace of mind as he broods on the mystery surrounding Eula Snopes. He takes on the role of spiritual and intellectual mentor to Linda, lending her books, manifesting an "avuncular" interest in her development. He wants to help her choose the right kind of college, but he has to reckon with Flem, who will not agree to let her leave Jefferson. Eula explains to him why this is so. She, too, tells him he does not know much about women. "Women aren't interested in poets' dreams. They are interested in facts. It doesn't even matter whether the facts are true or not, so long as they match the other facts without leaving a rough seam."[45] That is why Linda will refuse to believe Flem is not her father; she needs the support of respectability; she would deny the truth even if it were told her by Flem himself. It is then Eula urges Gavin to marry her daughter, even though he is many years her senior. That would solve the problem.

Gavin speculates on the nature of woman. If Flem's home has been violated, it was because his wife was prompted by the instincts of her sex. There was no question, he now realizes, of seduction.

She was seduced simply by herself: by a nymphomania not of the uterus: the hot unbearable otherwise unreachable itch and burn of the mare or heifer or sow or bitch in season, but by a nymphomania of a gland whose only ease was in creating a situation containing a recipient for gratitude, then supplying the gratitude.[46]

There was the fact of Manfred de Spain paying, as Gavin thinks, for the right to sleep with her. But Flem bides his own time and waits for the right moment to spring the trap, and the price he asks for not creating a public scandal is nothing less than the presidency of the bank.

Eula is caught in the trap. She commits suicide because that, as she realistically sees it, is the only way out. Flem gets control of the bank and Manfred de Spain is compelled, for a number of reasons, to leave Jefferson. According to Charles Mallison's interpretation, he had outraged the moral sensibility of the community:

[43] *Ibid.*, p. 94.
[44] *Ibid.*, p. 133.
[45] *Ibid.*, p. 226.
[46] *Ibid.*, p. 272.

He had not only flouted the morality of marriage which decreed that a man and a woman cant sleep together without a certificate from the police, he had outraged the economy of marriage which is the production of children, by making public display of the fact that you can be barren by choice with impunity; he had outraged the institution of marriage twice: not just his own but the Flem Snopes's too. So they already hated him twice: once for doing it, once for not getting caught at it for eighteen years.[47]

After Eula's death, the town forgives her carnal sin. Gavin had not been her lover and in that, according to public opinion, he was remiss; he had failed; he was now the bereaved one. He cannot understand what drove Eula to take her own life and, still blinded, accepts Ratliff's explanation that she was bored. " 'Yes,' he said. 'She was bored. She loved, had a capacity for love... to give and accept love.' " [48]

The Mansion, the last volume of the trilogy, goes over much of the same ground as *The Town,* except that it devotes a large amount of space to Mink Snopes and his long-brooding scheme of revenge against Flem. Linda comes back to Jefferson as a widow, still romantic in her conception of love. She continues to live in the house of Flem Snopes, through she now knows the part he played in marrying her mother. She knows how base he can be, the evil lengths to which he would be willing to go, and she plans to have him killed by his kinsman Mink.

Faulkner reveals the unacknowledged night life of the people of Jefferson, Mississippi, the men (and they are numerous) who patronize the studio set up by Montgomery Ward Snopes, where he exhibits dirty French postcards. He spins some raffish tales about Virgil Snopes and Fonzo Winbush, how they come to Memphis to enroll in a barber's college and mistake Reba Rivers' establishment as a respectable boarding house. They are innocent enough to look upon Miss Reba as motherly and Christian. It takes them a month before they fully realize where they are and what is going on in this part of the Memphis red-light district. The scenes in Reba's establishment that describe Virgil's exceptional phallic prowess are as good as any in Henry Miller's *Tropic of Cancer.* Steeped in the folk tradition of the tall tale, they constitute a brief, entertaining interlude in the grim saga of revenge by Mink Snopes. A thoroughly human character, Reba is confident that Montgomery Ward Snopes with his pornographic postcards cannot compete with what her girls are able to provide – the real thing.

Gavin is fifty by the time Linda returns. She wants to marry him but though he still loves her he refuses; he is too old for her. It is then that, like

[47] *Ibid.,* pp. 338–339.
[48] *Ibid.,* p. 359.

her mother, she offers to give herself to him, using the slang four-letter word, and he is frankly shocked by hearing it issue from her lips. *"No what shocks is when a woman uses it & is not shocked at all until she realizes I am."* [49] For him, the incurable idealist, the beauty of passion should not be defiled by that profane expression. Gavin wants a Platonic relationship, a love that has no need of the body.

It is difficult to sum up Faulkner in a single formula. His work is complex, instinct with irony, paradox, humor, compassion, and an abiding sense of the mystery and diversity of the human soul. His interpretation of the character of love is closely connected with his conception of the nature of man. He takes a pessimistic view of human nature, not as fallen or rooted in original sin but as ruled predominantly by instinct and passion rather than reason or morality and as perversely, often gratuitously, addicted to evil. If he believes in the integrity of the family, he is keenly aware of the strains and miseries of marital life. No love is lost between Mr. and Mrs. Compson in *The Sound and the Fury.* In *As I Lay Dying,* Addie Bundren does not think much of men and even less of her shiftless husband, Anse. If Faulkner paints the portrait of some splendid female heroines, he does not hesitate to show that the romantic aura surrounding woman, the idealization of her character, is largely the product of the male imagination.

In the symbolism that Faulkner uses in his exploration of the theme of love and sex, he tends to focus attention on the animalian heritage in man, to place emphasis on the demonic rather than the angelic aspect. Committed on the whole to a naturalistic framework of values, he projects a world that is corrupt, a world that has long ago lost its Edenic innocence. His novels come to grips with a human reality that is governed in large part by instinct. The appetites of the flesh again and again override the dictates of morality. If Faulkner is much concerned with the theme of sex, it is because Nature provides the norms to which his characters are compelled to defer. What is signally lacking in his fictional universe is an awareness of the possibility of achieving an harmonious and genuinely happy love relationship. In the world that he presents for our contemplation, love is a myth, an illusion, and sex is for the most part the dominant reality. Since Nature created man with all his physical passions, he cannot go against his instincts. But Faulkner's conception of Nature, as embodied in his novels, does not by any means justify "a sinking into nature." [50] Those who, like Flem Snopes, brutally violate and exploit Nature never enjoy what they possess. Flem succeeds in

---

[49] William Faulkner, *The Mansion.* New York: Random House, 1959, p. 239.
[50] Robert Penn Warren, "William Faulkner," in William Van O'Connor (ed.), *Forms of Modern Fiction.* Minneapolis: University of Minnesota Press, 1948, p. 134.

amassing wealth, but he is sexually impotent. Man is not subjugated by the clay of which he is made; he transcends himself by exercising the positive virtues of suffering and courage, compassion and endurance. Faulkner promulgates no mystique of sex, supports no redemptive or cynical philosophy of love. Like Malraux, he is a tragic writer who reports his version of the truth of the human condition.

PART THREE

THE MYSTIQUE OF SEX IN CONTEMPORARY

AMERICAN LITERATURE

SECTION A: SEX AS SALVATION

CHAPTER X

HENRY MILLER:
PROPHET OF THE SEXUAL REVOLUTION

Miller writes hundreds of pages describing in the minutest and clearest detail his exploits in bed. Every serious reader of erotica has remarked about Miller that he is probably the only author in history who writes about such things with complete ease and naturalness. Lawrence never quite rid himself of his puritanical consciousness, nor Joyce; both had too much religion in their veins . . . Miller's achievement is miraculous: he is screamingly funny without making fun of sex, the way Rabelais does . . . . Miller is accurate and poetic in the highest degree; there is not a smirk anywhere in his writings.[1]

When he deals with sex he seems to me to achieve a crudity unsurpassed except by the *graffiti* on the walls of public urinals, and the crudity is the more striking – and sometimes the more comic – because of the high-falutin to which it is juxtaposed. In my view, *Tropic of Cancer* is obscene in the simplest sense; but it is anything but pornographic: a book less aphrodisiac it is scarcely possible to find.[2]

He is most certainly not an obscene writer in the usual sense of the word.[3]

To charge a book like the *Tropic of Cancer* with pornography is like charging life itself with pornography. Is there anything pornographic about a man defecating? Anything pornographic about the sexual organs? All such processes and things just are . . . Life . . .[4]

In terms of chronology Henry Miller belongs to the group of writers such as O'Neill and Hemingway who dominated the twenties. We have decided to include him among the contemporaries because he is still productive, retaining the élan which characterizes the two major works, *Tropic of Cancer* and *Tropic of Capricorn,* he wrote while living as an expatriate in Paris

---

[1] Karl Shapiro, *In Defense of Ignorance.* New York: Random House, 1960, p. 324. In his essay, "The Greatest Living Author," Karl Shapiro refers to Henry Miller as a holy man – "Gandhi with a penis." *Ibid.,* p. 324.
[2] Walter Allen, *The Modern Novel.* New York: E. P. Dutton & Co., Inc., 1964, p. 181.
[3] Ludwig Marcuse, *Obscene.* Translated by Karen Gershon. London: Macgibbon & Kee, 1965, p. 258.
[4] Michael Fraenkel, *The Genesis of the Tropic of Cancer.* Berkeley, California: Ben Porter, 1946, p. 26.

during the thirties. Then, too, because of conditions of censorship which prevailed in the United States, he came relatively late on the native literary scene. Published abroad by the Obelisk Press, his two picaresque novels could not be put on sale in this country. It was not until recently that the Grove Press, bringing the case to court, won the legal right to issue an unexpurgated edition of these two works of fiction. Another reason why he deserves to be classified as a contemporary is that he still exercises a powerful influence on a number of avant-garde American writers. He was a pioneer intrepidly leading the way when the force of opposition was hard to overcome. His contribution made possible the sensational success of the sexual revolution in literary America. He transformed the Puritan heritage of shame and guilt associated with the sexual act into a thing of joy and laughter, stressing at one and the same time the indescribable pleasure that sex affords and the comic situations into which it plunges the human copulating animal.

Henry Miller has often been called and condemned as an obscene writer, but to be called that is not necessarily a mark of dishonor. He dramatized and therefore individualized the teeming world of sex, with all its wealth of physical and functional details. He carries out the dramatization with immense gusto, with unsparing realism. Copulation is a fact, a natural and pleasurable phenomenon, not something to snigger about or wax sentimental over. Miller is neither pornographic in method nor romantic in outlook. He does not make the attempt to spiritualize sex. And yet, despite the relish with which he focuses on the sexual act in all its limited yet lusty variety, he is assuredly not an obscene writer. He uses no fig-leaves which suggest more than they hide, no coy euphemisms, no discreet series of asterisks. He calls a spade a spade, not in the least embarrassed by the explicitness of his verbal references to the erotic behavior of the body. He will brook no restraints where the truth of life and the language of life are concerned, and he is confident he knows what the truth about man is.

Miller's supreme tenet is: Every kind of sexual stimulus is admitted, nothing is rejected. As for disorder – I am not afraid of it. – That is the root of serious obscenity. It is the most radical, the happiest rebellion. Its symbol is the liberation of the best-guarded prisoner: the body from the navel down.[5]

A pagan individualist, Miller holds the conventional taboos of the social order in sovereign contempt. He is the spokesman for the hitherto maligned instincts. He defies the gods of public opinion with an utter disregard for the consequences of his contumacy. He disposes of the traditional dualism of body and spirit.

[5] Ludwig Marcuse, *Obscene,* p. 264.

He shocks in order to liberate. When *Sexus* was being prosecuted in Oslo, Miller defended himself in a letter, dated February 27, 1959, against the charge that his book was obscene. He swept aside as irrelevant and absurd the judicial criteria applied. It was all nonsense. He was simply trying to make "sex pleasurable and innocent!"[6] He is in full opposition to all that society stands for, religion, politics, crime, especially its hypocritical and benighted attitude toward sex. His aim as a writer is to reveal everything about himself, no matter how shameful, to portray life nakedly in the form of a personal confession. Sex, he believes, can be a genuine source of joy, if only the repressive conventions that society imposes are removed. The experiences he describes are real, not contrived. *Sexus,* he insists, is not a dirty or evil book. "It is a dose of life which I administered to myself first, and which I not only survived but thrived on."[7] In defending his use of obscenity in his writing, he argues that when obscenity appears in literature

it usually functions as a technical device; the element of the deliberate which is there has nothing to do with sexual excitation, as in pornography. If there is an ulterior motive at work it is one which goes far beyond sex. Its purpose is to awaken, to usher in a sense of reality.[8]

The technical device, the stylistic method he employs is designed to provide an effective medium for his sexual manifesto in fiction. There is nothing tricky or flashy about it. In Freudian parlance, he simply knocks the censor over the head and proceeds to write about forbidden things – to tell *all* – in a disconcertingly forthright manner, each page a confession of the hitherto muzzled but now uninhibited libido.[9] He spruces up words conventionally regarded as vulgar and taboo, and brings them out smartly on parade, thus achieving an effect of daring originality, what Kenneth Burke calls perspective through incongruity. The solemn he treats with ribald mockery and iconoclastic disdain, the sublime with profane levity; the erotic, the sensual, the carnal – outlawed themes – he honors with lyrical fanfare and comic extravaganzas. Since the time of the Greeks sex in literature has been proscribed by Western civilization. Henry Miller considers it his mission to redress the balance, to restore sex to its rightful position of primacy.

Though a skeptic at heart, he has formulated his own code of transvalued values. Distrustful, like Hemingway, of big, inflated words like "love" and

---

[6] David Loth, *The Erotic in Literature.* New York: Julian Messner, Inc., 1961, p. 36.
[7] *Ibid.,* p. 37.
[8] Henry Miller, *Selected Prose.* London: Macgibbon & Kee, 1965, II, 364.
[9] This is a greatly enlarged and thoroughly revised version of an article by the present writer, "Henry Miller: Individualism in Extremis," *Southwest Review,* Summer, 1948, XXXIII, pp. 289–295.

"loyalty" and "sacred" and "idealism," he heaps fiery coals of contempt upon the heads of those who pay lip-service to these Pharisaical abstractions. His philosophy of life is that of an incorrigible individualist, lonely, rebellious, alienated. God is selfhood. His whole aim in life, he declares, "is to get near to God, that is, to get nearer to myself."[10] As a writer he is interested exclusively in himself, his career, his creative travail and fulfillment, his freedom, his integrity, his bodily appetites and their gratification. The world about him and the men and women in it are the raw material he exploits for his literary work. He beholds life as a spectacle, at present not a very edifying or diverting one. Society revolts him, for he detests its insane obsession with wealth, its crass falsification of values, its fatuous preoccupation with the trivial and the banal. From such a harsh, hideously distorted American reality he had fled to the Bohemian quarter in Paris where life, despite the burden of poverty he had to bear, was gay, sophisticated, insouciant, delightfully free from puritanic repressions. But the outbreak of the Second World War forced him to return to America, the air-conditioned nightmare he hates.

If he is not interested in society and in projects for its reform, that is because he has long ago abandoned all faith in economic panaceas. Salvation, if it is ever to be achieved, depends entirely upon the individual. Instead of discussing abstract toplofty ideas and espousing political causes of one kind or another, people should first come to terms with death and then decide how to lead their own lives. It is sheer folly to strive for material wealth and a greater abundance of mechanical conveniences. The artist revolts against such a shoddy and misguided fate. As artist he must not sacrifice his individuality for the sake of some artificial ideal like the brotherhood of man. That is why Henry Miller is opposed to revolutions. In the end they involve a return to the *status quo,* and the artist, the true revolutionary, is against the *status quo* at all times. Miller's ideal is to achieve an organic unity of life and art, to write about himself as best he can, without making any concessions to the arbitrary demands of society.[11] The rest is "literature."

He struggled desperately to emancipate himself from routine, the drudgery of work for pay, the irksome bonds of social responsibility. To be himself, to write, to be productive in his own way, to live as he pleased and in accordance with his convictions – that was the goal he set for himself. Why should he be everlastingly concerned about the distressed condition of humanity? He has his own problems to contend with. The world would go on even if he were to die at this moment. Why should he not be himself?

[10] Henry Miller, *Tropic of Cancer*. Paris: The Obelisk Press, 1939, p. 317.
[11] Henry Miller, *Tropic of Capricorn*. Paris: The Obelisk Press, 1939, p. 37.

Like Max Stirner in *The Ego and His Own,* he writes: 'The world would only begin to get something of value from me the moment I stopped being a serious member of society and became *—myself*." [12] He insists that life can be understood only in terms of individual experience; for him his own experience is the sole measure of truth. He must avoid formulas, systems of thought, utopian myths. He boasts proudly of the fact that he has never read a line of Karl Marx. The talk of the Marxist brethren makes him feel all the more convinced that he has missed nothing. The ideological drivel he hears about communism, capitalism, and Fascism sickens him. He is interested only in individuals, not in societies; in himself, not in the mass.

And having become himself, he was determined not to compromise. He would adventure in new directions, and that meant, as far as he was concerned, defying the social and moral taboos that surround the subject of sex. He would pursue his art and live his life without interference from others. And he had the courage, even at the beginning of his literary career, when he was desperately poor and utterly unknown, to refuse to make any damaging concessions. As an expatriate in Paris he was compelled to create a new life for himself; since he was cut off from his native roots, he had to nourish himself from within. His creative aim, which was to report the truth of experience in all its refractory, even unpleasant aspects, clearly called for the removal of all veils, thematic as well as verbal. Like Whitman by whom he was influenced, he would let forbidden voices speak through him: "Voices of sexes and lusts, voices veil'd and I remove the veil,/Voices indecent by me clarified and transfigured." As Henry Miller tells us in *The Cosmological Eye,* he had to become his own God. "Since I have become God I go the whole hog always." [13]

His admirers, puzzled by the militant pertinacity with which he plays the role of the prophet of sexuality, have surmised that there is a religious motivation behind his work. Lawrence Durrell, a close friend of Miller for many years, finds that what distinguishes Miller from the Marquis de Sade and Casanova is that his writings are informed with a religious intention, whether or not he is conscious of it. He is primarily a "religious" writer who "has effected an imaginative junction between the obscene and the holy . . . ." [14] This goes to show that in the case of a writer commonly regarded as the most aggressive and resourceful purveyor of obscenity in American litera-

---

[12] Henry Miller, *Sexus*. Paris: The Obelisk Press, 1949, p. 261.
[13] Henry Miller, *The Cosmological Eye*. Norfolk, Connecticut: New Directions, 1939, p. 3.
[14] *Art and Outrage: A Correspondence about Henry Miller between Lawrence Durrell and Alfred Perles*. New York: E. P. Dutton & Company, Inc., 1961, p. 23.

ture, the sex motif cannot be separated from the search for God, though this God manifests himself in the most grotesque erotic forms.

In novels like *Tropic of Cancer* and *Tropic of Capricorn,* Henry Miller explicitly states his creative purpose: to describe the sensual man as realistically as possible. From the very beginning, his ambition, like that of Thomas Wolfe, has been to devour all of experience, to include everything within the scope of his vision. Nothing human, however shocking, is to be concealed or glossed over. He is not concerned primarily with the psychology of sex. His object is rather to project in words the throbbing universe of sexuality, its anguish and aberrations, its ecstasies and disgusts: sex as spirit but chiefly sex as flesh incarnate, the base and the exalted, the inspired and the animalian. Throughout his fiction, however, the emphasis is placed not on the discredited emotion of love but on the raging, amoral libido, since this is closer to human nature as Henry Miller knows it. Man is represented as the personification of a will-driven, sex-demented, and sex-tormented sperm, while woman is no longer the vessel of the miracle of life's renewal, the high priestess in the sanctuary of love, but an organ for satisfying the inordinate sexual hunger of the male.

In the two novels mentioned above the nihilistic convictions of the author stand nakedly revealed. He believes in the primary instincts and their uninhibited fulfillment. The rest is so much hogwash – only he uses much stronger language to express his contempt for bourgeois morality. Man and woman, male and female, and their union in the flesh – this is alpha and omega, the aim and end of life. All other considerations are to be thrust aside as irrelevant and hypocritical. There is no God, beauty is a myth, idealism a patent fraud, justice a lie, love a sorry illusion. The secret of life lies wholly in sex. Here emerges the redemptive doctrine of the second lost generation, the religion divinely revealed by the numinous Priapus. Sex is the dynamism of life itself, the source of aliveness. Connected with it is the creative instinct: the ambition of the artist to perpetuate his ideas, to eternalize his genius, to hold up for contemplation a beautiful and intense moment of experience.

Henry Miller is the Bohemian nihilist who exploits the archetypes of God for his own profane purpose. He can, when it suits his mood, be properly blasphemous, spitting in the face of God. Like Salvador Dali, he is resolved to be uniquely and unregenerately himself. He will give birth to himself out of the grave of despair and he will elevate this despised and alienated self to the throne of God. He is an American who has jettisoned the whole cargo of religion, but he can speak in mystical accents of his unitive vision, his communion with the all-highest, God, but it is only a hyperbolic stance, a violent and for him appropiate literary metaphor. That represents his efforts to capture the heights of the sublime. His creative eye, when it is not contemplating the obscene, the disgusting, the excremental functions of the body, which are all parts of the divine creation, achieves states of ecstatic vision in which time present is obliterated and the poet is caught up in the artifice of eternity.

Like the mystics, Henry Miller deliberately seeks to focus on the most repulsive aspects of existence in order to recognize them as intrinsically beautiful, an organic part of the cosmic scheme of things. He glories in anality and thus, as Kingsley Widmer points out, transmutes the naturalistic fact, thus curiously brought into focus, into a metaphysical vision.[15] Like the Surrealists with whom he has much in common without swallowing their aesthetic as a whole, he finds everything in the world, the ugly, the hideous, the feculent, a source of wonder, a miracle in the making. Long before the beat writers made this transcendental discovery and intoned in rapt worship a hymn of praise for all things holy, Miller had included it as an integral part of his philosophy of being. For strange as it may seem, there is in this joyous nihilist a Transcendentalist echo. Like Emerson, he would look at Nature bare and see, actually see, the sun and the earth with the innocent eyes of a child. Like Emerson, he becomes "a transparent eyeball: I am nothing; I see all; the currents of the Universal Being circulate through me; I am part or parcel of God." [16]

But Miller is the type of author who resists all classification. He is a nihilist who rises above the slough of nihilism; a dedicated literary Bohemian who regards life as essentially more important than the writing of books. And he is a Transcendentalist with a difference, for he is never, not even in his most inspired epiphanies, reduced to nothing; he is always and intransigently himself, the rebellious individualist. If he invokes God, it is only the mysterious *persona* known as Miller raised to the highest degree. Thus he is able to capitalize on the dialectic of contradiction. He is saint and buffoon, iconoclast and man of God, blasphemer and *religieux*, devotee of the obscene and the sacred. He will revel in the dirt and muck of life, glory in the body and its secretions; he will project his nihilism in the spirit of hilarious fun, so that even his negation of what mankind has traditionally revered comes to seem a form of Dionysian acceptance. If there is any absolute to which Miller remains consistently faithful, it is the absolute of selfhood, the apotheosis of the God-usurping artist.

[15] Kingsley Widmer, *Henry Miller*. New York: Twayne Publishers, Inc., 1963, p. 23.
[16] *Selections from Ralph Waldo Emerson*. Edited by Stephen E. Whicher. Boston: Houghton Mifflin Company, 1957, p. 24.

His talk of God is counterpointed by his diagnosis of a civilization that has gone berserk, a world headed for the pit of destruction. Even sex has turned sour and frustrating. The possession of women offers no cure for the metaphysical sickness; it cannot heal the fractured being. The mystery of sex proves disenchanting, it is a nothing, a physiological illusion, and yet Miller's characters pursue it obsessively. Even at the culminating moment before the orgasm, the burden of loneliness is not lifted; and after the climax has been reached one remains cut off, spent, empty inside. Miller thus brings in sex as a strategic means to convey the demented, intolerable quality of contemporary life. Sex induces despair because of its very instinctual compulsion. It has become mechanized, a purely functional ritual unaccompanied by any genuine feeling.

But the conception of sex as stricken with the malaise of metaphysical despair, as doomed to post-coital disappointment, is not allowed to detract from the liberating, health-giving, life-affirming value of the sexual experience. What was once considered degrading is now regarded by writers like Henry Miller and Norman Mailer as the highest manifestation of the Life Force. To be spontaneously sexual, to achieve, in the language of Wilhelm Reich, orgastic potency, is to be truly alive; to deny the body and its instincts is to sign a covenant with death. Life is opposed to death, Eros to Thanatos, sexuality to spirituality and intellectualism. Nevertheless, this delirious overestimation of the sexual function is a symptom of spiritual despair because it concentrates all feelings, all sensations, in the genitalia and reduces man to the level of the beasts in the field. Ideals and aspirations do not count. The world of the spirit is a phantom world, bloodless, abstract, which has betrayed mankind, whereas the world of the flesh is tangible, palpitatingly real, and thoroughly satisfying. That, in general, is the central theme which runs through the work of such writers as Hemingway, Henry Miller, and Norman Mailer. Instinct, like sex, cannot go wrong, whereas ideas – and particularly ideals – lead us woefully astray and bring about various mental and nervous disorders. Therefore, sexuality is exalted as salvation. Once the curse of Puritanism is cast off, art will flourish and culture take a new lease on life. The human personality, happily sexualized, will become enriched and magnificently creative.

This literary defence of eroticism – and we shall encounter it again later on in the book – was based for the most part on a crude identification of sex with love. The American prophets of the new sex-*Anschauung* dismissed the age-old, folk-nurtured philosophy of love, which was nothing more, they contended, than a beguiling pretence that the two sexes are best united on ideal, spiritual grounds when the truth is that the real basis of union is sensual through and through. Sex is spirit, sex is love, sex is creation and finds sublimated expression in literature, music, and art. The world was peopled with sex, obsessed with sex, diseased with sex denied or wrongly used. The insurgents, up in arms against the moral sublimation of the sexual impulse, were convinced they had found a cure for what ailed mankind: we must accept the challenge of the sex instinct and then our neurotic obsession will simply disappear.

These prophets were fundamentally mistaken in their assumptions. Love and sexuality are closely related, but it is wrong to assume that love, since it is connected with the libido, is nothing but sex. Sexuality is an impersonal force of energy implanted in Nature, so that it can function, without the mediation of love, on a purely physiological level. But physical gratification alone is not enough to make a man happy.[17] For man does not wish to be possessed by instinct; he has no desire to be equated with the body and its appetites; he wants to be loved for his own sake. The belief that sex is all in all culminates in despair, and Henry Miller shows that this is so in the case of those characters in his fiction who act in accordance with this belief. Once the Dionysiac fury of lust is spent, what is left? Sex is, after all, but one beat in the cosmic rhythm, one part of life. To repress it brings about frustration and even neurotic breakdown; to suppress everything else in life in order to give it unrestrained expression entails an even more harmful deformation of the self.

D. H. Lawrence never fell into the lamentable error of considering sex more important than the creative purpose in life a man strives to fulfill; he warned his readers against making the dangerous mistake of confusing this purpose with sex.[18] "When man loses his deep sense of purposive, creative activity, he feels lost, and is lost. When he makes the sexual consummation the supreme consummation . . . he falls into the beginnings of despair."[18] The two issues, sex and the life-purpose, instinctual gratification and the pursuit of the ideal, must not be confused. "With sex as the one accepted prime motive, the world drifts into despair and anarchy."[19] America, according to Lawrence, has most to fear from lapsing into moral anarchy of this kind. Not that sex is to be repressed. By no means. If sex as an end in itself is a

---

[17] "Why is man unhappy and lonely in spite of an abundance of sexual opportunities? Why does fulfillment not necessarily generate gratitude and love but often produce hostility and hate?" Clemens E. Benda, *The Image of Love.* New York: The Free Press of Glencoe, Inc., 1961, p. 16.

[18] D. H. Lawrence, *Psychoanalysis and the Unconscious* and *Fantasia of the Unconscious.* New York: The Viking Press, 1960, p. 143.

[19] *Ibid.,* p. 144.

vice, "an ideal purpose which has no roots in the deep sea of passionate sex is a greater disaster still." [20]

Lawrence struggles to maintain a healthy moral attitude toward sex, but Henry Miller goes the whole hog.[21] He has gained the dubious distinction of being called the poet laureate of sexuality; he has thus far outstripped all other contemporary American writers (with the possible exception of James Jones in his recent novel, *Go to the Widow-Maker*) in uncensored freedom of sex-expression. He is a monomaniac on the subject. *Tropic of Cancer* and *Tropic of Capricorn,* both formerly banned in the United States, are enough to make one feel that the man is "mad." If Strindberg is "mad" in his misogynistic fixation, Henry Miller is equally "mad" in his grotesquely exaggerated interpretation of the lubricious nature of women. He debunks the myth of woman as the dangerous sex, a myth in which sex becomes closely associated with sin.[22] Practically all of Miller's female characters are perpetually in heat while the male characters are in a corresponding state of rutting frenzy. The talk of the men, their dreams, dwell predominantly on the theme of sex. The pursuit of woman, the sex-object, who in obedience to social convention puts up a token resistance or feigns unwillingness, lends the spice of dramatic excitement to an otherwise drab, intolerable existence. She is all body and all passion, but without individuality.[23] There is no

---

[20] *Ibid.,* p. 214.

[21] Henry Miller is incapable of the intuitive empathy Lawrence displays in his portrayal of the principal female characters in *The Rainbow* and *Women in Love.* Unlike Lawrence, he makes no pretence of acting according to any moral code. He stresses the prerogatives and the point of view of the lordly, conquering male. This male ethos, as Widmer shrewdly notes, "insistently, perhaps with overrated iconoclasm, emphasizes the physical to the exclusion of most subtleties of psychology and sentiment." (Kingsley Widmer, *Henry Miller,* p. 85.) In comparing Miller and Lawrence, Philip Rahv writes: "Miller is morally passive, whereas Lawrence . . . was sustained throughout by his supreme gift for moral activity . . . ." (Philip Rahv, "Sketches in Criticism: Henry Miller," in George Wickes (ed.), *Henry Miller and the Critics.* Carbondale: Southern Illinois University Press, 1963, p. 84.) Lawrence Durrell declares that the distinction between *Tropic of Cancer* and *Lady Chatterley's Lover* revolves around this controversial point of moral justification – "for Miller (who, unlike Lawrence, has thoroughly assimilated Freud) recognizes that sex is *both* a sacrament *and* also uproariously funny (not to mention silly, holy, and tiresome all in one . . . ." (Lawrence Durrell, "Studies in Genius," in *Ibid.,* p. 94.)

[22] "Under male dominance women have always accepted the roles which men have created for them. Having reduced them to the role of submissive dependents, men then criticized them for being submissively dependent." H. R. Hays, *The Dangerous Sex.* New York: G. P. Putnam's Sons, 1964, p. 179.

[23] Henry Miller has been severely criticized – and rightly so – for his imperceptive treatment of women in fiction. "Most of the sexual encounters in the *Tropics* and *The Rosy Crucifixion* are comic accidents . . . . The woman never emerges at all." Kenneth Rexroth, *Bird in the Bush.* New York: New Directions, 1959, p. 166.

marriage of true minds. Here at last is an American writer who dares to tell the unvarnished truth about the copulating animal known as man. What unbridled fantasies are spun by his aroused imagination, what prodigies of phallic valor, what stratagems and assaults, what wild pursuits, what Dionysian ecstasies – and what sad aftermaths!

Miller is too egocentric a novelist to do justice to the phenomenology of love or passion; hence he specializes in the physiology of sex. And it is his radical inability to believe in the genuineness of the experience of love that accounts in large measure for his concentration on the physical trappings of sexuality. The woman is only a sexual partner, always or almost always a willing and enthusiastic partner in the primal dance of passion. As Widmer says: "The physical acts of love in his writings invariably emphasize detachment and dehumanization – often hilariously so."[24] Henry Miller exposes the lie of love and only the fact of passion is left, but even that is a cheat.

Is this then a true picture of human reality in Paris or Brooklyn or anywhere else on earth, or a sheer nightmare of lust, the product of a perversely constituted imagination? Or is it essentially a *tour de force,* a Rabelaisian extravaganza in which the mechanics of sex are portrayed as comical as well as revolting? The curious feature about the whole business is that the author is all the time perfectly aware of the morbid implications of his obsession with sex. He links the unappeasable hunger of the flesh to the overwhelming consciousness of doom and death, and it is this shifting double perspective that makes his best work a contribution to literature rather than pornography. Like Hemingway, always at his back he hears time's chariot hurrying near. Sex, while it affirms life, is also one way of denying life. Henry Miller knows there is no escape from this dilemma; each moment leads inexorably to the ultimate of timelessness, but this perception does not drive him, as it did Aldous Huxley, to a mystical renunciation of instinct. Since he is doomed no matter what he does, he will not observe the moral code. He will cry out the horrible truth, even if he defiles Love and Beauty, Man and God. In the end time will conquer and chaos be enthroned, for behind the world there is chaos. Sex is Miller's chaos, his desperate method of running away from the doom of Time.

If he is convinced that the world is slowly dying of cancer, he is also convinced that the people who inhabit this world are wretched creatures, convulsed with lust and rage, decadent, ripe for suicide. Yet this vision of doomsday fills Miller with unaccountable elation. Let the deluge come, let the fire and brimstone consume Sodom and Gemorrah. The world for the past century has been dying; let it die. He would like to see it blown to

[24] Kingsley Widmer, *Henry Miller,* p. 76.

smithereens. "We are going to put it down – the evolution of the world which has died but which has not been buried. We are swimming in the face of time and all else has been drowned, is drowning, or will drown."[25] What is at the root of this cancer, what is dragging us down? The answer Miller gives is that men have deceived themselves too long with illusions and false ideals, and they have shed Niagaras of blood to preserve these illusions and false ideals.

Henry Miller, like D. H. Lawrence, has little faith in the power of reason. He draws a heavily weighted contrast between the life of ideas, which is sterile and stultifying, and the spontaneous, instinctive life, which makes for organic fulfillment. "Ideas have to be wedded to action," he declares; "if there is no sex in them, no vitality in them, there is no action. Ideas cannot exist alone in a vacuum of the mind."[26] In literature his object is to present "a resurrection of the emotions, to depict the conduct of a human being in the stratosphere of ideas, that is in the grip of delirium. To paint a pre-Socratic being, part goat, part Titan."[27] The superstructure of our world, we are told, rests on a rotten lie, with the result that humanity has deplorably declined in thought, feeling, and action.

When a hungry, desperate spirit appears and makes the guinea pigs squeal it is because he knows where to put the live wire of sex, because he knows that beneath the hard carapace of indifference there is concealed the ugly gash, the wound that never heals.[28]

There is the obscene horror that must be faced in all its compelling reality. Sex is at least very much alive, but inertia, inaction, ataraxia, paralysis of the will, these are worse than death. That is the fate of man: to endure the crucifixion – and the resurrection – of sex. There is no other way out. That is Miller's rationale of justification for seeking to portray a world of *natural* men and women, a world of teeming passions, dreams, perversions, madness. The aim is not merely to describe the instinct of sex in action but to deal with it truthfully, imaginatively, creatively.

What saves Henry Miller's fiction from being a dreadfully boring exercise in pornography is the personality of the man, life-loving, earth-rooted, and exuberantly joyous. Though he sexualizes the universe, he provides immensely rewarding moments when he confesses his inner secret, reveals his inner being, and rises to the plane of the universal. Then there is no mistaking the power and beauty of his utterance, even if we are irritated by his

[25] Henry Miller, *Tropic of Cancer*, p. 36.
[26] *Ibid.*, p. 245.
[27] *Ibid.*, p. 246.
[28] *Ibid.*, p. 252.

obtrusive and often irresponsible individualism. He will speak out and use the language of the body, no matter how revolting other people consider his revelations.

As a disciple of D. H. Lawrence,[29] though the pupil has surpassed the master in his treatment of the physiology of sex, he holds in profound contempt the ethics of Comstockery, the dogmatic viciousness which looks upon the sexual instinct as evil, and the brazen sanctimoniousness which insists on fig-leaved euphemisms or stringent avoidance of all sexual subjects as indecent. His sex morality, if such it can be called, proclaims itself to be beyond good and evil. Sexual fulfillment is the aim and end of life, and no scruple of conscience or spiritual nonsense should be allowed to stand in the way. His work is utterly free of sin or guilt. The erotic is the source of the divine. Sex, the universal instinct, the orgone energy that runs through all flesh and blood and mind, must be accepted for what it is, and any attempt to proscribe it on moral grounds is not only ineffectual but absurd. Just as well proscribe earthquakes or hurricanes on similar grounds. Like sex, they exist as tameless elemental forces. Sex *is*!

Henry Miller has written the testament of a sex-obsessed mind, based on the premise that all men's minds — and bodies, too — are sex-obsessed. What he was trying to do, as he confesses, was to dig a tunnel through the earth to get to the other side, "the ne plus ultra of the honeymoon of flesh." [30] The quest, fortunately, turns out to be metaphysical as well as physical in nature, mystical as well as sexual. Sex is used recurrently as a symbol of the search for meaning and fulfillment all men engage in. Woman is the incarnation of all that man hungers for, the embodied illusion of supreme felicity. Sex, too, harnessed to the motor of the imagination, re-enacts the death and resurrection of the body. All of which, according to Henry Miller, is a figurative way of talking about that which is really ineffable.

His outspokenness is part of his Ishmaelite complex; it rounds out his furious gesture of repudiation. He must affirm by first cultivating the extreme art of negation. In order to be reborn he has to die. Everything is perishable, in eternal flux. What is left? Only the capacity for sensual enjoyment. "I wanted," he declares, "to feel the blood running back into my

29 In "Creative Death," a fragment from a projected but unfinished work, *The World of Lawrence*, Miller pays high tribute to this visionary genius who penetrated the ultimate mystery of the cosmos. Lawrence is the artist who is forever reaching out to higher modes of being. Miller defines the artist in man as "the undying symbol of the union between his warring selves. Life has to be given a meaning because of the obvious fact that it has no meaning." (Henry Miller, *The Wisdom of the Heart*. Norfolk, Connecticut: New Directions, 1960, p. 5.) Literature is thus a mobilization of all the creative forces against the haunting terror of death.

30 Henry Miller, *Tropic of Capricorn*, p. 199.

veins, even at the cost of annihilation . . . . I wanted the dark fecundity of nature, the deep well of the womb, silence, or else the lapping of the dark waters of death." [31] But if he is to be reborn, if he is to be saved from death, then he must recover the pristine vitality of instinct, rediscover the meaning and power of sex. The ironic leitmotif of *Tropic of Capricorn* is given in the words of Kronski, who tells the narrator of the story: "Listen, that's what's the matter with you – you've got nothing but sex on the brain." [32]

Despite the many passages in Henry Miller's fiction on the aesthetics of sex, it is difficult to determine what his basic motives are, what daimon drives him, what he hopes to achieve by thus defiantly overemphasizing the erotic theme. Why should he regard the frank and full portrayal of sex relations in the novel as the crucial test of realism? Why is this to be established as the touchstone of truth? Why write as if sex constituted all of life? And why omit entirely the experience of love in or out of marriage? If his purpose is to startle the reader and break down his inhibitions, the method Miller employs – the repetition of the once forbidden four-letter word, the use of excrementitious epithets – succumbs before long to the law of diminishing returns; after a while these words lose their power to shock. Miller's persistent reliance on the shock value of obscenity is an indication of the extent to which he, like Joyce whose blasphemies in *Ulysses* are an expression of his emotional attachment to the Catholicism he has presumably cast aside, is still affected by the very conventions he would destroy.

If we reject, as we must, the assumption that Miller is writing pornography, then we must conclude that he harps so insistently on sex because he honestly believes that sex is the road to salvation. Not that he is unaware of the contradictions that such naturalistic sex mysticism generates. For time is his enemy as it is the enemy of all mankind, and it is not to be defeated by embracing a cult of biological hedonism. Not believing in God, the hero as dedicated sensualist must live feverishly in the present moment. Having abandoned both Heaven and Hell and the vision of the ideal inamorata, the Don Juans in Miller's fictional cosmos must turn to sex again and again as a means of combating the threat of eternity. For example, in *Tropic of Cancer,* what terrifies Van Norden more than anything else is the fear of being left alone, and he struggles to overcome this fear by forever chasing women. Yet, like Don Juan, he can never "possess" the women he seduces. Even when he is with them, at the most poignant moment of sexual intimacy, he cannot lose himself. A divided being, perpetually spying upon himself, he resorts to sex because that is the one way of obliterating for a brief

[31] *Ibid.,* p. 81.
[32] *Ibid.,* p. 91.

moment the hatefully obtrusive self. No woman, however, can cure him of his sickly self-absorption nor can sexual indulgence rid him of his ferocious self-contempt. This seems to lend support to Miller's contention that his books are not about sex but about the quest for self-liberation. Concerning *Tropic of Cancer* he says: "Liberally larded with the sexual as was that work, the concern of its author was not with sex, nor with religion, but with the problem of self-liberation." [33]

If Henry Miller concentrates attention on those physical appetencies that American culture has hitherto outlawed in print, namely sex, he does so because it enables him to make some remarkable discoveries about the night-side of human nature; desires unacknowledged, thoughts screened or suppressed, erotic fantasies hidden in the dark of the unconscious, are all brought to light. He exploits the sexual myth because he is convinced everything else about modern man is dead. A primitivist in many respects like Sherwood Anderson and D. H. Lawrence, he believes that civilization has robbed our instincts of their purity of expression, transforming us into cerebrated, intellectualized, but passionless creatures. The only thing that interests him vitally as a writer, Miller announces, is "the recording of all that which is omitted in books." [34] He would redress the balance. In short, he specializes in the erotic because he hopes in this way to overcome the anesthesia of modern life. Man has been betrayed by the better part of his nature. And what is the solution? To make the word flesh again, to live joyously in the present. "I am only spiritually dead," Miller writes. "Physically I am alive. Morally I am free." [35]

This quotation affords a fitting description of Miller's heroes, who are spiritually dead but morally free and physically very much alive. And it is sex, we are assured, which is the only experience capable of bringing them back to life. Sex gives them a moment of orgasmic beatitude, but then comes the inevitable reaction of the aftermath: the disillusionment, the weariness, the satiety, the disgust. The cycle of desire and disenchantment never stops. They embody, these amoral nihilists, the truth of Shakespeare's definition in Sonnet CXXIX of lust in action: "The expense of spirit in a waste of shame," except that they never feel a sense of shame, only the ache of emptiness. Perhaps the next experience will be different. Hence their urge to seek new varieties of erotic sensation. Though they suspect that it is all a species of illusion, they can fix their mind on nothing else but sex. "All that

---

[33] *The Henry Miller Reader.* Edited by Lawrence Durrell. Norfolk, Connecticut: New Directions, 1959, p. 356.
[34] Henry Miller, *Tropic of Cancer*, p. 21.
[35] *Ibid.*, p. 107.

mystery about sex and then you discover that it's nothing – just a blank." [36]
Sex without love, though Miller rarely uses that compromising word, is
utterly without meaning.

The sexual scenes in *Tropic of Cancer* alternate with eloquent apostro-
phes to Matisse, with passages of soaring vision when the body of this death
is transcended and the feverish compulsion of sex is for the moment forgotten and the imaginative artist speaks of his loneliness and the meaning of
his pilgrimage on earth. Since all the roads of life lead to the one terminus:
death, he is determined to reveal the whole truth about life, the dark, festering places of the human heart, the mystery of sex.

If anyone knew what it meant to read the riddle of that thing which to-day is
called a "crack" or a "hole", if anyone had the least feeling of mystery about
the phenomena which are labelled "obscene", this world would crack asunder.
It is the obscene horror, the dry, fucked-out aspect of things which makes this
crazy civilization look like a crater . . . . When a hungry, desperate spirit appears
and makes the guinea pigs squeal it is because he knows where to put the live
wire of sex . . . . And he puts the live wire right between the legs . . . . The dry,
fucked-out crater is obscene. More obscene than anything is inertia. [37]

Henry Miller's work forces upon the critic the enormously difficult task
of trying to determine the difference between pornography and literature. It
is hard to formulate the difference with precision, but the difference is
perceptibly there. *Lady Chatterley's Lover* and *Tropic of Cancer,* when
judged as a whole and not by isolated offensive passages taken out of context, are by no means pornographic in content. The current standard of
public taste generally decides the issue of what is permissible in print. Is
there any way then of distinguishing between pornography and obscenity?
Is the first morally objectionable at a given time while the other is permitted
on the ground that it is a realistic rendition of life? [38] The fight against re-

---

[36] *Ibid.,* pp. 147–148.

[37] *Ibid.,* p. 252.

[38] Alfred Perles, in his eulogistic biography of Henry Miller, takes up the problem
of pornography. "There are about a dozen words in the English language – in any
language, for that matter – which the censor takes exception to. Miller uses them, but
without being pornographic." (Alfred Perles, *My Friend Henry Miller.* New York: Day,
1956, p. 106.) Geoffrey Gorer, the British anthropologist, points out what is perfectly
true, that a literary work may be pornographic in content without directly employing
obscene words. Pornography, Gorer holds, "is defined by its subject and its attitude
thereto. The subject matter is sexual activity of any overt kind, which is depicted as
inherently desirable and exciting . . . it is a fiction, in prose or verse, narrative or
dialogue, mainly or entirely concerned with the sexual activities of the imagined characters." (C. H. Rolph (ed.), *Does Pornography Matter?* London: Routledge & Kegan
Paul, 1961, pp. 29–30.) Pornography, Gorer goes on to say, has been progressively
narrowed in scope until at the present time it is left "with little but the description of
the activities of various sets of genitals." (*Ibid.,* p. 30.)

pressive censorship has in recent years been won in the courts and need not be rehashed at this point. It is now acknowledged that serious writers like Joyce, D. H. Lawrence, Henry Miller, and Norman Mailer are justified in exploring the night-side of the personality, its irrational and libidinal components. Sex is as much a part of life as the aspirations of the spirit, and the language of sex is as legitimate a part of literature as the vocabulary of idealism.

And yet there are times when Henry Miller oversteps the bounds of decency and produces fiction that must be judged as pornographic in content. His worship of Pan turns into a carefully staged *Walpurgisnacht*. The image of sexual love is dragged in the mud. A case in point is *Sexus*, the first part of the trilogy, *The Rosy Crucifixion*, in which scenes of riotous lust are brought in for their own sake. The novel is of sex all compact, deliriously absorbed in descriptions of the physiology of coition. Though the power of mystical perception is still present, this is offset by an overemphasis on what Lawrence Durrell, a friend and admirer of Miller, calls "lavatory filth." [39] He roundly accuses Miller "of finger-painting in his own excrement rather than producing art." [40] The contents of the book alternate between passages of poignant self-analysis and long sections that are devoted to a minutely detailed account of the hero's sexual exploits. What we are given is the pseudo-romanticism of sex, the mechanics of copulation, the whole business incredibly exaggerated, though Miller, in replying to Durrell's charge, defends himself on the ground that he was trying to recapture the truth of his experience of the past, just as it happened. The protagonist, again the Miller *persona,* has but one aim in life: to sleep with as many women as he can seduce. His policy is to follow his "natural" sexual impulses to the limit.

Yet this sex-conqueror, this dreamer, thirty-three years old, takes himself with fundamental seriousness; he broods on his uniqueness, his indisputable, if still unrecognized, genius. He is seeking to find himself, to enter upon his career as a writer. Unfortunately he has not been able to escape from the air-conditioned nightmare that is America. Employed as a manager in a telegraph company (this was before his flight to Paris), he finds the world around him ugly and detestable, a reality that negates all he desires and secretly yearns for. The city is a vast cemetery, smelling rankly of death. Repeatedly, in this as in his previous novels, Miller draws a lurid, repellent picture of our frenetic, anxiety-ridden, money-mad civilization. Then he reaffirms once more his redemptive message: the only thing that can restore

---

[39] *Lawrence Durrell and Henry Miller: A Private Correspondence.* Edited by George Wickes. New York: E. P. Dutton & Co., Inc., 1963, p. 265.
[40] *Art and Outrage,* p. 53.

man to life is the elixir of sex – sex and the life of dreams. He is amazed by the paradox of the mystery of sex: that it should generate such exorbitant desires and produce such disappointing results. Suddenly he delivers his blasphemous and ironic annunciation of faith:

I believe in God the Father, in Jesus Christ his only begotten Son, in the blessed Virgin Mary, the Holy Ghost, in Adam Cadmium, in chrome nickel, the oxides and the mercurochromes, in water-fowls and water-cress, in epileptoid seizures, in bubonic plagues, in Devachan, in planetary conjunctions, in chicken tracks and stick throwing, in revolutions, in stock crashes, in wars, earthquakes, cyclones, in Kali Yuga and in hula-hula. *I believe. I believe.* I believe because not to believe is to become as lead, to lie prone and rigid, forever inert, to waste away . . . .[41]

Like Whitman, he mystically accepts everything in the world: the divine and the demonic, the good and the evil, the ugly and the beautiful, the obscene and the sublime.

But surrounding him is the effluvia of industrialism run amok, spelling desolation and death. He is a wage-slave incarcerated within this prison of stone and steel. Hence, Miller argues, it is understandable that his thoughts should dwell on woman as the means of his emancipation, on sex as salvation. All he knows is that in the darkest moments of failure and despair there are reserve funds of energy which carry a man along and sustain him – that is, if he wishes to be saved. There, at any rate, is the portrait of the nihilistic, sexually-committed hero Miller paints for us. He labors to make us believe that the only thing which can rouse this protagonist to flights of creative inspiration is sex; it is sex that makes it possible for him to view the crazy world around him in proper perspective. It is Mara who awakens in him the dormant ambition to write.

He spends many pages, in each of the three novels that make up the trilogy, in analyzing this impulse to write, why it arises, how it functions. The best writing, Miller feels, is automatic, born of the unconscious, without the collaboration of the conscious will.

A man writes to throw off the poison which has accumulated because of his false way of life. He is trying to recapture his innocence, yet all he succeeds in doing (by writing) is to inoculate the world with the virus of his disillusionment. No man would set a word down on paper if he had the courage to live out what he believed in.[42]

It is passages like these which reward the reader who has the patience to wade through this lengthy pornographic novel: these illuminating reflections on the non-conformist character of the writer and on the art of writing

---

[41] Henry Miller, *Sexus,* pp. 14–15.
[42] *Ibid.,* pp. 24–25.

which reveal the appalling gap that separates the creative intention from the words that finally come forth.

Words, sentences, ideas, no matter how subtle or ingenious, the maddest flights of poetry, the most profound dreams, the most hallucinating visions, are but crude hieroglyphs chiselled in pain and sorrow to commemorate an event which is untransmissible.[43]

These interludes, however brilliantly written, are not enough to save the book, which depends upon a simplistic psychology of sex. The assumption throughout, blatantly underlined, is that men are the insatiable hunters, undeterred by moral scruples of any kind, concerned solely with enjoying as many orgiastic experiences as possible with as many different women as possible, and that the women, if properly tempted and aroused, will respond with eager, shameless abandon. Henry Miller cannot curb his inordinate interest in the sex life of his characters. Whether deliberate or not, *Sexus* is a concoction of pornography, which reduces the male to the lowest common denominator of promiscuous sexuality. Happy marriages do not exist; monogamy is a myth; infidelity is the rule among both men and women.

But this is to put a moral gloss on his fiction, and that is perhaps a wrong approach. His work as a whole is informed with an eldritch humor, product of an imagination that beholds the world and the behavior of the men and women in it from an original, thoroughly unconventional point of view. Himself an "original" character, he has an alert and sympathetic eye for the quirks of nonconformity in others, their streaks of wildness, the methods they use to overcome the inevitable frustrations and tedium of life. Some drink to forget their wretchedness, some take up fantastic hobbies, some lead "double lives," some pursue the dream of sex as if it could lift them above the rut of routine, some are veritable cranks, self-appointed evangelists of salvation and damnation, true believers, prophets, mystics, visionaries, holy madmen. Miller observes all of them with objective curiosity, listens to their ravings, seeks to penetrate the secret of their being, but remains intrinsically himself, unaffected by their lives or their preachment. And it is because he cannot be shaken out of his orbit by the conjunction of other planetary influences, that he is able to discern the sad but often hilarious oddity of the human animal, the disparity between semblance and reality, between the public mask and the grotesquely distorted face of suffering desperation it is intended to hide. What Miller at his best reveals is a streak of black humor, an irony that is surprised by nothing, a realism of insight, though not without its comic counterpoint, that is hardened to expect the worst of human nature. He is essentially a comic writer. "To Miller,

[43] *Ibid.,* p. 27.

sex is not an instrument of power and degradation but a howling joke, and the most comic of all created things is the female sex organ as observed by his own oddly objective, though properly concupiscent eye."[44]

To sum up: A twentieth-century Bohemian, Miller is painfully aware of his alienation from society. He remains individualistic in an age of techno-logical coordination because he believes that the modern artist can win his freedom and maintain his integrity only by accentuating the uniqueness of his ego. Only in this way can he come organically close to reality, without being drugged and desensitized by the opiate of routine, work, habit, politics, stereotyped religion. Spontaneity is the very law of our being. His mission, he feels, is not to submit or to rebel but to remain incorruptibly himself. His work is the testament of a creative spirit who believes it his duty to reveal the truth about man, however unpalatable it may seem to his generation. He is convinced that life in all its totality must be accepted, the carnal as well as the spiritual. Though he has occasionally produced pornographic fiction, he is no pornographer by vocation. His glorification of sex is actually a Dionysian celebration of life in its most dynamic manifestations. He asks the ultimate metaphysical question: what shall a man live for? And the answer he gives, in no sentimental terms, is: sexual love; reunion with the godhead, the limitless expansion of consciousness. His message to mankind is sounded by one of his characters in *Plexus*: "*Let us become fully alive, that is what I have been trying to say.*"[45]

His signal limitation is that he rarely goes beyond the physical realm. Despite his excesses in the art of erotica, he will be remembered in the an-nals of American literature as one of the experimental writers who initiated, like Sherwood Anderson and Ernest Hemingway, a return to primitivistic starkness of expression, as a novelist who endeavored to leave no expe-rience of man, however sordidly sexual or illicit, unrecorded. He will be remembered, too, as one of the patron saints of the beat generation who developed still further his revolutionary sex ideology.

---

[44] Leslie A. Fiedler, *Waiting for the End*. New York: Stein and Day, 1964, p. 39.
[45] Henry Miller, *Plexus*. London: Weidenfeld and Nicolson, 1963, p. 373.

CHAPTER XI

THE SEXUALIZED WORLD OF THE BEAT GENERATION

A single hour of blazing carnal sensuality makes up for a whole month during which one has asked oneself daily: "In such circumstances, is life worth
living?" [1]

Today, the modern novelist, announcing a realistic physical man, has spawned
a fetal thing whose brains and bones cause us . . . to put rue into our nostrils.
We are, finally, so defiled that we have to shriek at the Uncleanness of our
organs and functions in a cloacal, naturalistic literature. [2]

Is it "honesty" to report of human nature only what lies between the legs? Is it
"courage" to dive into a cesspool, and then come up dripping with ordure? [3]

The cult of passionate love has been so far *democratized* as to have lost its
esthetic virtues together with its spiritual and tragic values . . . . [4]

There is no longer any place in present-day civilized life for a simple natural
love between two human beings. [5]

1. The Transvaluation of Values [6]

In his essay, "Eroticism in Literature," Alberto Moravia, the Italian novelist, declares that the signal victory won in the field of literary expression
marked a welcome release from the trammels of social convention, a triumph over the tyranny of taboo. Sex is no longer shocking when is appears

[1] Henry de Montherlant, *Selected Essays.* Translated by John Weightman. New
York: The Macmillan Company, 1961, p. 244.
[2] Edward Dahlberg, *Can These Bones Live.* New York: New Directions, 1960,
pp. 65–66.
[3] Robert Elliot Fitch, *The Decline and Fall of Sex.* New York: Harcourt, Brace and
Company, 1957, p. 109.
[4] Denis de Rougemont, *Love in the Western World.* New York: Harcourt, Brace and
Company, 1940, p. 14.
[5] Sigmund Freud, *Collected Papers.* London: Hogarth Press, 1950, IV, p. 210.
Quoted in Herbert Marcuse, *Eros and Civilization.* Boston: The Beacon Press, 1955,
p. 264.
[6] A small part of this chapter is based on an article by Charles I. Glicksberg, "Sex
in Literature." *The Colorado Quarterly,* IX, Winter, 1961, pp. 277–287.

as a central subject in literature. The fig leaf has been dropped. There is no further need for euphemistic discourse or the cautious strategy of evasion. "Today, for the first time for many centuries," Moravia goes on to say, "the sexual act can be represented directly, explicitly, realistically and poetically in a literary work, whenever the work itself makes this necessary."[7] To the question whether it is necessary to dwell on the sexual act, he replies that it is not always necessary but when it is necessary it must be dealt with, and to avoid it becomes a problem of art, not of morals. If sex is talked about so often in modern literature, that is because sex in our time is equated with love. The prohibitions and inhibitions of the past have been broken down. Psychoanalysis has stepped into the picture as the arbiter of moral values.

This summary diagnosis of eroticism in European literature holds equally true of conditions in literary America. There is one difference, though: the sexual revolution that has erupted in some literary quarters in the United States has been conducted under the auspices of Wilhelm Reich rather than those of Sigmund Freud. The beatniks and hipsters who are seeking to overthrow what they regard as the morally repellent and repressive tradition of American culture in matters of sex are too radical in their thinking and style of life to accept the advice or even require the services of an orthodox psychoanalyst. Convinced that the society they live in is abnormally constituted, they militantly refuse to conform to what they consider its life-negating standards. Like Henry Miller, their conception of love is based not on spiritualized feelings of communion but on glorified instinct. Biology is king. The orgone box is the holy of holies. The new categorical imperative reads as follows: the foul demons of repression must be exorcised, the folly of asceticism inherent in the Puritan system of ethics must be overcome and this can best be accomplished by surrendering in all Dionysian innocence and ecstasy – and without benefit of moral casuistry – to the call of sex. It is desire that is sovereign, desire that liberates and exalts. That is how to get rid of the insidious neurotic fixation on the dogma of original sin.[8] This is the goal of Reichian primitivism they sought to reach: to fuse with the elemental flux of orgone energy that is Nature.

Their programmatic intention of exploring fully the meaning of sexual experience in order to comprehend the nature of man in its totality is, from

---

[7] Alberto Moravia, *Man as an End*. Translated by Bernard Wall. New York: Farrar Straus & Giroux, 1965, p. 228.

[8] Kierkegaard associates original sin with sexuality. Sin came into the world and "sexuality was posited – the one being inseparable from the other." (Sören Kierkegaard *The Concept of Dread*. Translated by Walter Lowrie. Princeton: Princeton University Press, 1946, p. 44.) It is because man is spirit, a synthesis of soul and body, that Kierkegaard couples sexuality with sinfulness.

an aesthetic point of view, unassailable. They might, in theoretical defence of their position, proclaim as their motto: *Nihil humanum a mihi alienum puto.* It is difficult, however, at first glance, to discover any close connection between sexuality, as they interpret it, and literature. Their manifesto simply calls for an experimental advance that was largely carried through by such pioneers as Joyce, Sherwood Anderson, Hemingway, D. H. Lawrence, and Henry Miller. But with the exception of Henry Miller, who gave the beat generation his paternal blessing, none of these writers ever maintained that sex was the be-all and end-all of existence. As we have seen, what happened after the disillusioning experience of the First World War and the rapid spread of Freudian doctrine was that the imperative of physical passion gradually replaced the sentiment of love. Sex became the dominant force in life among the younger generation of intelligentsia; sex was its own excuse for being. The identification of love with sex was made in explicit terms. Down with marriage, down with monogamy, down with sex designed solely for procreative purposes [9] – that was the rallying cry raised, and it was now being renewed with greater stridency and force of conviction by the creative spokesmen of the beat generation. [10]

The twentieth-century writer, especially in the United States, is frankly fascinated by the irrationality as well as the mystery of the sexual instinct. He attempts to study each of its complex manifestations, the abnormal as well as the normal. He will not be deterred by social interdiction or moral taboos from examining the character of sexual love, since it plays so important a part in human life. He is interested in finding out how and why passion overwhelms the resistance of reason and the moral sense. What is

[9] One "radical" psychiatrist finds fault with his age on the ground that the sexual revolution it advocates has never really been carried out. The notion that our age is peculiarly enlightened and liberal in matters of sexual behavior is, he charges, without foundation in fact. The glib and presumably "free" and knowledgeable talk does not hide a fundamental falseness and fear of sex. The anomalies of sexual behavior, the repressions, the neurotic suffering, are as intense as ever before. "French bathing suits, the literature of menstrual hygiene, the open sale of contraceptives, the use of four-letter words in literature and daily speech, the questionnaires that call a spade a spade – notwithstanding all these, we live in an era of sexual darkness and primitiveness." (Robert Lindner, *Prescription for Rebellion.* New York & London: Rinehart & Co., Inc., 1952, p. 81.) Lindner denounces the widespread belief that sex exists specifically and primarily for purposes of reproduction and that to use it for any other purpose – for pleasure, for example – is immoral. Physiologically and psychologically it is a fact, he argues, that the exercise of sexuality does yield pleasure soon after birth and long before puberty supervenes.

[10] "At the same time, to be 'promiscuous' was to assert the validity of sexual experience in and for itself." Norman Podhoretz, "The Know-Nothing Bohemians," in Thomas Parkinson (ed.), *A Casebook of the Beat.* New York: Thomas Y. Crowell Company, 1961, p. 205.

the nature of this compulsion which is so overpowering that nothing can withstand it? What is "romantic love," the malady which Flaubert imaginatively diagnosed in *Madame Bovary,* and exactly how is it related to the sexual instinct? Is every attachment man feels for a woman to be subsumed under the all-inclusive category of sex? Is there no such thing as falling in love or is this a respectably sublimated disguise for the operation of sexual desire? Modern writers give different answers to these questions, though most of them are concerned to show that instinct almost invariably overrides the protests of reason and the dictates of public morality. The transvaluation of values in the field of sexual behavior, as exemplified in contemporary American fiction, is richly documented by John O'Hara in such novels as *A Rage to Live, Butterfield 8,* and *Ten North Frederick.* Relying on the hard-boiled, naturalistic method perfected by Hemingway, he shows that every city and town, while carefully maintaining a facade of virtue, has its quota of scandals, sinners, adulteries, promiscuities, and perversions. He gives us an honest picture of changing mores in the first half of the twentieth century, of a new sexual morality in the making. In *Butterfield 8* he makes the point that love can be differently defined and has curiously different effects. "It can happen to be pure when for one reason or more, two people do not go to bed together; and sometimes it is enough, and better, that they do not go to bed together." [11] But love, whatever else it might connote, "is sleeping together." [12]

Thus the theme of sexuality has of late become the dominant motif in American fiction. In England, too, the same impulse manifests itself, though on a less obsessive scale in serious fiction.[13] Lawrence Durrell conceives of Eros as "being the motive force in man: an animal Eros-powered and Eros-

---

[11] John O'Hara, *Butterfield 8.* New York: Random House, 1955, p. 131.

[12] *Ibid.,* p. 131.

[13] The results in England are appallingly evident in the sex-cum-violence novels that are produced in such large numbers. The new style in English sex-novels has since the thirties been patterned after the American model, inspired by such books as *The Postman Always Rings Twice* (1934), by James M. Cain, and the works of that eminently popular and prolific author, Mickey Spillane. The "heroes" are tough, brutal, with no sentimental nonsense about them, and the women are seductively sensual in physique, large of thigh, their breasts straining. Sex is thrilling only when it is sadistic. This type of sadistic literature "is not produced for a small and perverse set such as made their own use of the works of the Marquis de Sade. It has a wider appeal at its own level." (Richard Hoggart, *The Uses of Literacy.* London: Chatto and Windus, 1957, p. 213). In this cruel, monstrous world of sex, moral values scarcely exist. Richard Hoggart reports that there is no longer any concern with such old-fashioned reactions as shame, sin, remorse, retribution. Popular books of this sensational character point up the spiritual emptiness that has settled over the masses of the megalopolis. Only sex is real in a world devoid of meaning and value.

dowered,"[14] but he portrays sex as symbolic of the human condition. Though the *Alexandria Quartet* treats the subject of love in all its ranges, from the normal to the abnormal, Durrell never exploits sex for its own sake.[15] But in the United States the prevalent tendency in the fifties and sixties was to follow Henry Miller's example and go the whole hog. A goodly portion of contemporary American fiction dedicated itself to the full-throated affirmation that surrender to instinct was somehow good for the soul, the supreme blessedness of existence. Love is sex, sex is love, the two are one and inseparable. But the writer discovered, as he labored to incorporate the sexual motif imaginatively within the body of his work, that he had to contend with the recalcitrance of language to express his meaning. How could mere words hope to convey the intensity of a consummatory experience that was, as both D. H. Lawrence and Henry Miller maintained, beyond the reach of language or even the grasp of consciousness? Sex as integrated within the structure of a novel was something qualitatively different from the actual experience: it was psychically distanced, remembrance[16] wrested out of the limbo of time[17] and fitted within an organically unified art-form.

But sex remembered is not sex experienced. The physical relationship between men and women as portrayed in the *Alexandria Quartet* is subjectively conditioned. The lines of force in the magnetic field shift their elective affinities suddenly, sometimes unpredictably, but the erotic force itself, the thrust and pull of passion, the tumultuous upsurge of desire, is generated by the imagination. Love is a fiction, a psychological projection, a subjective enhancement of the female object desired or "possessed," but once this is understood the phenomenon of love becomes even more of an impenetrable

[14] Harry T. Moore (ed.), *The World of Lawrence Durrell*. Carbondale, Illinois: Southern Illinois University Press, 1962, p. 162.

[15] "The respect Durrell shows for all human coupling prevents the *Quartet* from being sensational and emphasizes his conviction that the ultimate value of sex is what it can teach us about ourselves." *Ibid.*, p. 206.

[16] Citing the example of Proust, Herbert Marcuse brilliantly analyzes the relationship between Eros and time. "Remembrance retrieves the *temps perdu*, which was the time of gratification and fulfillment. Eros, penetrating into consciousness, is moved by remembrance .... But in so far as time retains its power over Eros, happiness is essentially a thing of the *past* .... Time loses its power when remembrance redeems the past." (Herbert Marcuse, *Eros and Civilization*, p. 233.) But this defeat of time, since it is achieved by means of art, is only spurious and reinforces the realization that time is the deadly enemy of Eros.

[17] "In art sex is involved, of course. But it does not function as sex functions outside, it does not elicit either our moral or our erotic response." (Eliseo Vivas, *D. H. Lawrence: The Failure and the Triumph of Art*. Evanston, Illinois: Northwestern University Press, 1960, p. 144.) Indeed, it is pornographic literature of the kind Richard Hoggart describes, which aims to induce the same erogenous excitement as sex does.

mystery. When the imagination actively begins to consider what is "possessed" in the act of love, it perceives that the mind is not only the great mother of desire, the fertile ground of romantic passion, but also the seat of treachery and betrayal. There is no assurance of steadfast faith in love, no guarantee that one is loved with the same ardor and degree of fidelity that one happens to feel; above all, there is no permanence in love. It is as volatile as mercury, as impalpable as air, as full of grotesque and surprising contradictions as life itself.

The focus of interest in literature consequently shifts, in the case of the more profoundly perceptive novelists, from the portrayal of the primal scene to an analysis of the psychology of love in all its ambivalent dimensions of being. Durrell, like Proust, interprets passion as a trick of the senses. Katherine Anne Porter, in *Ship of Fools,* exhibits love as an illusion, precious indeed but not to be trusted too implicitly. The hard-boiled lover of today, however, as represented in American fiction, is unabashedly physical in his desires and generally promiscuous in his erotic pursuits. Like Lieutenant Frederick Henry in *A Farewell to Arms,* he tries to steer clear of messy personal relationships with women; it is only, or chiefly, the pleasure of their body that he craves; to fall in love is a form of emotional bondage too painful to be borne. In a cruel and chaotic world in which life may be snuffed out at any moment by the outbreak of global warfare or an atomic holocaust, love is an impossibility. Nothing lasts. All the more reason, then, for living a life of pure sensations and investing the mechanical ritual of sex with the elements of the sacred.

That is why so many novels of the fifties stress so insistently the pervasive importance of sex in life. A striking example is Vance Bourjaily's *The Violated* (1958). Everyone in the novel is caught up in the rhythm of the sexual cycle. Infidelity is the rule, adultery a common pastime. The more sex the merrier. Even Tom Benziger, the Christlike figure, is drawn into the net. In addition, the author introduces a number of homosexuals.[18] The most sexually precocious character is the adolescent Guy, from Mexico, beautiful and fabulously wealthy. He is initiated into sex by the lascivious Angelica; he possesses her as soon as he attains potency at the age of twelve and then he makes her young daughter pregnant. From that time he devotes himself seriously to the sport of seducing young women and keeping a statistical

---

[18] The homosexual theme is a recurrent object of interest to a number of modern novelists: John Horne Burns, Gore Vidal, Calder Willingham, and Truman Capote. The theme has symbolic value as expressive not only of deviation but also of revolt. Whatever the cause, sexual maladjustment seems to be steadily growing. The subject is no longer taboo. In the theater, the playwright is no longer under the frustrating necessity of stating a homosexual theme in terms of heterosexual situations.

record of his conquests. He perfects his technique of seduction, adapting it to suit each of his girl victims. At one point in the novel he has reached the magnificent score of 205, but by that time sex is beginning to bore him. He confesses that he is "less interested in sex than in statistics."[19] He grows tired of these women he possesses, tired of their personalities as well as their bodies. He hopes to reach his goal of 350 conquests and set a record. It was, he realized, an absurd ambition, but it was worth all his efforts precisely because it was so absurd. In this way he was secretly getting his revenge on life.

For sex was a comic act taken seriously, the male organ a piece of physiological buffoonery, the female organ, hiding behind its funny muff of hair, equally absurd, a slot in the body, hence the placing of one in the other, and rubbing to produce gratification was all travesty, a humorless burlesque of what bodies can do that has grace and strength....[20]

And yet he cannot give up this absurd vocation. Otherwise, what would become of him? How would he spend his time? For him sex is a desperate but ineffectual means of trying to escape this sickness unto death.

There, once more, we behold the metaphysical dilemma on the horns of which the metaphysical novelist is impaled: if he invokes Nature as his controlling metaphor, he thereby often reduces his protagonist to the condition of an animal, a Caliban basely bound by the cords of physical appetite. He may attempt to assure himself that these tides of instinctual desire are beautiful and perfectly justified in or out of marriage, and yet he cannot help but feel that man is more than a copulating animal. Whether or not this is born of illusion, his sex-conquering heroes must somehow make the effort to humanize and ennoble what is purely instinctive. Sex can become meaningful to them only if they look upon their partner as a personality to be respected in her own right, though never fully known or "possessed." Their being is enriched by sex only if it is combined with the emotion of love. Otherwise, they remain embittered, disillusioned, lost.

Modern American fiction, however, gives expression on the whole to a rooted distrust of the phenomenon of love. Woman is the enemy, physically desired and yet feared and despised. Sex is sought with urgent singleness of purpose and yet is regarded by many as something shameful and sordid. Strindberg led the way by depicting the relation between the two sexes as one of irreconcilable conflict. The misogynist, who cannot live without the love of woman, continues to brand her an inferior creature, hostile to his

[19] Vance Bourjaily, *The Violated*. New York: The Dial Press, 1958, p. 303.
[20] *Ibid.*, p. 420.

spiritual needs, the cunning foe who seeks to trap him in marriage and finally destroys him. This gives rise to an erotic cynicism unrelieved by any genuine insight into the fundamental meaning of the experience of love.

Not that this crude psychology of sex makes itself felt in literature as formal ideology. The unique value of fiction at its best is that it is not in the least doctrinaire. It endeavors to present and interpret the human condition, of which sexual love is only a part, in all its complexity and infinite variety. It shows by means of dialogue and its developing action how snarled in ambiguity is the problem of motivation. Hence, at its best, its portrayal of characters in love is never grossly simplified, reduced to a single physical pattern of causation. Though situated within an established framework of social values, these characters must decide for themselves what is good and evil, and their decision in many instances of moral conflict may be a terribly difficult one to make. For no emotion is pure; good is not easily to be distinguished from evil in a corrupt world; falling in love is not an automatic guarantee of future happiness. Perceptions of this subtle and profound order inform Katherine Anne Porter's fictional analysis of the phenomenology of modern love.

T. *Katherine Anne Porter's Version of Modern Love*

In that fable of a journey by ship, *Ship of Fools,* which records the picaresque adventures of a group of passengers on board the German freighter *Vera* that is sailing from Mexico toward Germany, the author makes the reader tensely aware of the insidious power of evil in man. Love, as is vividly illustrated by the troubled relationship between Jenny Brown and David Scott, is instinct with cruelty and conflict. Katherine Anne Porter portrays the human animal as oscillating between the two poles of affection and antagonism, sensual union and fractious separateness. The male is governed by the desire to dominate; he wishes to lord it over the female. The conflict of wills goes on all the time, each partner struggling hard against the fate of being absorbed by the other. Each one seeks a way out of his subjective prison of loneliness, each craves the beatitude of love, but few in this novel are capable of the loyalty, the devotion, and the sacrifice of self that love demands. Dr. Schumann, the German physician on board the ship, who is suffering from an ailing heart that may suddenly end his life, observes the singular follies of the passengers, their manias, their proneness to evil, but is himself, despite his scientific medical training and his Catholic faith, exposed to the temptation of irrational desire. Though he has never been unfaithful to his wife at home, in his old age he falls in love with La Condessa.

Katherine Anne Porter views the comedy of love from a number of contrasting perspectives. William Denny, the Texan, knows what women are like and how "prostitutes" should be treated. Sex is all there is to love, and it can always be bought for a price. More representative of the tensions and torments of modern love is the story of David and Jenny, their quarrels and reconciliations. They love each other, they need each other, but their free union (they are not married) is one long martyrdom. David, the son of Methodist parents, cannot break outside himself; he distrusts her female mind; in her he senses an enemy and resists what he considers her attempt to "possess" him.

The feeling of resentment is there, the desire to get even, and David tries to pay her off for every hurt, fancied or real, she inflicts on him. Jenny is by nature disposed to respond warmly, but she has learned to be suspicious of him, since he depreciated any sign of sentimental softness on her part. When she confides that she loves him and hopes thus to tear down his barriers of reserve, he is not to be caught off guard. Exercising an author's privilege of omniscience, Katherine Anne Porter points out that they were

both ashamed of the evil natures they exposed in each other; each in the first days of their love had hoped to be the ideal image of the other, for they were desperately romantic, and their fear of exposing themselves, of showing and learning unlovely things about each other, made them dishonest and cruel. In their moments of truce both believed that the love between them was very pure and generous, as they wished it to be; there needed only to be . . . needed only to be what, exactly, they both wondered, secretly and separately, and found no answer.[21]

This is the burden of their anguish. In their rare moments of reconciliation, they made "vague vows to themselves and to each other, to keep faith – faith with what? to love each other . . . ."[22] But they cannot sustain the fragile illusion of love.

Jenny must be watchful over every word she utters in his presence. David, typically modern in his, supposedly, enlightened skepticism, did not care for such "spiritual" expressions as God, soul, virtue, love. "He could translate them into obscene terms and pronounce them with a sexual fervor of enjoyment . . . ."[23] And Jenny is offended by this trait in him. Between them there is only hostility. She loves to caress and to be caressed whereas he wants to make love violently, grimly, and get it over with. Even when they sleep together, they quarrel. If she is temporarily attracted to Wilhelm Frey-

[21] Katherine Anne Porter, *Ship of Fools*. Boston and Toronto: Little, Brown and Company, 1962, p. 44.

[22] *Ibid.,* p. 44.

[23] *Ibid.,* p. 55.

tag, it is because, as she reflects: "I'm just starved and frozen out; my man won't share with me, he wants everything to himself." [24]

Her conception of love is full of bitterness. She remembers the scene she had once beheld of a man and a woman locked in a death battle, the man's raised hand carrying a long knife, the woman's breast and stomach pierced, the blood streaming down her body, while the woman beat the man on the head with a jagged stone, his features hidden in rivulets of blood, each bent vengefully on this one purpose, "to kill each other." [25] This scene recurs fitfully in her dreams, and then the dream shifts, the features of the couple change, and the faces become David's and her own! There it is symbolically presented, the cruelty that is love, the mystery of love and hate, love and death, intertwined.

If Katherine Anne Porter demystifies the myth of romantic love, she is equally unsparing in her treatment of the essentially modern myth of "free love." She describes with poignant insight the self-caused suffering this couple have to endure. The path of freedom they chose proves to be a constant painful source of friction.

They had agreed in the beginning not to marry because they must be free, marriage was a bond cramping and humiliating to civilized beings: yet what was this tie between them but marriage, and marriage of the worst sort, with all the restraints and jealousies and burdens, buit with none of its dignity, none of its warmth and protection, no honest acknowledgment of faith and intention.[26]

Soon shattered was the illusion that they would manage to make their free union a lasting one, for David fought against the emotion of love "as if it were an evil force outside of them both, instead of a force of life they both possessed and exchanged with each other . . . ."[27]

The German conception of the woman's role is that she be kept subordinate to her husband, who supports the family. Freytag, who is married to a Jewish woman, believes in legal rights only, the rights accorded the man by the marriage contract, the right to abuse his wife up to a certain point, but without this contract no woman (and he is thinking here of Jenny) should put up with the tyranny of the male. When he spouts his ideal of love as consisting of everlasting fidelity and goes on to assert that a single act of unfaithfulness destroys the whole past of genuine devotion, Jenny sharply retorts that this is not so: "to be unfaithful once is to be unfaithful once, and you can be repentant and get back in the fold . . . ."[28] When Freytag voices

[24] *Ibid.*, p. 92.
[25] *Ibid.*, p. 144.
[26] *Ibid.*, p. 145.
[27] *Ibid.*, p. 146.
[28] *Ibid.*, p. 168.

his sentimentalized version of love, she is tempted to believe in it since it reflects the dream of her own deluded heart, but she knows it is false.

"I think it is a booby trap," she said, with a violence that made her shake all over. "I hate it and I always did. It makes such filthy liars of everybody. But I keep falling into it just the same."

"With all the wrong people," he said flatly, but in a covert tone of triumph which annoyed her at once, "and what you fall into isn't love."

"I know, I know," said Jenny, intolerantly, "it's only Sex, you'll be telling me next. How do you manage to keep True Love and Sex separated?" [29]

She ends the conversational bout with Freytag by remarking ironically that the ship is simmering with love. Freytag, whose flesh is secretly itching with desire, persuades himself that at heart he is the most faithful of men.

Love, as Katherine Anne Porter delineates it in this episodic novel, is suffering and strife, anguish and misunderstanding. The irrational compulsion of sexual hunger is largely the cause. In some men, like Denny, the gratification of their lust is the principal object of their quest. For the sake of sleeping with Concha, the gypsy, Johann is cruel to the old dying man, Herr Graf, and even considers murdering him. Each one yields to his favorite temptation of the flesh. Dr. Schumann believes in original sin while La Condessa, who has no use for theological discussions, rejects the myth of the Fall of Man. The young, she knows, behave like animals. The gypsies on board the boat illustrate the unconscionable shamelessness of animal passion. For Amparo sex is a commodity to be sold at a price while her love is reserved for Pepe, who beats her. We are given this detailed description of their violent love-making.

They sniffed, nibbled, bit, licked and sucked each other's flesh with small moans of pleasure, exploring for odors and savors and sensations in all its parts, their bodies going obediently through a repertory as complicated as a ballet, in the rhythms of a slow-motion film. He never wished to make love to her except when she had just come from another man, full of strange smells and heats, roused and disturbed, ready for him and his special ways with her. [30]

Here is another example of the perversity of love, the beast-like ballet in which sadism and the pleasures of love-making go together. Love is an animalian frenzy in which pleasure and pain are oddly commingled.

Dr. Schumann, who feels guilty because of his sinful love for La Condessa, is bitter about "the sex that brought confusion into everything, religion, law, marriage; all its duplicities, its love of secret bypaths, its instinct

[29] *Ibid.,* p. 168.
[30] *Ibid.,* p. 224.

for darkness and all mischiefs done in darkness." [31] What vile things the term "love" covers! And he is not the only one to feel that way about the utter shamefulness of sexual intercourse. David recalls how after a sexual experience with a woman in a mining camp, he felt a "deep qualm of loathing and intolerable sexual fury, a poisonous mingling of sickness and deathlike pleasure . . . ." [32] In his early relationship with Jenny he had tried to make her understand that

this aftertaste of bitter disgust had cleansed him, restored him untouched to the wholeness of his manhood. He was glad to be able to say he was sick of the thought of sex for a good while after such nights. He had felt superior to his acts and to his partners in them, and altogether redeemed and separated from their vileness by that purifying contempt. [33]

But Jenny, who suffers from none of these scrupulosities of conscience, diagnoses David's reaction as a typical Methodist hangover. Katherine Anne Porter spares us none of the illusions of the copulating human animal who strives to clothe his lust in the high-sounding rhetoric of love. *Ship of Fools* seems specially designed to bear out the truth of Freud's remark: "There is no longer any place in present-day civilized life for a simple natural love between two human beings." [34]

A. *The Sex-Ethic of the Beat Generation*

Katherine Anne Porter's novel sums up comprehensively – and not without a pronounced shudder of revulsion – many of the attitudes toward sex expressive of the modern generation. She carries on the tradition – but in how disenchanted a manner – established by the leading American novelists of the twenties. Sherwood Anderson had shown how those people who denied, or were forced to deny, the needs of their sexual drives paid the penalty by harvesting a crop of "queer" neurotic symptoms. Sexual energy could in part be sublimated but it could not be completely repressed without endangering the health of the organism. The truth of Freud's teaching was vindicated, though he had never preached the necessity of unconditional sexual fulfillment, without due regard for the demands of culture. Through the ages of civilization mankind has learned the painful wisdom of bringing the sexual instinct under some form of social control. Even Hemingway, for all his efforts to formulate a naturalistic morality, never held that sex was

[31] *Ibid.*, p. 237.
[32] *Ibid.*, p. 281.
[33] *Ibid.*, p. 281.
[34] See footnote 5.

all in all. D. H. Lawrence protested vehemently against the overestimation of the importance of sex. Though sex in some form or other enters into all human activity, it was fantastic, he declared, to explain everything in terms of sex. "All is *not* sex," he insisted.[35]

But for the beat generation all *is* sex. Nothing is more revealing of the way of life and the literary productions of this group than their attitude toward sex. For the beatnik, like the hipster, is in opposition to a society that is based on the repression of the sex instinct. He has elevated Sex – not Eros or libido but pure, spontaneous, uninhibited Sex – to the rank of the godhead; it is Astarte, Ishtar, Venus, Dionysus, Christ; it is the source of the mysterious and divine orgone energy flowing through the body of the universe. Jazz is sex, marijuana is a stimulus to sex, the beat tempo is adjusted to the orgiastic release of the sexual impulse. Lawrence Lipton, in *The Holy Barbarians,* stresses that for the beat generation sex is more than a fountainhead of pleasure; it is a mystique, and their private language is rich in the multivalent ambiguities of reference so that they dwell in a sexualized universe of discourse. The singular uncompromising force of their revolt against the odious cult of restraint is illustrated by their refusal to dance in a public place. The social dance is but a disguised ritual for the expression of ungratified sexual desire. For this reason, too, their language is more forthright and earthy. The beatniks crave a sexual experience in which their whole being participates.

It is therefore not surprising to find that they resist the lure of marriage and the baited trap of domesticity, for like cats they are determined not to tame their sexual energy. They withdraw to the underground of the slums where they can defy the precepts of legalized propriety. Unlike the heroes and flappers of the lost generation in the twenties, they disdain the art of "necking" and "petting." That is reserved for "the squares." If they avoid the use of the outlawed four-letter word it is because in their eyes it is taboo; it is sacred. As Lipton, the prophet of the beat generation, declares: "In the sexual act, the beat are filled with mana, the divine power. This is far from the vulgar, leering sexuality of the middle-class square in heat."[36] This is the Holy Grail these knights of pure sensation are in quest of, this is the cosmic urge to which they respond.

If Wilhelm Reich is the Moses who led them out of the Egyptland of sexual repression, Dylan Thomas is the poet who offers them the dialectic of justification for their indulgence in liquor, marijuana, jazz, and sex. Henry

---

[35] D. H. Lawrence, *Psychoanalysis and the Unconscious* and *Fantasia of the Unconscious.* New York: The Viking Press, 1960, p. 59.
[36] Lawrence Lipton, *The Holy Barbarians.* New York: Julian Messner, 1959, p. 158.

Miller is their literary patron saint whose fictional testament gave inspired expression to the new religion of sex. In addition, they have been converted to Zen Buddhism, with its glorification of all that is "natural" and mysteriously alive, its awareness that everything in the world is flowing. They make no attempt, in their novels or their critical proclamations, to reconcile Zen with their determined quest for the beatific bliss of the orgasm. Logic is not one of the virtues they admire or care to practice. That is how they rebel against the stultifying uses of intelligence. Since they refuse to think straight, they are free to assume the most paradoxical and contradictory positions. They are by sex obsessed, but they also resort to religious metaphors: they are in search of mana, the numinous, the spiritual, but not anything connected with formal religion.[37] What they are after is the beatific vision.

But whatever form their metaphysical quest for ultimate meaning may take, the "religious" consummation they seek is never separated from sex. The style of life adopted by the beat generation as uniquely their own is designed to enhance the primal value of the sexual experience. Jazz is good not only because it promotes wholeness of being but, specifically, because of its decided sexual effect. Jazz is the musical language of sex, the vocabulary of the orgasm; indeed, it is maintained that the sexual element in jazz, by freeing the listener of his inhibitions, can have therapeutic value. That is why, so the argument runs, the squares are so fearful of jazz and yet perversely fascinated by it. Instead of surrendering themselves to the orgiastic release jazz gives them, the squares undergo psychoanalysis or flirt with mysticism or turn to prostitutes for satisfaction. Thus the beat brotherhood transmute jazz into something holy. Jazz, like sex, is a mystique. It is not a sublimation (hateful word!), a substitute for sex, but a dynamic expression of the creative impulse in the uninhibited man.

The mystique of sex, combined with marijuana, jazz, and Zen, is meant to provide a design for living. Those who are sexually liberated can become creatively alive and free, their instincts placed at the service of the imagination. Like Henry Miller but without his remarkable gift for comical counterpointing, the beat spokesmen righteously denounce all that makes for death; they bid all men become cool cats; let them learn to "swing" freely, to let go,

---

[37] Like a character stepped out of Sartre's Existentialist fiction or drama, one beat declares, as quoted by Lawrence Lipton: "Man no longer exists – God has become an atheist and no longer believes in the existence of man. God no longer exists – there is no man to invent him." (*Ibid.*, p. 119.) These are the trite blasphemies the beat representatives hurl forth. They condemn everything in modern civilization, especially in America, as a fraud, and reject religion as the worst fraud of all. The beat identify themselves not with the priest or rabbi but with the outcast, the outlaw, the desperado, the saloon keeper, the whore.

to become authentically themselves, and then perhaps there is a good chance that Western civilization will be saved. Seceding from a society that is can- cerously infected with a deathward drive, the beatnik is concerned wholly with his personal salvation in the living present. If he is indeed the child of nothingness, the predestined victim of an age of atomic warfare, then he will go beyond good and evil and consult only his physical needs. He will not curb his instinctual desires but discharge the sexual energy within him that makes him feel fully and truly alive, even if it is only for this brief moment before the apocalypse of annihilation explodes on earth.

That is why the members of the beat generation proudly assume the title of the holy barbarians; they will raze to the ground the shrines, temples, museums, and churches of the state that is the enemy of the kind of life they believe in. Apart from the categorical imperative of the orgasm and, a later addition, the metaphysics of Zen, the only affirmation they are capable of making is that art is their only refuge. Their writing, born of their experi- ments in marijuana and untrammeled sexuality, reflects the extremity of their existential alienation. Their ethic of radical non-conformity culminates, frequently, in a nihilism that drains them of the vital energy necessary for any sustained creative effort. The mind, they feel, has betrayed them, reason is the foe of life; hence they will trust only their physical sensations, the wisdom of the body, the sacred promptings of the unconscious. With lyrical intensity they reveal what they hate, their rage of repudiation, but their faith in sexual love, inspired by the revolutionary rhythms of jazz, finds its climax and consummation in the orgasm. Their creative work, as exhibited in *Naked Lunch,* mirrors the nightmarish mentality of the psychopath, rootless and irresponsible. Their rebellion against authoritarian society is not far removed from the violence of revolt characteristic of the juvenile delinquent.

The life they lead is undisciplined and therefore, not surprisingly, un- productive for the most part, even though they make a fetish of devoting themselves to some creative pursuit – writing, painting, music. Non-con- formists on principle, they exalt "madness" as a way of attaining the highest degree of illumination. When they express themselves, however, it is incan- descent hatred that grips them, the fury of negation. And it is sex that is at the heart of their aesthetic. Principally it is the sexual experience that they worship as the Way and the Life, the Glory and the Kingdom. What they discuss with utter seriousness as if it were the most profound and urgent philosophical issue in the world is the degree to which sex, rightly used of course, can inspire the Muse. Monogamy is the peculiar vice from which the abjectly fearful middle class continue to suffer, whereas the dedicated beat- nik has the courage to break out of that prisonhouse of respectability. Promiscuity is the order of the day. There is no need for signing any marita contract. When "a Bohemian man and woman are fond of each other, sooner or later they will live together." [38] One girl, in describing her past, he succession of broken marriages, the abortions she had to undergo, confesses that she loves sex and sees no reason why she must justify her passion. If i is an honest feeling that impels her, then why should she not yield to it? "*Most* often," she says, "it's the *monogamous* relationship that is *dishonest*." [39] There is nothing holy in wedlock. This girl soon dropped the "bourgeois" psychiatrist who disapproved of her mode of life. She found married life stifling and every prolonged sexual relationship unbearably monotonous. Variety for her was the essential spice of sex.

This is perhaps an extreme case of nymphomania but it illustrates the neurotic types who are drawn to the movement, which regards men largely as a means of providing sexual gratification. Whereas some members of the beat colony in San Fransisco recognize "that pure sensuality is no substitute for love," [40] most of the rebels are strongly attracted by the promise of sexual freedom. And yet the freedom they seize upon so avidly fails to yield them the happiness they had hoped for and before long they are exposed to the ravages of disillusionment. Sex for the San Fransisco group is "a source of disappointment, disillusionment, or dissatisfaction as well as grief and regret, but not guilt." [41] They engage in no enduring relationships. They are so immersed in their own subjective problems that they fail to respond either warmly or understandingly to the needs of others. And the psychic conflicts that plague them adversely affects their creative ambition. They dream, they nurse grandiose visions of creative fulfillment, but their enthusiasm does not last "their work habits are erratic; and their artistic output irregular. They are usually incapable of *sustained* effort in their work because they are concerned with their problems; they are too easily led astray by momentary diversions." [42]

These rebels are full of internal contradictions, and their revolt frequently takes the form of passivity. Who are the recruits magnetically drawn to this movement? Junkies, nymphomaniacs, Lesbians, homosexuals, alcoholics, the weak, the irresolute, the despairing, the derelicts and outcasts of society. The men embrace a life of independent poverty, but usually with a "shack-up" partner who will help to support them. One beatnik got the woman he

---

[38] Francis J. Rigney and L. Douglas Smith, *The Real Bohemia*. New York: Basic Books, Inc., 1961, p. 47.
[39] Lawrence Lipton, *The Holy Barbarians*, p. 30.
[40] Francis J. Rigney and L. Douglas Smith, *The Real Bohemia*, p. 49.
[41] *Ibid.*, p. 72.
[42] *Ibid.*, pp. 70–71.

was living with so involved in drugs and self-analysis and all-night sessions of sex that she was beginning to crack up. What obsessions had she picked up during these long feverish nights of talk and love-making? Sex as the creative principle of the universe, the secret of primitive religions, the vital force in the life of myth. Everything in the final analysis reduced itself to sexual symbolism. In his chapter in *The Holy Barbarians* on "The Love-ways of the Beat Generation," Lipton spares the reader none of the sordid details. No one in West Venice asks questions about the "free" union of the sexes so long as the partners share the same libertarian attitudes of the group.   ,

The women who come to West Venice, having forsaken the cause of radicalism, are interested, like the men, in living only for the moment, in being constantly on the move. Those who are sexual deviates are naturally impelled to join this community. Part of the ritual of sex is the use of marijuana.

The Eros is felt in the magic circle of marijuana with far greater force, as a unifying principle in human relationships, than at any other time except, perhaps, in the mutual metaphysical orgasm. The magic circle is, in fact, a symbol of and preparation for the metaphysical orgasm.[43]

Under the influence of marijuana the beat devotee experiences a wonderfully enhanced sense of self as if he had discovered the open sesame to the universe of being. Carried high on this "charge," he composes "magical" poetry that is supposed to capture in words the organic rhythms of Nature. If he thus achieves a dreamlike, drugged intensity, he pays the price for this indulgence by producing work – Allen Ginsberg's *Howl* is a notable example of this tendency – that is Dionysian and disoriented, but without either depth or Apollonian control. Neither sex nor drugs in themselves furnish a royal road to creativity.

4. The Sex Motif in Beat Fiction

In *Nothing More to Declare,* Clellon Holmes assesses what he calls the "Revolution Below the Belt." He feels that though the sexual revolution of our time has gained some ground, it marks only the victory of minor liberal reforms. Writers can be more outspoken today and call a spade a spade. Books by previously banned and damned writers – D. H. Lawrence, Henry Miller, and William S. Burroughs – can now be bought at the corner drug store. Sexuality has come into its own. The conviction has now been accepted that sexuality

[43] Lawrence Lipton, *The Holy Barbarians,* p. 171.

is not so much a specific emotion directed at a specific person, as it is an objectless, steadily coursing flow of energy out from the centers of the Being which, like an underground stream, can surface in an infinite variety of places, in an infinite number of ways.[44]

The Era of the Orgy, he confidently declares, "may finally be here, but what it evidences is neither a moral collapse nor a Late Empire Decadence; rather it is a sign of an existential crisis, a crisis of ultimate personal identity, a specifically religious spasm in a godless world."[45] It is interesting to note his identification of sexuality with religion. He is explicit on this score. "Thus sexuality, in this godless age, has become a religion . . . ."[46]

If love, as Ortega y Gasset believes, reflects the nature of man, if the person in love betrays what he is by his behavior in love, then the writers of the beat generation, by their celebration of the pseudo-religious cult of sexuality, are creating what is virtually a new literary genre. For them not love but sex is the creative force that permeates every sphere of life. Whereas love traditionally remains forever beyond satisfaction and seeks to pass beyond the narrow boundaries of the self, the orgiastic love of the beat is meant to heighten the sense of life. The beat hero draws no distinction between sexual love and the sexual instinct. Love is sex and nothing but sex. In *On the Road,* by Jack Kerouac, the male characters burn with an impure, gemlike flame, passionately interested in drugs, drink, jazz, and sex. Dean Moriarty, the best saint, is singleminded in his devotion to the religion of sex: "to him sex was the one and only and important thing in life . . . ."[47] His consuming passion is to "dig" life, to absorb the entire beauty of the universe, to know the meaning of time, to fulfill himself by experiencing sex in *all* its dimensions.

How are the sex ethic and the aesthetic of the beat generation portrayed in fiction?[48] The blurb for the paperbound edition of *On the Road* mentions marijuana, jazz, and Zen as the boosters of the beat generation, and it speaks of the two main characters, Sal Paradise and Dean Moriarty, as revolutionaries who seek intensity of sensation, profoundly moving experiences, and the way to truth and God. The novel relates the picaresque odyssey of their adventures across the American continent. It presents the exploits of a generation that feels defeated, inwardly dead, and that is

[44] John Clellon Holmes, *Nothing More to Declare.* New York: E. P. Dutton & Co., Inc., 1967, p. 167.
[45] *Ibid.,* p. 175.
[46] *Ibid.,* p. 179.
[47] Jack Kerouac, *On the Road.* New York: The New American Library, 1960, p. 49.
[48] Part of this section is based on the article by Charles I. Glicksberg, "The Rage of Repudiation: Polemic of the Beats," *Southwest Review,* Autumn, 1960, XLV, pp. 342–353.

driven to the desperate expedient of being forever on the move, wandering restlessly from city to city, place to place, in quest of stronger wine, madder music, the magical mood that marijuana is capable of inducing, and the sheer ecstasy of sex. Every moment must furnish a new thrill, but since each moment vanishes as it is savored these characters must be perpetually on the go, using up their nervous energy to the last spark, until they fall asleep from sheer exhaustion. Dean, the hipster, the saint of sensuality, is supposed to exemplify the hedonistic faith summed up in the line: "for life is holy and every moment is precious."[49] His sense of the holiness of life and the preciousness of every moment takes the form of stealing cars, driving across the breadth of the land with maniacal speed, taking drugs, and having sexual intercourse with countless girls. Sal Paradise is drawn to him because he represents a type he extravagantly admires:

because the only people for me are the mad ones, the ones who are mad to live, mad to talk, mad to be saved, desirous of everything at the same time, the ones who never yawn or say a commonplace thing, but burn, burn like fabulous roman yellow candles exploding like spiders across the stars....[50]

Here we have set forth the cult of experience for its own sake. To live without restraint, to defeat the curse of time and overcome the deadly blight of boredom – that is the heart of the beat desire, the justification of the madness that has seized hold of these leaders of the sexual revolution. Kerouac glorifies these psychopathic outlaws (Dean Moriarty winds up in Bellevue Hospital), but he glorifies them without at the same time revealing their basic limitations. He romanticizes these rebels against the social order, treating the rest of the unredeemed world as inhabited by either fools or hypocrites, Golems who walk in darkness.

The characters in *On the Road* reach a stage of desperation when they explode: they get riotously drunk, they consume powerful doses of marijuana, cured or uncured, and then the visions come. That is how they manage to say yes to life, by gratifying their desires, however perverse, of the moment; they care about nothing else but that. Everything is to be enjoyed – everything! That is characteristic of Dean Moriarty, the fool of life, the legendary hero of the beat generation, who is the soul of the Beatific. Kerouac declares that he is the originator of the term "beat." For him the word means beatific. But according to others, the word has a different connotation. These beat rebels actually look upon themselves as defeated, emotionally disturbed, chronically depressed, neurotically unbalanced, filled with despair. This is really the meaning of the term.

[49] Jack Kerouac, *On the Road*, p. 49.
[50] *Ibid.*, p. 9.

In *Big Sur* Kerouac reveals the price the beat characters must pay for their license, their heavy drinking, their reckless pursuit of the will-o'-the-wisp of pleasure. Inevitably, especially when they are thrown upon their own resources and must endure a period of solitude, they confront the vision of death, and the vision of death, when the initiate is not prepared to face it, brings on the horrors. Drink will not drive these horrors away; it will only make them more terrifying. Nor will travel do the trick either; one cannot flee from himself. So that when the King of the Beatniks, the self-pitying Jack Duluoz, who is the *persona* of the author himself, begins to drink steadily he is overcome by the madness he is trying to run away from.

Kerouac again introduces the hero of *On the Road*, Dean Moriarty, now given the name of Cody, who has served a stint in prison and at present has a job, but his character has not changed. He is still the champion fornicator, the great lover, irresistible to women. He must work at recapping tires to support his family (though he is not legally married) and must make periodic parole visits, but he is still involved with a variety of adoring mistresses. He turns one of them, Billie Dabney, over to Jack, and she is nothing loath. Kerouac ushers in a number of other beat characters: Joey Rosenberg, a youngster who wishes to taste all of experience, a sort of beat Jesus; Romana Swartz, a Rumanian Jewess who loves to walk around practically naked and is the sexual partner of Dave Wain; and George Basso, the Japanese youth who expounds a new theory of the sexual excesses Buddha engaged in before he had his vision of nirvanic blessedness. There is a poet, McLear, who composes a poem that describes in elaborate detail every part of his body and his wife's body in the act of sexual intercourse.

Does this fixation on sex explain why Kerouac has become a "fashion-able" writer? He is proud of his reputation as King of the Beat and he has striven strenuously, to his own cost as a serious novelist, to live up to his reputation. His aesthetic, his creative method, his subject matter, his style, these have all been affected by his unchallenged position as spokesman for the disaffiliated, the rebellious, the "mad" members of the beat generation. Kerouac is typical of the American writer who, unlike his European coun-terpart, tries to be "original," "profound," and "primitive" without first having assimilated the fruits of a rich culture that would undergird and bring into proper perspective his attempt at formulating an orgiastic and mystical way of life. The trouble with his fiction — and it is characteristic of the kind of life the beat hero leads for better or worse — is that it is essentially undisciplined and immature. The two go together, just as the author makes no secret of the fact that he is completely identified with his protagonist, Jack Duluoz.

Immature in his mystical seizures and frenzies of despair, in his rapid and extreme alternations of mood, he fails to reach the dizzy heights or penetrate the depths of the tragic vision. Cutting himself off from the major sources of the Western literary tradition except for the few gods he professes to worship (Blake, Baudelaire, Céline, and Whitman), he makes discoveries that are not at all new. The philosophical insights that inform his work are a confused and crude amalgam of anarchism and the worst features of neo-romanticism. When he falls into one of his beatific trances, he beholds as beautiful and sacred everything in the universe, the microcosmic as well as the macrocosmic, the leaf twirling on the tree, the ball of dung, the water in the creek, the waves pounding on the shore whose music he tries to translate in an onomatopoetic Ur-poem, the light of the sun, the bluejay, the mouse, the beetle, and the bat. Everything is holy, instinct with numinous beauty – that is the reiterated ineffable message. He struggles to give expression to an undiscriminating pantheistic ecstasy.

Unfortunately, for all his diatribes against reason and the uses of the intellect, his Zen Buddhism is self-conscious, intellectualized, and therefore unconvincing. Unable to contain his soul in peace or sustain this Buddhist vision of supernal ecstasy, he sinks into a state of despair. Hence his flight from solitude and the ephemeral joy of contemplation; taking to drink, drugs, and sex, he repudiates the Zen perspective. Now he is haunted by the thought of the evanescence of things, the inexorable march of time, the fatality of death, and his wails of anguished disenchantment sound adolescent in tone. He has been misled by his cult of youth and sexual freedom. Now the years are catching up with him and he must face the problem of dying, he must enter upon the quest for the ultimate meaning of life.

But his search for an absolute, like his search for God, does not change his position as prophet of the beat world. He is still opposed to everything that is: the established, the conventional, the traditional. He must swing, "go," travel back and forth on the continent (travel, significantly, plays a large role in beat fiction, for movement and change of place are expressive of the spiritual restlessness of the beat generation), become gloriously drunk, "high." Unfortunately, the road of excess does not, in art, lead to the palace of wisdom. Whatever libertarian code the literary rebel tries to live by, he cannot afford to neglect his obligations as an artist.

But Kerouac is too impatient to heed such "square" counsel in the field of aesthetics. He writes rapidly, trusting in the demonic powers of improvisation. He dashes off *On the Road* in the space of three weeks. He has only scorn for the meticulous labors of revision, the sensuous and elaborately wrought prose of a Walter Pater. Though he declares that he avoids idea-words, his besetting sin is to substitute emotive expressions for the precise and evocative sensory image. The result is that on many occasions he overstates his case with a plethora of emotively charged adjectives: sad, mournful, wonderful, beautiful. Since everything in the world is beautiful, he has but to announce that a scene in *Big Sur* is beautiful and presto, it is so.

His style is therefore unpruned, prolix, rhapsodic. He seeks to emulate the rhythms of jazz by doing without periods to separate his sentences, thus producing a lax, mannered sprawl. Disdaining the time-honored, indispensable principle of selectivity, he trusts to the treacherous technique of free association. He will take no necessary pause to dredge up the proper word but allow his mind to build up his word order freely, spontaneously, permitting no afterthoughts to mar his inspired originality. There is to be no taint of craft in his work of fiction. This is the gospel of Surrealism in writing, the cultivation of a splendid, unmediated frenzy. In "Essentials of Spontaneous Prose," Kerouac writes: "If possible write 'without consciousness' in semi-trance . . . allowing subconscious to admit in own uninhibited interesting necessary and so "modern" language what conscious art would censor, and write excitedly, swiftly . . . in accordance . . . with laws of orgasm . . . ."[51]

As might be expected, this extreme dependence on the deep wells of the subconscious makes for a highly self-conscious, disordered prose, marred by attitudinizing. Kerouac is constantly aware of his role as prophet, novelist, King of the Beat, and the creative yogi. He writes autobiographical novels which dispense with the trappings of plot and the necessity for motivating the actions of his chief characters. He writes dithyrambs, the narrative of his turbulent life, the record of his thoughts, feeling, and spiritual states: his bouts of drunkenness, his sexual exploits, his experiments in solitude and meditation. He writes exclusively about himself.

In *Big Sur,* the hero has reached the age of forty and there is stormy weather ahead of him on his life's journey. He must break out of his drunken condition, and so off he goes to San Fransisco and from there to a cabin on Sur. He will make his home in the woods, like the bhikku he fancies himself as being, but after three weeks of plain and solitary living he feels the call to return to the haunts of his boon companions. Then comes the onset of madness. But wherever he travels, he carries his notebook and pencil with him. Drunk or sober, mad or sane, bored or inspired, he must set down his impressions. He describes his experiences alone in that cabin, his observations of ocean and beach, rock and wind and clouds. This hero

[51] Thomas Parkinson (ed.), *A Casebook on the Beats,* p. 67.

tells us about his theological preoccupations, but fails to give us the underlying reasons for this spiritual crisis.

The novel strikes a false note in that it furnishes no correlation between
the mystical moods, the Buddhist visions, and either the sexual interludes
or the outbreak of madness. The story, subjective and confessional in content, is full of internal inconsistencies. Jack's obsession with death is not
motivated, unless Kerouac means to say (and this would be the rankest
heresy) that the hedonistic ethic of experiencing everything, drinking the cup
of life to the lees, enjoying women, consuming endless quantities of alcohol,
leads only to the dead end of despair. No wonder these beat men and women
grow weary and neurotic. It is not alcoholism or excessive indulgence in sex
that does them in but their sudden frightening perception of the aimlessness
and sorry waste of their lives.[52]

The section describing how Cody turns his mistress Willamine over to his
friend is in the worst (debased) romantic tradition. Catholics both, Jack and
Cody are so devoted to each other that they are able to share a girl together
without jealousy or strife. Jack remarks (it is the author speaking) that this
represents the emergence of a new ideal in the world where two men can
be staunch friends and not fight possessively over girls. Cody, who is still
portrayed as the beat saint, has no need to become a writer "because life is
so holy for him there's no need to do anything but live it." [53] The author in
the form of his narrator (the two are one) would have us believe that this
new "love" between Willamine and Jack is filled with innocence. This is the
sentimental streak in Kerouac that vitiates his work; he fails to distinguish
between love and sex.

For with sad musical Billie in my arms . . . and Cody has given his consent in
a way, we go roaming the Genghis Khan clouds of soft love and hope and anybody who's never done this is crazy – Because a new love affair always gives
hope, the irrational mortal loneliness is always crowned . . . .[53]

In the name of "love" everything is justified. Heaven is reached

in the mere fact of the taking off of clothes and clashing wits and bodies in the
inexpressibly nervously sad delight of love – Dont let no old fogies tell you
otherwise, and on top of that nobody in the world even ever dares to write the
true story of love, it's awful, we're stuck with a 50% imcomplete literature and
drama – Lying mouth to mouth, kiss to kiss in the pillow dark, loin to loin in
unbelievable surrendering sweetness so distant from all our mental fearful abstractions it makes you wonder why men have termed God antisexual somehow.[54]

---

[52] Jack Kerouac, *Big Sur*. New York: Farrar, Straus and Cudahy, 1962, p. 141.
[53] *Ibid.,* p. 147.
[54] *Ibid.,* pp. 147–148.

This is a fairly representative sample of the sloppy kind of writing Kerouac produces when he deals with the subject of sex. Though it is rooted in the tradition of romantic love, its fundamental values are turned upside down: it is the body, not the soul, that brings one nearer to God.

The affair with Billie (Willamine) does not help to cure Jack of his growing state of madness. There is actually nothing much for them to do except to make love. When Jack is not sexually engaged, he drinks; he has no other outlets for his energies. He has put his writing completely aside. At this point he raises the big question: "What are we gonna do with our lives?"[55] It is perfectly clear what the answer will be: they will continue to rush about from place to place, indulge in other affairs, and drown their misery in booze or drugs. The penalty for getting high is to fall into depression and the only way out of the blues is to swing again to another peak of euphoria.

If Jack comes to realize that he does not love Billie, it is because he is tired of the whole business; boredom has set in, and the next stage is madness. Billie desires to sleep with him, wishes to marry him, but in his paranoiac condition he will have no part of her. Suddenly he realizes that all his talk about sutras and Zen is but playing with empty words. He finally does make love to Billie, but sex is by this time beginning to poison his system; he hates himself and derives no relief from the orgasm. He is too badly stricken by his vision of death. It is the Devil who is tormenting him, but in his agony – he is Catholic, after all, as well as a Zen disciple – he sees the Cross and is saved. 'I lie there in cold sweat wondering what's come over me for years my Buddhist studies and pipesmoking assured meditations on emptiness and all of a sudden the Cross is manifested to me –"[56] Through the mediation of the Cross he is restored to life: to drink and sex and Zen.

The Dharma Bums also takes up the archetypal theme of the quest for ultimate meaning and self-realization. The hero, who is, as usual, the *persona* of the author, acts and speaks as if he were the first one to discover the wisdom of Buddhism, particularly of Zen Buddhism, and the virtues of solitary meditation. Another important ingredient in this so-called novel (it has no formal structure, no pattern of progression) is a fixation on sex; there is little talk of love; the girls are more than willing to give themselves without the preliminary assurance of love. And by sex Kerouac means "natural," down-to-earth, orgasmic sex, with no nonsense about it.

The hero who spins the tale is repeatedly quoting from the Sutras, practicing his devotions, and stressing his conception of beat as beatific. Here

---

[55] *Ibid.*, p. 164.
[56] *Ibid.*, pp. 205–206.

is the yogi, the guru American style, on the move, travelling from New York to San Francisco, seeking to emulate the example of Buddha. Then he meets Japhy Ryder and learns about the Dharma Bums. Japhy Ryder is someone of special distinction, a creature of the woods, steeped in animal lore, a student of Indian myth, studying Chinese and Japanese in order to become an Oriental scholar. Here we get the Beat-Zen-Nature hero, who enjoys nothing more than propounding koans.

Besides being an Oriental scholar and an expert on Zen Buddhism, Japhy is also – and inevitably – an expert on girls; he attracts them with magnetic power but none of them has any power over him. He has his cottage where he practices with Princess, one of the girls who have fallen in love with him, the difficult art of concentration. Ray watches the ritual as Japhy and Princess, both stark naked, sit facing each other, keeping silent.

Japhy wasn't at all nervous and embarrassed and just sat there in perfect form just as he was supposed to do. "This is what they do in the temples of Tibet. It's a holy ceremony, it's done just like this in front of chanting priests. People pray and recite Om Mani Pahdme Hum, which means Amen the Thunderbolt in the Dark Void. I'm the Thunderbolt and the Princess is the dark void, you see."

"But what's she thinking?" I yelled almost in despair, I'd had such idealistic longings for that girl in that past year and had conscience-stricken hours wondering if I should seduce her because she was so young and all.

"Oh this is lovely," said Princess. "Come on and try it."

"But I can 't sit crosslegged like that." Japhy was sitting in the full lotus position, it's called, with both ankles over both thighs. Alvah was sitting on the mattress trying to yank his ankles over his thighs to do it. Finally Japhy's legs began to hurt and they just tumbled over on the mattress where both Alvah and Japhy began to explore the territory. I still couldn't believe it.

"Take your clothes off and join in, Smith!" But on top of all that, the feelings about Princess. I'd also gone through an entire year of celibacy based on my feeling that lust was the direct cause of birth which was the direct cause of suffering and death and I had really no lie come to a point where I regarded lust as offensive and even cruel.[57]

We get some insight into the nature of this "religious" experience when we learn that Princess, only twenty years old, is sex-mad and man-crazy and loves to play this erotic game of "yabbum." Ray Smith, the narrator, his Buddhist asceticism by now utterly forgotten, is induced to play the game. Japhy tells Smith: "I distrust any kind of Buddhism or *any* kinda philosophy or social system that puts down sex."[58] This is a key line: it affords a clue to the values underlined in the novel: sex (that always comes

---

[57] Jack Kerouac, *The Dharma Bums*. New York: The Viking Press, 1958, pp. 18–19.
[58] *Ibid.,* p. 30.

first) plus Zen Buddhism equals the beatific. While Ray and Princess take a warm bath together, Alvah and Japhy in the other room discuss "Zen Free Love Lunacy orgies."

This sets the pervading tone of *The Dharma Bums*: "yabbum," mixed bathing in naked bliss, Zen Free Love Lunacy orgies, together with the more than obliging Princess who says that she feels like the mother of all things and has to take care of her "little children." We are supposed to believe that by her indulgence in these "mystical" practices she is striving, like Japhy, to become a Bodhisattva. Japhy knows everything there is to know about these practices; "there was no question," as he points out," of what to do about sex which is what I always liked about Oriental religion." [59] Japhy Ryder is, as Alvah calls him admiringly, "a great new hero of American culture." [60] He is the mad saint, the Zen lunatic, who is enjoying life in the void.

Sex, yabbum, mountain-climbing – it is all part of the void. This is the discipline the new gospel preaches – mountain-climbing, solitude, meditation, renunciation, but also free love. What we get in this religion of the Zen Lunatics, of which Japhy is the prophet, is a strange mixture of incompatible elements: Whitman, Thoreau, the return to Nature, Buddhism, sexual freedom. Alas, the separate parts refuse to blend. Ray Smith makes the point that he cannot explain the Dharma to people, the notion of the unreality of the so-called real world, the transcendence of all fear, the attainment of the bliss of Nirvana. "Everything is possible," Ray reflects. "I am God, I am Buddha, I am imperfect Ray Smith, all at the same time, I am empty space, I am all things." [61] Occasionally Kerouac strikes a note of depression or metaphysical disillusionment or mystical illumination, but it is only a passing mood. Soon these Beatific Bums are back on the old erotic track.

This is enough to suggest what Kerouac is up to. It should make clear, too, the distinction between the beat movement as a proposed way of life and the literary expression of this movement. The only reason the movement has attracted so much attention, apart from its brushes with the law and its deliberate defiance of community mores, is that a few of its members have achieved recognition as writers. One of its truly talented spokesmen is Clellon Holmes, whose novel, *Go,* owes much to Dostoevski. Holmes understands the beat characters he portrays and is able to view them objectively; within the framework of the novel he provides the dramatic con-

[59] *Ibid.,* p. 31.
[60] *Ibid.,* p. 32.
[61] *Ibid.,* p. 122.

trasts and conflicts which reveal the self-defeating absurdity of the movement. He reveals that these members of the beat generation are spiritually
bankrupt; they can find nothing worth living for. Hobbes, the narrator, himself a novelist, serves an admirable function in his double role of intellectually defending the actions of these beat characters while emotionally
recognizing them for what they are. He perceives the shortcomings of his
friends and the demented world they live in.

It was a world of dingy backstairs, "pads," Times Square cafeterias, be-bop
joints nightlong wanderings, meetings on street corners, hitchhiking, a myriad
of "hip" bars all over the city, and the streets themselves. I was inhabited by
people "hungup" with drugs and other habits, searching out a new degree of
craziness; and connected by the invisible threads of need, petty crimes of long
ago, or a strange recognition of affinity. They kept going all the time, living by
night, rushing around to "make contact," suddenly disappearing into jail or on
the road only to turn up again and search one another out. They had a view of
life that was underground, mysterious, and they seemed unaware of anything
outside the realities of deals, a pad to stay in, "digging the frantic jazz," and
keeping everything going.[62]

This is the disorder which has taken possession of a whole generation,
Stofsky, the homosexual character in the novel, has drawn up a mystical
slogan for himself: "The way to salvation is to dig, give up, go mad!"[63] For
Pasternak, the writer, the only important problem is death, so he decides
that life is holy in itself. Nothing else matters. There is the single affirmation
of the holy barbarians: the belief that life is beautiful and sacred.

As Holmes describes them, whenever they are on the move through the
night of the city, the cry that impels them onward is "Go! Go!" In the night
through which they rush blindly and feverishly, searching for a goal which
they are unable to define, they find no surcease, for if time is their enemy it
is not to be defeated by jazz or whiskey or marijuana or indiscriminate sex.
There is much in the behavior of the beat generation, as Holmes delineates
it with sardonic compassion, that is downright revolting. They are devoid
of a moral sense, seemingly not in the least concerned at whose expense they
get their thrills. The third section of Go, appropriately called "Hell," pictures men and women who are stricken with a terrible flaw, spiritually hol-
low, corrupt, lost, doomed to live without hope, beaten down, not at all
beatific.

With the exception of Clellon Holmes, Jack Kerouac, and Ken Kesey,
the original model for Dean Moriarty and Cody, who is the author of two
novels, One Flew Over the Cuckoo's Nest and Sometimes a Great Notion,

[62] Clellon Holmes, Go. New York: Charles Scribner's Sons, 1952, p. 35.
[63] Ibid., p. 109.

the beat novelists lack the patience and the power of sustained application of will that artistic creation demands. Their epiphanies are born of drugs, jazz, promiscuous sex, neurosis, and metaphysical despair. There is no promise of fulfillment in a literature that springs spasmodically from psychopathic negation. One of the friendly critics of the movement, Kenneth Rexroth, declares that Allen Ginsberg's *Howl,* a clinical confession in free verse, is "the confession of faith in the generation that is going to be running the world in 1965 and 1975 – if it's still there to be run." [64] It is this oppressive premonition of disaster which explains, though it does not justify, the immersion of the beat writers in subjectivity, their irresponsible attitude toward social conventions, their professions of contempt for the difficult and exacting discipline that art requires, and their celebration of orgiastic sex.

[64] *Evergreen Review,* 1957, I, p. 11.

CHAPTER XII

NORMAN MAILER:
SALVATION AND THE APOCALYPTIC ORGASM

Ineffectual in their attempt to formulate an aesthetic based on states of sexual hyperaesthesia, the gifted and productive members of the beat generation launched a literary revolt that seems mildly "leftist" when compared to the ultra-revolutionary mood of the hipsters, who are all-out nihilists.[1] For Hip is the philosophy of the apocalyptic orgasm, and Norman Mailer is its self-appointed prophet. As an underground man, defiant of the laws of society, the hipster is on his own; he responds only to the impulse of the moment. He might equally well be called the outsider, the American Existentialist who has gone the limit. He identifies himself with the Negro, the marginal man, who bears in his soul the mark of oppression. Hip, like beat, derives from the Bohemian world of jazz; it draws ideological sustenance from such a mixed grab bag of influences as D. H. Lawrence, Henry Miller, and Wilhelm Reich, but its uniquely distinguishing trait is the militancy of its adherence to the mystique of the apocalyptic orgasm. As a quasi-Existentialist, the hipster is a mystical psychopath who does not reason but feel. Norman Mailer estimates that there are probably not more than one hundred thousand men and women – a surprisingly high percentage – who regard themselves as hipsters, psychopaths who can view their abnormality without guilt and with a kind of aesthetic detachment.

---

[1] Hipsters and beatniks have much in common: both share the love of marijuana and jazz, both take, as it were, the vow of poverty, both are antagonistic to a society that is repressive. What are the differences? They do not run deep. While the beatnik retains his faith in the salvationary value of the orgasm, he is limited in his fund of sexual energy. Whereas the beatnik is oriented toward Zen and uses sex as a means of achieving _satori,_ the hipster, though he respects Zen, prefers to get his mystical illumination directly from the body of a woman. The hipster is thus the extremist, the man dauntlessly in quest of the fullness of life, while the beatnik "wants to get out of reality more than he wants to change it . . . ." (Norman Mailer, _Advertisements for Myself._ New York: G. P. Putnam's Sons, 1959, p. 374.) The beatnik winds up in a mental hospital; the hipster may land in jail but he does not fall into a psychosis.

One is Hip or one is Square (the alternative which each new generation coming into American life is beginning to feel), one is a rebel or one conforms, one is a frontiersman in the Wild West of American night life, or else a Square cell in the totalitarian tissues of American society . . . .[2]

Like the beatniks, these rebels disdain the services of psychoanalysis; they refuse to adjust. Aware of their own sources of strength as well as their limitations, they are sure of one thing: they know that whatever is wrong with them can be cured only through the therapy of the orgasm. That is the compulsion under which the hipster labors. His quest for "the good orgasm," which expands his creative possibilities, leads him to violate the regnant taboos of society. He becomes a sexual outlaw because that role offers him the only chance of remaining physically alive, throbbing with the elemental energy of creation. The war for sexual freedom, Mailer announces, has been won. The movement could not be halted, for it was supported by people

who were sincere about sex, and idealistic, naive no doubt like a good many of us, innocent sexual totalitarians, we felt sex is good, sex has to be defended, sex has to be fought for, sex has to be liberated. So we liberated sex.[3]

In *Advertisements for Myself,* Norman Mailer voices the hope that out of the radical nihilism of Hip and the sexual revolution it brought about a process of rebirth will take place.

Norman Mailer gives us an elaborate analysis of the character of the psychopathic hipster, even of his impulse to murder. Then he moves on to an interpretation of the orgasm as therapy, the salvation wrought by the apocalyptic orgasm. In this way, through the blessed release the good orgasm provides, the hipster manages to remain fundamentally healthy instead of being, like the square, frustrated, impotent, and wretched all his life long. The pilgrim in resolute search of sexual fulfillment, the hipster realizes how sexually deprived he is in a repressive social order but he does something about his condition; he is prepared to fight for the miracle of growth. That is how, open to all varieties of experience, he reaches out toward the feeling of power and self-renewal. Here, then, in brief, is the Mailer manifesto of sexual freedom, with its secular theology of justification.

But Hip, when it is examined critically not for its revolutionary sex ideo-

[2] Norman Mailer, "The White Negro," in Gene Feldman and Max Gartenberg (eds.), *The Beat Generation and the Angry Young Men.* New York: Dell Publishing Co., Inc., 1958, p. 373.

[3] Norman Mailer, *The Presidential Papers.* New York: G. P. Putnam's Sons, 1963, p. 130. But if he helped to liberate sex, he seems of late to have moved suspiciously close to the "conservative" position. He is not in favor of birth control or planned parenthood. The reproductive instinct must not be thwarted. It is criminal not to allow life to be born.

logy but for its creative expression, amounts to very little. With the single exception of Norman Mailer, the writers who belong to the Hip movement (who are they?) are singularly unproductive. American Existentialism based on Hip is thus far largely theory, speculation, vision, not yet – if it will ever be – a fruitful working enterprise. The hipsters – and they resemble the beatniks in this respect – are too fiercely wedded to their subjectivity, their rebellious egotism, and their driving need for sexual expression, to have sufficient energy left for the concentrated labor of creation.[4] It is not the case that the hipster hero really desires to be himself, for he does not know who he is, and his experiments in sexual excess are not designed to bring about the fulfillment of his creative needs.[5] That is not too important, however, as far as he is concerned. First things come first. Sex transcends art in the order of Hip priority. Essentially the revolt of the hipster resolves itself into a militant demand for sexual license. As Mailer says:

The point is that, so long as one has a determinedly atheistic and rational approach to life, then the only thing that makes sense is the most comprehensive promiscuous sex you can find.[6]

It is unfortunate for the development of a writer when he gives hostages to fortune by committing himself fanatically to some ideology or philosophical outlook, for then he runs the danger of becoming a true believer, and the energy of vision that should go into the making of his books is dissipated in evangelical exhortation. What he gains in strength and unity of conviction he loses in negative capability, in readiness of imaginative response to aspects of experience that do not fall within the scope of his formed beliefs. By giving himself wholly to one point of view, he shuts off possibilities of awareness not to be seen from that fixed angle of vision. Mailer already suffers markedly from this self-imposed restriction. In his defence of Hip, the new "religion" of modern man, he becomes shrilly argumentative – a

---

[4] "The hipster's life ... became schizoid; whenever possible, he escaped into the richer world of tea, for the helpless and humiliating image of a beetle floating on its back, he could substitute one of himself floating or flying, 'high' in spirits, dreamily dissociated, in contrast to the ceaseless pressure exerted on him in real life." Anatole Broyard, "A Portrait of the Hipster," in Chandler Brossard (ed.), The Scene Before You. New York and Toronto: Rinehart and Company, Incorporated, 1955, p. 118.

[5] Though Nietzsche recognized the sexual origins of art, his discovery anticipating the findings of Freud, he pointed out that the true artist does not give free rein to his sexual instinct. "The force that one expends in artistic conception is the same as that expended in the sexual act. ... An artist betrays himself ... if he squanders himself here ... it can be a sign of decadence. ..." Friedrich Nietzsche, The Will to Power. Translated by Walter Kaufmann and R. J. Hollingdale. Edited by Walter Kaufmann. New York: Random House, 1967, p. 432.

[6] "An Impolite Interview with Norman Mailer," The Realist, December, 1962, No. 50, p. 21.

bad sign, surely, in an imaginative writer whose function is to reveal and not to judge. What extra-literary crusades did Joyce or Hemingway or Faulkner engage in? Hip as a program for salvation is actually the antithesis of art. What, after all, has it to do with literature? That is the question. Mailer believes, of course, that Hip is capable of calling forth wonderful sensations and revelations. Hip is experience in all its intensity and plenitude, Hip is the splendor and consummation of sex. The hipster is willing to gamble on his faith in redemption through the flesh, even if he suffers eternal damnation for his "sins," but all this fails to make clear how the literature of Hip, such as it is, deepens the sensibility or moral consciousness of people.

Mailer assures the reader that his "Notes toward a Psychology of the Orgy" constitutes the heart of *Advertisements for Myself,* a programmatic commitment to Hip. In the list of descriptive terms he draws up by way of definition, Hip is associated with, among other things, the spontaneous and the instinctive, the perverse and the nihilistic, with sex and the body electric, with Wilhelm Reich and Trotsky and the Negro, with marijuana, skepticism, murder, and seduction by touch. The Catholic essence, according to this jumbled list of dualistic categories, belongs with Hip; the Protestant ethic with Square. American Protestantism is oriented toward the machine whereas the Catholic Church, more pliant and accommodating in its creed, does not deny the needs of the body. The Catholic, therefore, has to undergo less of a wrench to comprehend the universe of Hip. The mind in that religion is not cut off from the body whereas Protestantism, Mailer, the novelist turned theologian, alleges, forces the flesh to function within strictly prescribed and rigidly enforced institutional limits. The body is incorporated within the efficient operation of a gigantic social machine. In order to fit into this coercive acculturating process, man had to tame his god-given instincts. That is why, as a form of protest, many are drawn to the cult of the orgy, but it is precisely this Dionysian revolt that the contemporary rulers of society are determined to put down. They are afraid of this explosion of violence, the outbreak of the orgiastic. Nevertheless, despite all the power elite can do to prevent it, the age is obsessed with sex. The obsession takes a curiously distorted form: sex as orgy, sex as rape, and sex as murder.[7] In

---

[7] It was Otto Weininger who in *Sex and Character* held that sexual intercourse is related to murder. There is, he asserted, an element of cruelty in eroticism. "Love is murder." (Quoted in David Abrahamsen, *The Mind and Death of a Genius.* New York: Columbia University Press, 1946, p. 176.) For a study of the underlying connection between sex and sadism, between sex and the desire to mutilate and murder the female, see Colin Wilson, *The Origins of the Sexual Impulse* and his novel, *Ritual in the Dark.* In his chapter on "Sadism and the Criminal Mentality," Wilson argues that in our time "the typical psychopathic crime is often the 'crime of boredom,' the crime that appears

An American Dream, Mailer portrays a hero, Rojack, who is driven, because of the sexual frustration he experiences in his marriage, to murder
his wife. "Murder, after all," he declares, "has exhilaration within it . . . The
exhilaration comes I suppose from possessing such strength. Besides, murder offers the promise of a vast relief. It is never unsexual." [8] Modern man,
the indictment reads, has transformed his commodities into sexual symbols
and these dominate his system of production. This, Mailer charges, inevitably induces an increment of biological guilt, "for the urge to mate is dying
in us and we need the spice of a dead object." [9] These are the psychotic
symptoms, the headlong gravitation toward death, that are making themselves felt in our mechanized mass society.

It was the severe struggle Mailer passed through in composing *The Deer
Park* and finally getting it published in the face of concerted opposition that
turned him into a sexual rebel.[10] His novel, a nightmarish study of characters caught in the corrupt world of Hollywood, deals primarily with sex,
but in this, we are told, lies its controlling moral content. All the characters
are infected by the prevailing spirit of corruption: columnists, movie producers, script writers, actors and actresses, hangers-on, pimps, and call
girls. With the exception of Sergius O'Shaugnessy, not a single one of them
displays any decent impulses or moral courage. Craven, depraved, pitiful
creatures, each of them can be bought for a price. Even the gifted Charles
Eitel is brought to his knees by a Senate Investigating Committee. This is
the modern Sodom which Mailer paints on a broad canvas: the nightly bouts
of drinking, the carnality, the perversions, the degeneracy, the triumph of
evil, the rank nihilism. This is the oppressive motif the novel sounds: the
leading characters, defeated by life, are spiritually lost.

Though conforming to the method of naturalistic objectivity, Mailer obviously wrote *The Deer Park* in a mood of unrelieved disgust. The realism
with which the picture is drawn is part of the author's plan to tell the unvarnished truth about this sector of reality. He reveals the changing moods

to have no particular motive, but to spring out of 'too much freedom' and total lack
of a sense of purpose." (Colin Wilson, *The Origins of the Sexual Impulse.* New York:
G. P. Putnam's Sons, 1963, p. 195.) Sex crimes become increasingly frequent in an
age of moral bankruptcy. One specialist in the literature and folklore of eroticism,
G. Legman, declares that Americans prefer sadism in their popular arts. Sadism is
"installed as the substituted outlet for a forbidden sexuality . . . ." (G. Legman, *Love
and Death.* New York: Breaking Point, 1949, p. 62.)

[8] Norman Mailer, *An American Dream.* New York: The Dial Press, 1965, p. 8.

[9] Norman Mailer, *Advertisements for Myself,* p. 432.

[10] See Charles I. Glicksberg, "Norman Mailer: The Angry Young Novelist in
America," *Wisconsin Studies in Contemporary Literature,* Spring–Summer, 1960, I,
pp. 28–34.

and inner motivation of his characters, their intemperate thirst for power, their love that turns into hate, their capacity for wallowing in the sink of corruption. This unsparing delineation induces a cumulative sense of horror, not redeemed by any vision of higher values. What we get is a panorama, a weird phantasmagoria, etched in depth, of rottenness and putrefaction, the lowest hell of degradation to which people can fall. Sergius, a writer, is the only one in pursuit of meaning. Preparing himself for his profession as a writer, he explores the mystery of the unknown, the insoluble complexities of life, whereas Charles Eitel is shown to be a failure because he weakly compromises and betrays his love of the art of films. Sergius will not sell out; it is probably for this reason that Mailer for a time intended to make him the hero of his next Hip novel, *The Time of Her Time,* a fragment of which appears in *Advertisements for Myself.*

The composition of *The Deer Park* marked a turning point in the literary career of the bitter and embattled Mailer. The novel had been accepted by Rinehart and been put in page proofs, but he was told he would have to excise six objectionable lines. When he refused to do so, publication was stopped. He sought to find a new publisher but that was not easy. The search ended when G. P. Putnam's agreed to bring out the novel without demanding a single change. But this vindication of his stand was not enough to heal the wound that had been inflicted. He had already learned his lesson: he was being rejected as a menace to society; his view of life was being condemned as nasty and perverted. He would not submit to this conspiracy of intimidation. Only by fighting more recklessly for the things he believed in would he be able to survive as a writer. He opened the flood gates of his wrath and became God's angry man. Gradually he became convinced that he was by nature a psychic outlaw, and he accepted this truth about himself. He turned for "kicks" to marijuana, which possessed he found, the wonderful power of opening his senses, "the door back to sex, which had become again all I had and all I wanted." [11] Unfortunately his experiment with marijuana had a weakening effect on his mind.

When the page proofs from Putnam's began to come in, Mailer found that the present version of the novel did not satisfy him; it would have to be changed drastically, not to soften its offensive outspokenness but only to improve its structure and style so as to gain the approval of his artistic conscience. He set about the task of revision under the influence of drugs, his unconscious controlling the process, and before long he was in reality sentence by sentence, shaping the body of an entirely new novel. He went

[11] Norman Mailer, *Advertisements for Myself,* p. 278.

on doggedly with the work of revision, "bombed and sapped and charged and stoned with lush, pot, with benny, saggy, Milltown, coffee, and two packs a day . . . ."[12] He was driving himself furiously, rushing from drug to drug, fearful of failure. He wrote in the first person, imbuing O'Shaugnessy with greater vitality, so much so that the protagonist was more and more taking on the lineaments of his begetter.

Mailer dwells circumstantially on these details relating to the composition of *The Deer Park* because he wishes to show how he fought the good fight as the champion of freedom of expression in the United States. His revision made no concessions to social conventions. In fact, the new version accentuated the sexual motif; he had not muted the underlying theme but conscientiously heightened it. Now *The Deer Park* represented a savage indictment of a guilty society. The novel, though it sold fairly well, enjoyed no sensational success. Though he was depressed by all this, he now had the courage to face his detractors. He resolved to remake himself, for he was convinced that the life within was more important for the spiritual survival and growth of the writer than his work itself. He would write a fourth novel, with O'Shaugnessy as one of his heroes, and this time he would not hold himself back in the least. He would keep the rebel in his nature more truly alive instead of trying to stifle him. In this way he hoped to reach people and influence the history of his time. He does not deny that *The Deer Park* is concerned overwhelmingly with sex, but it is also preoccupied with the question of moral values. In this country, he contends, the writer cannot deal with one without having to call in the aid of the other.[13]

Mailer is thus committed to the aim of ushering in a revolutionary change in the consciousness of man. He resembles D. H. Lawrence in this respect, but how different is his method of approach – egotistic, blustering, brash. He is confident that the fiction he produces in the future will have the deepest influence of any work being done by the other American novelists of his age. Here is prophecy informed with the dynamism of a personal faith that is by no means modest, but this is perfectly in keeping with the dominant tone of *Advertisements for Myself*. He puts into action the depressing moral that in order to get ahead the young writer in America must enter the lists and strenuously advertise himself. In this sense he is playing the game of publicity. This is the approved way, as Daniel J. Boorstin points out in *The Image,* of becoming a celebrity in America, not of achieving fame. Though he indulges in braggadocio, he remains intransi-

---

[12] *Ibid.,* p. 243.
[13] When questioned about *The Deer Park,* Mailer did not deny but rather affirmed that it was "totally about sex. And it is also totally about morality." *Ibid.,* p. 270.

gent in his stance of nonconformity. He will prove his creative usefulness by continuing his essential work of demolition. In his brain-blasting rage he relies on what he calls his secret weapon: marijuana. It will serve him faithfully in his campaign to become the leader of Hip.

In a column, "The Hip and the Square," he wrote for *The Village Voice*, he composes a fervid eulogy of the intuitive knowledge the hipster gains: his insight that every desire, however abnormal, is part of the dynamic urge of life. Mailer's Existentialism, which has little in common with Sartrean Existentialism, is based on a mysticism of the flesh. Its origins, according to Mailer,

can be traced back into all the undercurrents and underworlds of American life, back into the instinctive apprehension and appreciation of existence which one finds in the Negro and the soldier, in the criminal psychopath and the dope addict and jazz musician, in the prostitute, in the actor, in the – if one can visualize such a possibility – in the marriage of the call-girl and the psychoanalyst.[14]

This is the orgiastic philosophy of the revolution in consciousness which will have its triumph in the future.

Such prophetic pronouncements in *Advertisements for Myself* add little, if anything, to Mailer's stature as a novelist. Indeed, they may provoke legitimate doubts as to his rank in the hierarchy of American writers of fiction. He would have been better off in his new role as creative prophet of Hip if he had followed Camus' example and written his orgasmic Existentialist novels first and then produced books on the order of *The Myth of Sisyphus* and *The Rebel* to clarify his views as a thinker. Mailer argues too much; he uses up in the passion of polemics precious energy that should be conserved for his creative struggle.

His approach to a problem, as in his strident advocacy of Hip, is to run to extremes. In "The White Negro," which he feels is one of the best things he has written, he openly espouses the cause of the rebel and identifies with the underworld of the hipster, the man who welcomes the psychopathic element in his being as a means of liberating himself from a society that has surrendered to the death instinct and is thereby enabled to return to life, even if he has to resort to criminal deeds in order to achieve his end. The hipster, who has taken over the code of the outlawed and oppressed man, the Negro, knows the full intensity of his desires, whatever they may be, and takes what he considers appropriate measures to satisfy them, without being deterred by conventional notions of good and evil. In complete rapport with the imperatives of his unconscious, he trusts only what he experiences, his

[14] *Ibid.*, p. 314.

living consciousness of the present, and his experiences are rooted in the final truth of sex and subjectivity.

Mailer handily disposes of the logical objection often raised that the hipster is, after all, a psychopath and not a model to emulate. By leading the kind of life he does, the hipster transcends his psychopathic handicap; he rebels against the repressions tyrannically imposed by a sick society. Thus he rises above the neurotic contradictions and the reactionary terrors of his age. Mailer then comes to the crux of his Hip manifesto: he formulates his Existentialist philosophy of the orgasm as therapy, the apocalyptic orgasm that is the quintessence of life and the seed and soul of art. In this proclamation of sexual freedom, the marginal Negro plays a messianic role. What Mailer never comes to grips with – and he should (he commands our attention as a professional novelist, not as the founder of a sexual cult) – is the fundamental question of how Hip provides a viable aesthetic for the writer of fiction. No such aesthetic is forthcoming for a very good reason. Sex, like marijuana or alcohol, does not give birth to art. Mailer, in short, is calling for a sexual, not a literary, revolution.

The hipster may be, as Mailer insists, the Faustian underground hero of the twentieth century, the outlaw in search of the unspoiled fullness of life, wrestling with the destiny of his nervous system and gambling with death, but one fails to see what all this has to do with Mailer's own growth and development as a writer or how the metaphysic of Hip will fructify American literature and art. Why should a serious novelist – and Mailer is basically that in intention – affiliate himself with a psychopathic, lawless group like the hipsters? Hip may lead (though one is inclined to doubt it) to the discovery of deeper insights and greater sharpness and intensity of experience, but this constitutes at best a promise of pseudo-religious salvation or therapeutic relief. It is not the same thing as opening magically the blocked road to creative fulfillment. Mailer's confused and negative theology of sex will not promote his career as a novelist. Hip has no direct bearing on the formidably complex problem the writer faces when he undertakes the task of composing a novel. There is no such mythical creature as a Hip novelist. There are only good or bad novelists.

Mailer, in *Advertisements for Myself,* assures us he is working on a project that may take him ten years to complete, a novel which will break down all the established inhibitions and taboos, but the selection he offers, "The Time of Her Time," from this work in progress does little to arouse hope for a masterpiece like *Ulysses.* We are given, in this brief extract, the story of Sergius O'Shaugnessy, the protagonist of *The Deer Park,* and his determined efforts to bring a stubbornly resistant Jewish girl to a sexual climax. In his "Prologue to a Long Novel," Mailer states that his aim is to destroy innocence, to strip aside the foul, ulcerous lies that infect the live body of love, but this "Prologue" does not carry much conviction. It is largely an outline of his metaphysic of time as growth and of time as orgasm.

To repeat: The blunt, debunking truth is that the putative aesthetic of the orgasm offers no guarantee that the writer who adopts it will be able to fulfill himself creatively. All human experiences, the unconscious and the superconscious, heaven and hell, love and sex, dream and reality, life and death, are open to the art of fiction, but the ideological assumption that by exploring the orgasmic theme in all its electrifying implications the novelist can make a uniquely new and original contribution is sheer nonsense. In *The Deer Park* the scenes devoted to sexual experimentation of the most perversely varied kind are, like the elaborately detailed scenes of sadism in *The 120 Days of Sodom* by the Marquis de Sade, unrelieved in their dullness, whereas the chapters which portray the existential anguish of disillusionment, the dead weariness of the flesh after it has undergone the crucifixion of seeking God through the orgasm, the frantic search for meaning and value that elude these wanderers in the inferno of lust and corruption that is Hollywood – all this strikes an authentic note of tragic loss and defeat.

We are now witnessing the rise of a school of sex-obsessed fiction led by such an epic of eroticism as *Go to the Widow-Maker* by James Jones: novels dealing profusely with sexual symbolism, promiscuity, perversions, and ingenious variations on the theme of orgastic ecstasy.[15] In them instinct will be enthroned and sex reduced to physiology. Robert Elliot Fitch, in *The Decline and Fall of Sex,* is perfectly correct in his contention that the whole issue of the treatment of sexuality in literature, the depiction of human beings as animals in hot quest of the metaphysical or apocalyptic orgasm, relates to the writer's conception of the nature of man. The writers of the

---

[15] One symptom of the reaction that in some quarters has set in against this tendency is the publication of the novel, *The Chapman Report,* by Irving Wallace, a topical satire on the twentieth-century mania for gathering statistical information about the sexual life of Americans, in this case American women. Dr. Chapman is the scientific crusader, a take-off presumably on Dr. Kinsey, the man with a sacred mission in life, which is to remove the miasma of ignorance concerning the *vita sexualis.* To lend the power of dramatic conflict to his modern "fable," the author creates a Devil's advocate, Dr. Jonas, an adversary of the highest integrity, who is opposed to the reduction of the love-life of man to a series of physiological reflexes, a process that can be objectively measured. "All your diagrams, graphs, tables, are devoted to the physical act – quantity, frequency, how much, how often – yet this doesn't tell these married women a damn thing about love or happiness. This is separating sex from affection, warmth, tenderness, devotion, and I don't think it should." (Irving Wallace, *The Chapman Report.* New York: The New American Library, 1960, p. 153.)

beat generation and particularly the devotees of Hip worship the divine Priapus: "Sex is Life. Sex is the Self. Sex is the Resurrection and the Life." [16] This is the pass to which much of contemporary fiction has come. Mailer proudly declares that he intends to explore the psychology of murder and suicide (as he does in *An American Dream*), incest and orgy, orgasm and time. That is the glorious destiny he hopes to carry out as the first philosopher of Hip.

The beat writers and the hipsters have decided with Blake that to desire but act not breeds pestilence, but what does it breed in terms of literature? What is true of life is not necessarily true of art. The hipster is free to damn braces, but the writer needs them urgently. Man lives in a world of culture. The call for a return to primitivism is doomed. The windows of perception must be cleansed but that will not be accomplished by resorting to drugs. The body of the flesh must be affirmed and not denied, but the affirmation is in itself not an instinctive response but an act of spirit, a creative transcendence. If modern writers wish to worship the god of sexuality that is their privilege, but as writers their work will be judged by its form and content and not by its revolutionary sex mystique.

[16] Robert Elliot Fitch, *The Decline and Fall of Sex*. New York: Harcourt, Brace and Company, 1957. p. 14.

SECTION B: THE DIALECTIC OF THE SEX MYSTIQUE

CHAPTER XIII

THE DEATH OF LOVE

The question: What is sex? And the concomitant questions as to what is obscene, impure, is *(sic)* not asked, let alone answered, precisely because of barriers of semantic anxiety which precludes our free or, I think, objective scientific examination of scientific phenomena. How can these phenomena be studied if one is forbidden to write or think about them? [1]

I wondered why Americans must be taught how to love. Perhaps it's because in our country there is felt to be something shameful in two human beings taking their pleasure together. In America I remember a tension between the sexes. Human love is a disease for the isolation ward, not at all nice. Thus love in America is often divided into the classification of Having Sex and Getting Married. Neither has much to do with love. It was the Having Sex which began to strike us in Naples as being so cold-blooded. What caused this? The Italian scenery? The Neapolitan women? But after a while I and many other Americans ceased to be satisfied with passion without affection. I'd known Americans who'd lost their virginity without ever kissing or making love in the old sense of the word. So we came to look upon this Having Sex, this ejaculation without tenderness as the orgasm of a frigidaire. There was no place for it in the scheme of human love. It wasn't so much bestial as meaningless. For Having Sex meant that the two bodies involved never really knew one another. They just rolled and arose strangers, each loathing the other.[2]

Why should it be considered an unfaithfulness, a betrayal, to love more than one woman or more than one man? Nothing sillier could be conceived. It's preposterous. We love constantly, love everywhere. We love in all sorts of degrees and ways.[3]

[1] William S. Burroughs, *Naked Lunch*. New York: Grove Press, Inc., 1966, pp. xxxiv–xxxv.
[2] John Horne Burns, *The Gallery*. New York and London: Harper & Brothers, 1947, pp. 303–304.
[3] Conrad Aiken, *Blue Voyage*, in *The Collected Novels of Conrad Aiken*. New York and Chicago: Holt, Rinehart and Winston, 1964, p. 95.

1. Prelude

In order to study the dialectic of the sex mystique in contemporary American fiction, we chose from a host of offerings in the growing literature of erotica a group of novels that reflect, critically or admiringly, the changing Sex-*Anschauung* of our time; novels that are all the work of serious-minded and talented writers. They picture for us the new pattern of moral values that has been or is being instituted. Though some pay excessive attention to the physical-mechanical aspects of the sexual relationship and attach too much importance to sexual fulfillment, identifying love with the experience of orgasmic consummation, they are not engaged in producing pornography. What is of signal interest in the novelists whose work we have selected for analysis is their characteristically different interpretation of the nature and existential meaning of human sexuality.

What emerges from this flood of fiction dealing with various phases of the sexual life – fornication, adultery, promiscuity, rape, the aberration of love, nymphomania and satyriasis – is the problem of value. Writers have taken advantage of the relatively greater freedom granted them by the courts to focus frankly and fully on some compelling aspect of this once stringently forbidden theme. Their defence, when they are brought under attack, is that they are, like Kinsey and his associates in their scientific inquiry into the sex life of the American male and female, doing no more than imaginatively reporting the truth about their sex-obsessed characters. They are not to be identified with the immoral views or evil acts of their protagonists, though, of course, they are, as authors, directly responsible for everything they include in their vision of life.[4]

Writing about sex in fiction is today a flourishing and highly successful enterprise. Books with some legitimate claim to literary distinction that belong to the genre of erotica, are legion, and their number increases every publishing season. A critical review, however brief, of the leading specimens of contemporary erotic fiction would have swelled this book to prohibitive size. We have had to select a few representative novels that would illustrate from a variety of perspectives the growth and spread of a mystique, the drastic changes brought about in the morality of modern love and marriage, the emergence of the belief that sex without the emotional entanglement of love is all to the good, the overcoming of the taboo against the free use of what has long been called the dirtiest word in the English language. We

---

[4] One literary critic contends that "The creation . . . of art can never be a completely neutral activity." Wayne C. Booth, *The Rhetoric of Fiction*. Chicago: The University of Chicago Press, 1961, p. 329.

have chosen to write about the work of Mary McCarthy, Vladimar Nabokov, William Styron, Leslie A. Fiedler, James Purdy, John Barth, and
James Jones. If there is no common ideological bond uniting this group of
representative novelists, except perhaps their belief that sex is an intensely
fascinating and rewarding subject, a new means of exploring the nature of
the human animal, what they do seem to bear witness to, sometimes sadly,
sometimes ironically, is the death of love.

2. Mary McCarthy: The Comedy of Sex without Love[5]

Making love, we are all more alike than we are when we are talking or acting.
In the climax of the sexual act, moreover, we forget ourselves; that is commonly
felt to be one of its recommendations. Sex annihilates identity, and the space
given to sex in the contemporary novels is an avowal of the absence of character.[6]

Mary McCarthy has left her mark upon this generation. She appears in a
variety of roles – enfant terrible, journalist, iconoclast, dramatic critic, war
correspondent, and writer of short stories and novels – all of them revealing
the kind of personality and versatile talent she possesses. She enjoys telling
the unvarnished truth as it appears to her. From which it follows that what
she writes is bound to be unpalatable, for she refuses to be diplomatic or
discreet. That is why she succeeds in shocking so many people.

In her fiction she usually begins with the general conception, the germinal
idea, and then proceeds to embody it in a group of representative characters.
She concentrates on experiences she has known, she presents people she
has met, using, for example in The Groves of Academe and The Group, the
impressions she gleaned while attending Vassar and while teaching at Bard
and Sarah Lawrence.[7] She betrays a persistent hostility to the male of the
species, a tendency to look upon sex with revulsion. Her later fiction presents sex in a ludicrous light.

Her fiction is the best antidote for the orgasmic bravado, the Hip apotheosis of sex. Her unrelenting honesty of perception, her piercing wit, and
her power of satiric deflation, have made her the most devastating critic of

---

[5] According to Elizabeth Hardwick, "it is part of Mary McCarthy's originality to
have written from the woman's point of view, the comedy of Sex." Elizabeth Hardwick, A View of My Own. New York: Farrar, Straus and Cudahy, 1962, p. 36.
[6] Mary McCarthy, On the Contrary. New York: Farrar, Straus and Cudahy, 1961,
p. 276.
[7] "... Mary McCarthy's approach to fiction is that of the essayist ... the nucleus
of truth or idea in her fiction is the essential element ...." Doris Grumbach, The
Company She Keeps. New York: Coward-McCann, Inc., 1967, p. 31.

the sex mystique. Not for her the dizzy flights of rhetoric male novelists usually indulge in when they describe the act of sexual intercourse. Not that her heroines are opposed to sex. Far from it. They may at first resist the too ardent advances of the male but by their provocative behavior they connive at their own seduction. They surrender the fort, but even as they give in their minds are active, their eyes keenly observant, and what they see is enough not only to disillusion them but to make them feel somewhat ashamed. For them the physiology of sex, together with all that accompanies it, is disappointing and disturbingly absurd. Mary McCarthy is not in the least squeamish; she paints the primal scene with controlled objectivity; she points no moral, though the moral effect is implicit in the context of the story she narrates; but her will to truth leads her to strip the aura of romance from the sexual act. Hence she portrays for us the comedy of sex without love.

Promiscuity and adultery, these are for many of Mary McCarthy's female characters the mark of an emancipated person. The emancipation, however, is never complete. The feminine mind still adheres to what it considers regressive, ethical principles that stress the need for fidelity, so that conscience is harrowed by a sense of guilt. The problem is further complicated by the war between the sexes. In the story, "Cruel and Barbarous Treatment," the unfaithful wife is unwilling to hurt her husband: she will not discuss with him her affair with the Young Man, her lover. This is how the author analyzes the difficulties that arise in the course of a romantic adultery. With honorable courtship the social ritual was clearly formulated.

But with the extramarital courtship, the deception was prolonged where it had been ephemeral, necessary where it had been frivolous, conspiratorial where it had been lonely. It was, in short, serious where it had been dilettantish. That it was accompanied by feelings of guilt, by sharp and genuine revulsions, only complicated and deepened its delights, by abrading the sensibilities, and by imposing a sense of outlawry and consequent mutual dependence upon the lovers.[8]

Mary McCarthy is adept in exposing the duplicitous motives that enter into this drama of deception. It made the heroine feel superior. She had no desire to put horns on her husband's head and she failed to see the comedy of his situation. "It was as if by the mere act of betraying her husband, she had adequately bested him . . . ."[9] It is a thrilling, if forbidden, experience she is enjoying, and she is enjoying it precisely because it is sinful and forbidden.

The drama has to move on to its next stage. The truth must come out, but

---

[8] Mary McCarthy, *The Company She Keeps*. New York: Harcourt, Brace and Company, 1942, p. 4.
[9] *Ibid.*, p. 4.

the real reason for the wife's decision to disclose the truth to her husband is that she does not relish keeping her affair a secret. She craves publicity, the limelight. She will go through with the divorce. On her trip to Reno she realizes that she will never marry the Young Man, her lover. She must now face the future in the unenviable role of a spinster. "Cruel and Barbarous Treatment" is a satiric allegory highlighting the changed social attitude toward adultery and divorce. Far from being a stigma, a source of scandal and shame, divorce, like adultery, is accepted as a way of life.

In "The Man in the Brooks Brothers Shirt," Mary McCarthy deftly dramatizes the game of seduction. Margaret Sanger finds herself reluctantly accepting the invitation of a man for a drink in his compartment on the train. Before she knows what happened she is telling this stranger the intimate details of her former marriage. She is getting drunk. The next morning she wakes up in bed, naked, next to the body of the man. Dimly she recalls the events of last night and then the full force of memory strikes her: the four-letter words he had forced her to repeat, the resounding, bruising blows he had rained on her bare buttocks. Even after her immediate reaction and her vomiting, she allows him to make love to her again, though she considers it an act of charity on her part. What stands out in this encounter is "the sexual passivity of her heroine. Miss McCarthy's typical female character usually finds herself being pushed rather unwillingly into bed. And, even during sexual intercourse, the heroine does not stop thinking . . . ." [10]

A Charmed Life reflects the moral or rather amoral values of the community: the promiscuity, the permissiveness of the code, the alcoholism, the outcropping of violence in domestic life. It reveals the fitful struggle to make life meaningful and productive, the fragility of love, the escape into sex and party-going and drinking. Martha realizes the danger of drink in this Bohemian colony, New Leeds, consisting of non-conformists, misfits, would-be artists and writers. We hear the story of how Martha first met Miles (who is supposed to represent Edmund Wilson, Mary McCarthy's second husband) and went to bed with him and was willing to become his mistress but he insisted on marriage, and how he dominated her life as long as the marriage lasted. Why had she yielded to him in the first place? She must have wanted it to happen.

And yet when she meets him again – they have both remarried – the old magnetism of his affects her strongly. The people at the party talk about religion, adultery, love, art, literature, and psychoanalysis. In the scene in

[10] Barbara McKenzie, Mary McCarthy. New York: Twayne Publishers, Inc., 1966, pp. 91–92.

which the group gathers for the reading of a play by Racine, Miles discourses brilliantly as he compares Racine with Shakespeare, and Martha, who had majored in philosophy, joins in the discussion. Intellectually gifted, she knows the mystery of epistemology: how can we know that we know? How can we trust our sense data and then our moral perceptions? What is wrong, what is right? Martha declares: "Nobody can stay in the right – I mean in real life – and that's the terrible thing . . . . If you think you're in the right for more than a few seconds, you'll find that you're in the wrong." [11] Evil is somehow unavoidable. Whatever we do, we become smutched with guilt.

After the party at which they had consumed a great deal of liquor, Miles takes Martha home and makes love to her on the sofa in her parlor, "playing the beast with two backs," [12] while her husband is away in Boston. At first she fought him off, but his desire for her she considers a compliment. Her struggle becomes less intense, and she finally allows him to have his way. It is soon over. "It had been like an exercise in gluttony; they had both grasped for a morsel they did not really want." [13] She feels disgusted with herself. But during the wrestling match, while she was resisting him, she had thought to herself that one more time could not possibly matter when she had slept with him so many times in the past? The real problem is, what is she to tell John?

A Charmed Life is a mild study in sexual misconduct and its tragic consequences compared to the more panoramic and daring novel, *The Group*. In this narrative of eight Vassar girls, class of 1933, running from the early years of the depression to the outbreak of the Second World War, Mary McCarthy portrays with incisive ironic strokes the radical moral changes that have come over the younger generation. She delineates the fate that befalls the members of this group in their revolt against the standards of their elders. They aspire to be free, unfettered, unconventional, independent-minded; they will put their progressive ideas into action, but the results unfortunately do not turn out as they had confidently anticipated.

The novel opens with the scene of the marriage of Kay, one of the leading spirits of the group, to Harald. Her college mates are startled at this wedding ceremony in church, for Kay had declared herself to be a scientific atheist. The girls also knew that Kay had "lived with" Harald before their union

[11] MaryMcCarthy, *A Charmed Life*. New York: Harcourt, Brace and Company, 1955, p. 194.
[12] *Ibid.*, p. 197.
[13] *Ibid.*, p. 205.

was religiously sanctioned. The wedding provides an opportunity for introducing each of the characters who will play a part in the story.

The Group is outspoken in its disclosure of the intimate details of the
sexual life of the characters: seduction, Lesbianism, homosexuality, defloration, contraception. The new sexual ethic is summed up in this passage
about Dottie Renfrew, twenty-three, still a virgin, though an avid reader of
D. H. Lawrence:

> She and Mother had talked it over and agreed that if you were in love and
> engaged to a nice young man you perhaps ought to have relations once to make
> sure of a happy adjustment. Mother, who was very youthful and modern, knew
> of some very sad cases within her own circle of friends where the man and the
> woman just didn't fit down there and ought never to have been married. Not
> believing in divorce, Dottie thought it very important to arrange that side of
> marriage properly; a defloration, which the girls were always joking about in
> the smoking room, frightened her. Kay had had an awful time with Harald;
> five times, she insisted, before she was penetrated, and this in spite of basketball
> and a great deal of riding out West.[14]

This is comic realism at its best, worlds removed from the prudish
reticence that marks William Dean Howells' delineation of love. Indiscreetly
honest in its observations yet unmistakably satiric in tone, this passage
strikes a new note, entirely different from the sexual vitalism of Henry
Miller or the glorification of the orgasm in Norman Mailer. Mary McCarthy
neither idealizes nor debunks sex. She is interested primarily in examining
the values these girls profess to live by, their quixotic faith in progress, their
confused search for happiness and fulfillment, their earnest resolve to liberate themselves from the outworn taboos and moral prejudices of the older
generation. Hence their preoccupation with the physiology of sex; to be
knowledgeable and experienced in this area is the mark of the new emancipated woman.

When Dottie is intiated into the mysteries of sex, she is filled with awe.
She is alone with a man in his flat, an attic room. She hardly knew this man,
a friend of Harald, whom she had met at the wedding reception. He drank
to excess and was clearly not in love with her. Then it happened and we are
told how he undressed her and made love to her, though he made no preliminary declaration of love for her. That was not part of the ritual. We are
given a detailed description of her defloration, the movements of copulation, her enjoyment of the act, her explosive orgasm. She has now become a
woman, though in her ignorance she fears she has not lived up to his expectations. All she knew about sex she had gleaned from reading Krafft-

[14] Mary McCarthy, *The Group*. New York: Harcourt, Brace and Company, 1963,
pp. 23–24.

Ebing, who "most described nasty things like men making love to hens, and even then did not explain how it was done." [15] She is fearful of being made pregnant but he reassures her on this score, explaining the technique of *coitus interruptus* to her. He informs her that she has come to a sexual climax and pays her the compliment of saying that she is probably highly sexed. She blushes furiously.

According to Kay, a climax was something very unusual, something the husband brought about by carefully studying his wife's desires and by patient manual manipulation . . . . Yet even Mother hinted that satisfaction was something that came after a good deal of experience and that love made a big difference. [16]

She is getting her education in the arcana of sexual technique. Dick, her present lover, tells her that to be highly sexed "is an excellent thing in a woman. You mustn't be ashamed." [17] But it is sex without the troublesome element of love entering in; "there had been no thought of love on either side." [18] Ingenuously she tells Dick:

My generation is a little different from Mother's. I feel – all of us feel – that love and sex can be two different things. They don't have to be, but they can be. You mustn't force sex to do the work of love or love to do the work of sex . . . .[19]

The next morning, when Dottie leaves Dick's room, he orders her to get herself a pessary and she agrees to carry out his bidding. The new woman is prepared for any sacrifice in order to satisfy her lover. He is willing to give her sex on his terms, without any of the responsibilities or emotional complications that love brings. Dick has no intention of being forced to settle down and limit himself to the possession of one woman. He warns Dottie there is to be no foolishness on her part, no falling in love. Undeterred by his warning, she goes ahead blithely with her plan to be fitted with a pessary. She visits a birth-control clinic and is given the name of a doctor who will take care of her, together with "a sheaf of pamphlets that described a myriad of devices – tampons, sponges, collar-button, wishbone, and butterfly pessaries, thimbles, silk rings, and coils – and the virtues and drawbacks of each." [20] Mary McCarthy dwells with realistic fullness of detail on the medical examination Dottie undergoes and how the contraption is inserted in her vagina.

What is remarkable in all this is not the nature of the material, hitherto

---

[15] *Ibid.*, p. 34.
[16] *Ibid.*, p. 37.
[17] *Ibid.*, p. 38.
[18] *Ibid.*, p. 42.
[19] *Ibid.*, p. 43.
[20] *Ibid.*, p. 51.

taboo in American fiction, but the tone of factual, no-nonsense realism the author employs, as if she were describing a tooth being filled. She uses no genteel euphemisms. She seeks neither to heighten nor underplay her effects, and she does not have to do so. She drives home the point that today in the United States sex has become largely a matter of technique. Though not overtly a moralist, she is impelled by her decided gift for satire and her need to be unswervingly honest in depicting the character of modern love to reveal the consequences that follow upon this much vaunted relationship of sex without sentiment. These girls in "the group" staked their life upon the latest scientific information, the sexual enlightenment, the supposedly liberating insights of psychoanalysis.

Mary McCarthy is picturing the values of American society in the thirties in examining what is called "the etiquette of contraception, which . . . was, like any other etiquette – the code of manners rising out of social realities." [21] In a dry satiric manner she discusses the economic aspect of contraception in a love affair. No man would put a girl like Dottie to all this trouble and expense unless he planned to sleep with her a long time. Harald, who voices this view, analyzes the difficulties raised by owning an apparatus of this kind. The man had to keep the equipment for the girl's sake, and the object served as a sacral reminder of the girl for whom it was intended.

In the same way, a married woman pledged her devotion by committing her second pessary to her lover's care; only a married woman of very coarse fiber would use the same pessary for both husband and lover. So long as the lover had charge of the pessary . . . he could feel she was true to him. Though this could be a mistake.[22]

The scene in which Dottie waits for her lover to return home – and waits in vain – so that she can deposit the pessary safely in his room, is instinct with the pathos of humor. She worries about what to do with the contraption once the affair is over. She recalls Kay's views on the subject, which sound cynical to her. According to Kay, the authority on such matters, there were

women of the lower sort, divorcees and unattached secretaries and office workers living in their own apartments, who equipped themselves independently and kept their douche bags hanging on the back of their bathroom door for anybody to see who wandered in to pee during a cocktail party. One friend of Harald's, a veteran stage manager, always made it a point to look over a girl's bathroom before starting anything; if the bag was on the door, it was nine to one he would make her on the first try.[23]

---

[21] *Ibid.,* p. 54.
[22] *Ibid.,* p. 55.
[23] *Ibid.,* pp. 56–57.

Mary McCarthy, in *The Group,* follows in the tradition of Flaubert, shattering the romantic illusions of her ultra-sophisticated female characters. Each one reaches out frantically for a happiness that, alas, eludes her. In the end the members of the group come up against the realization of their limitations; the years of experience brought them less than they had dreamed of or bargained for. Kay has never been sure of her hold on her husband, who talks about love in chemical and mystical terms. She is determined to keep him, but trouble soon breaks in on their marriage. We discover that he is unfaithful to his wife; he is currently having an affair with Norine, whose husband, Put, is impotent. Norine learns the medical truth about her husband's condition; his trouble is functional; he is "capable of full erection, but only with whores and fallen women."[24] She reveals the medical history and his sordid experiences with whores and factory girls in Pittsfield.

They'd pull up their skirts, in an alley or a doorway, and he'd ejaculate, sometimes at the first contact, before he got his penis all the way in. He'd never made love to a good woman and never seen a woman naked. I'm a good woman; that's why he can't make it with me. He feels he's fornicating with his mother. That's what Freudians think; the Behaviorists would claim that it was a conditioned reflex .... It's been an awful blow to him. I excite him but I can't satisfy him. His penis just wilts at the approach to intercourse.[25]

These are the comic and pathetic disclosures of the miseries of sexual maladjustment Mary McCarthy has no hesitation in furnishing the reader. Norine goes on to tell more about her unhappy married life. One neurologist shoos her out of his office when she declares she does not want to have children. In his professional opinion, sex wasn't necessary for a woman. A general practitioner gave her some original and constructive advice. He suggested that she "buy some black chiffon underwear and long black silk stockings and some cheap perfume. So that Put would associate me with a whore. And to try to get him to take me that way, with all my clothes on . . . ."[26] She follows the prescription faithfully and even puts out a polar-bear rug for the rape scene, but Put ejaculates prematurely and then blames her for spending all that money on such luxuries. Put has considerately offered to divorce her, but she will not run away from the struggle. There is nothing wrong with Put except his sexual incapacity. Then she philosophically rationalizes her decision:

But sex isn't the only thing in marriage. Take the average couple. They have intercourse once a week, on Saturday night. Let's say that's five minutes a week,

[24] *Ibid.,* p. 129.
[25] *Ibid.,* p. 130.
[26] *Ibid.,* p. 130.

not counting the preliminaries. Five minutes out of 10,080. I figured it out in percentages – less than .05 per cent. Supposing Put were to spend five minutes a week with a whore – the time it takes him to shave? Why should I mind?[27]

There speaks the advanced, statistics-spouting modern woman. She bravely faces the music.

As for Harald, she has no intention of breaking up Kay's marriage, but she cannot give up. They have been lovers for some time. Nor is she his first conquest; he has had affairs with other women that Kay knows nothing about. There are times when she feels jealous of Kay, but she consoles herself with the thought "that every experience is unique; what he does with her can't alter what he does with me. And vice versa. I'm not taking anything away from her. Most married men perform better with their wives if they have a mistress."[28]

In relating the story of the eight members of this group of Vassar girls, Mary McCarthy gives us a satiric cross-section of radically changing moral values and standards of sexual conduct during the depression years. The characters come alive. The satire is brilliantly sustained. Dottie Renfrew and her mother discuss the problem of what to do about her daughter's still lingering feeling of love for Dick, the man who had deflowered her. The mother, strangely enough, wants her to go back to Dick even if it means delaying her engagement to an older man or breaking it off, but Dottie realistically decides she will go ahead with the plans for her marriage. She tells her mother about the contraceptive Dick had bidden her to supply herself with and then points out that her mother's romantic interpretation of the episode is fantastically out of line with the truth. She had not been seduced. That supposition is old hat, the make-believe of the older generation.

Mary McCarthy dwells pointedly on the gulf that separates the two generations. Mrs. Renfrew recalls a discussion that had taken place at her class reunion;

one of the faculty members of Mrs. Renfrew's class had stated it as a generalization that this new crop of girls was far less idealistic, less disinterested, as a body of educated women, than their mothers had been. Mrs. Renfrew had not believed it, noting to herself that Dottie and her friends were all going out to work, most at voluntary jobs, and were not trammeled by any of the fears and social constraints that had beset her own generation.[29]

[27] *Ibid.*, p. 131.
[28] *Ibid.*, p. 135.
[29] *Ibid.*, p. 177.

In an ironic reversal of roles, she tries to make clear to her daughter that it was perfectly all right for Dottie to sacrifice her pride in seeing Dick again, but Dottie replies that a new age has come into being. It was no longer necessary for women to make sacrifices. "Sacrifice is a dated idea.... What society is aiming at now is the full development of the individual." [30]

Then we learn that Kay has been committed to the psychiatric ward by her husband. Her marriage had broken down. She had reached a point in her long-suffering relationship with Harald when she no longer loved him. But if she obtained a divorce then she was acknowledging that her life was a dead failure, and that realization was intolerable. Norine, glib as usual, is able to sum up Kay's difficulties neatly. She was too competitive, she suffered from repressed Lesbian tendencies and thwarted social drives, and therefore transferred her ambitious striving to her husband. "And all the time she was driving him to make money, she was ruthlessly undercutting him because of her penis-envy." [31] Then comes the shocking news: Kay dies by falling or jumping from a window. The novel ends with her funeral.

Mary McCarthy debunks the romance of sex by focusing attention on its mechanical aspects. It is her studied objectivity, her detachment, that heightens the comic satiric mood she builds up. There is no faking in her prose, no orgiastic passages celebrating the joys of sex. Her feminine characters do not lose their identity or their consciousness during sexual intercourse; both observers and participants, they watch themselves do the dance of the sheets and are both amused and ashamed by what they see. The trouble is they tend to intellectualize their experience; they try to understand what they are passing through, to bring the technology of sex fully into consciousness. Woman is portrayed as the victim of the joyless hoax of love; she discovers, in *The Group,* that men are heartless; poseurs, impotents, philanderers, promiscuously inclined, they are interested in sex alone, incapable of tenderness or unwilling to give it. [32]

3. Nabokov and the Nymphet Syndrome

If Mary McCarthy mercilessly presents the comedy of sex without love, Vladimar Nabokov in *Lolita* punctures the mystique of sex by reducing it to absurdity. Originally published in Paris before it gained legal acceptance in the United States, *Lolita* is a curiously chaste masterpiece of erotica. From

[30] *Ibid.,* p. 178.
[31] *Ibid.,* p. 346.
[32] The men in *The Group* "are selfish, malicious, loveless, and obsessed with their own psychological problems." Louis Auchincloss, *Pioneers & Caretakers.* Minneapolis: University of Minnesota Press, 1965, p. 183.

the start we are made to realize that this is a sordid and extremely pathetic tale but not without flashes of oblique humor. Here is a fictional account of a sexual abnormality, the hero's passion for pre-pubertal girls, that steers clear of obscenity. The language is ornate, romantically colored. Humbert Humbert (the name itself suggests the satiric intent of the author), who tells his own story, is not the kind of man who would indulge in four-letter words. The fictitious editor of the manuscript Humbert Humbert left behind him when he died of a coronary thrombosis while in prison, defends his right to publish the text of the manuscript unexpurgated, for those scenes that might be considered most reprehensibly aphrodisiac "are the most strictly functional ones in the development of a tragic tale tending unswervingly to nothing less than a moral apotheosis."[33]

The novel unquestionably contains a moral ending. The obsessed hero suffers because of his nympholepsy; he knows he is committing a crime against Lolita, corrupting her life, but he cannot help himself. His sensual appetite is stronger than his prudence or sense of conscience. As the putative editor remarks, he has no intention of glorifying the character of the incredible Humbert. "No doubt, he is horrible, he is abject, he is a shining example of moral leprosy, a mixture of ferocity and jocularity that betrays supreme misery perhaps, but is not conducive to attractiveness."[34] He is abnormal, but Nabokov wisely omits the clinical details and the psychoanalytic jargon in describing his condition. The author enjoys recording Humbert's inflated rhetoric, his flights of enraptured fancy, and it is these passages that betray not only the egregious folly of the hero but the unconscious humorous effects his lyrical confession produces.

He is writing this confession while under psychiatric observation. From the beginning of his sexual awakening he has been attracted to nymphets. He makes repeated allusions to Poe's fixation, his poetic love for Annabel Lee. He frankly acknowledges and defends his singular passion for girls between the ages of nine and fourteen, whom he calls "nymphets." Not that all girls within this age bracket belong to the enchanted group of nymphets. A nympholept knows how to make the proper anatomical distinctions, and Humbert proceeds to enlighten us as to the character and attributes of the true nymphet. Only the artist and madman can discern by infallible signs the one who is entitled to be selected as a nymphet. Then, too, the man who falls under her spell must be older, at least ten years or more.

Humbert, a European, is repelled by so-called normal relationships with nature women. His heart goes out to nymphets whenever they pass him in

[33] Vladimar Nabokov, *Lolita*. New York: G. P. Putnam's Sons, 1955, p. 7.
[34] *Ibid.*, p. 7.

the street, but he must disguise his shameful yearning for the unattainable
The mating call moves him not. He has caught glimpses "of an incompara-
bly more poignant bliss." [35] For him this is more tempting than the most
gloriously embellished adventure in adultery. But he cannot yield to his importunate desires. At first he does not comprehend the nature of his furious
longing; his mind resists the urgency of his need.

While my body knew what it craved, my mind rejected my body's every plea.
One moment I was ashamed and frightened, another recklessly optimistic. Taboos strangulated me. Psychoanalysts wooed me with pseudodeliberations of
pseudolibidoes.[36]

He recognizes the symptoms that will later plunge him into insanity. Like
his begetter, he enjoys poking fun at the solemn diagnostic nonsense spouted
by psychoanalysts. His mind continues to dwell on the one theme: his
craving to possess a nymphet sexually.

He fights against his besetting temptation. He marries Valeria and thus
hopes to purge himself of his "degrading and dangerous desires." [37] The
marriage turns out unhappily. After the Second World War breaks out, he
succeeds in reaching the United States and then suffers a recurrent attack
of insanity. His contempt for psychoanalytic quackery is evident in his
description of how he recovered his sanity while being treated at an expensive sanatorium.

I discovered there was an endless source of robust enjoyment in trifling with
psychiatrists: cunningly leading them on; never letting them see that you know
all the tricks of the trade; inventing for them elaborate dreams, pure classics in
style (which make *them,* the dream-extortionists, dream and wake up shrieking);
teasing them with fake "primal scenes"; and never allowing them the slightest
glimpse of one's real sexual predicament.[38]

He delights in misleading them, in throwing them off the scent. He has
nothing but amused scorn for the variety of psychiatrists, each with his
special type of interpretation.[39]

[35] *Ibid.,* p. 20.
[36] *Ibid.,* p. 20.
[37] *Ibid.,* p. 26.
[38] *Ibid.,* p. 36.
[39] For reasons that he makes sufficiently clear in his novels Nabokov is opposed to
the Freudian system, including, though with less acerbity, Jung's psychology in his
sweep of rejection. "A mordant skeptic of myths and archetypes, he is continually
poking fun at the 'Viennese witch doctor' and the stereotyped thinking of his disciples."
(Page Stegner, *Escape into Aesthetics.* New York: The Dial Press, 1966, pp. 16–17.)
It is, he believes, too easy a method for the psychoanalysts and the psychoanalytically-
oriented critics to identify fictional characters with the infantile complexes of their
author. As a literary artist Nabokov disdains theories, ideologies, labels, and programs.
In his autobiography he states that he completely rejects "the vulgar, shabby, funda-

He decides to go off to the New England countryside and finds lodging with a widow, Mrs. Dorothy Haze, where he meets his ideal nymphet, the adorable Lolita, who takes him captive at once. He composes a madrigal "to the soot-black lashes of her pale-gray vacant eyes, to the five symmetrical freckles of her bobbed nose, to the blond down of her brown limbs...."[40] He is badly smitten, haunted by her physical image, observing with the delight of a connoisseur every gesture, every movement of her body. He is afraid of suffering another breakdown if he remains a boarder in this house, but he cannot leave. It is as if Lolita had cast him under a spell.

He marries Mrs. Haze in order to be closer to Lolita. She is killed in an accident and that clears the way for his "elopement" with Lolita. A rhetorician, a sentimentalist, he furnishes a scrupulously detailed account of his attempt to seduce Lolita, but as it turns out it is she who seduces him. In composing his *apologia pro vita sua,* Humbert, the egregious romantic, is bent on proving that he is not a scoundrel. He avoids describing the first night of lovemaking in which Lolita played the role of teacher and he the part of stupid but willing pupil. "I am not," he writes, "concerned with so-called 'sex' at all. Anybody can imagine those elements of animality. A greater endeavor lures me on: to fix once for all the perilous magic of nymphets."[41]

They are off on their honeymoon flight across the face of America. He learns that he was not her first lover. He did not deflower her. She had been initiated in the rites of Venus before she met him. But this does not dampen his infatuated hunger for her. From motel to motel they wander, "ideal places for sleep, argument, reconciliation, insatiable illicit love."[42] His difficulties begin on this trip; he is fearful she will blab, as indeed she threatens to do. He has to frighten her and bribe her into submission. He is always afraid of inquiries, the curiosity of strangers met on the way. Though he is surrounded by danger, though Lolita proves a cruel and capricious mistress, he is unutterably happy. An incorrigible sentimentalist, he addresses the reader in this mawkish fashion:

Reader must understand that in the possession and thralldom of a nymphet the enchanted traveler stands, as it were, *beyond happiness.* For there is no bliss on earth comparable to that of fondling a nymphet.[43]

mentally medieval world of Freud, with its crankish quest for sexual symbols...."
Vladimar Nabokov, *Speak, Memory*. New York: G. P. Putnam's Sons, 1966, p. 20.
40 Vladimir Nabokov, *Lolita*, p. 46.
41 *Ibid.,* p. 136.
42 *Ibid.,* p. 147.
43 *Ibid.,* p. 168.

The flight of Humbert is told in a retrospective vein. He suspects that he is being followed by a red convertible. His pubescent sweetheart is acting suspiciously. He has a pistol and is prepared to use it. His act of murder at the end is foreshadowed in these nostalgic reminiscences. He betrays no sign of repentance or regret. His chief stock of humorous references comes from his detestation of Freudian symbolism. "We must remember that a pistol is the Freudian symbol of the Ur-father's central forelimb."[44] When Lolita vanishes without leaving a trace, he undertakes the pursuit, checking the registers of hotels and motels, only to discover that his hated rival was using ingenious literary pseudonyms as if both to mock him and lead him on. He winds up again in a sanatorium. He is not cured of his pederosis. The only palliative he can resort to for the treatment of his misery is that of art.

Nabokov is throughout in complete command of his material; he is both fascinated and amused by his hero's sexual obsession. The novel preaches no sexological message. *Lolita,* like Nabokov's other novels, is not meant to point a moral. He studies abnormality but does not probe its psychogenic roots. For him the true artist is not at the mercy of some neurotic compulsion or sex mystique. Nabokov is free of the ideological fixation on sex to be found in such novelists as Norman Mailer.

4. William Styron: Sex and Nihilism

We have selected *Set This House on Fire* for a brief discussion not only because it relates the current apotheosis of sex to its roots in nihilistic despair but also because it presents a protagonist who bears a suspiciously close resemblance to Norman Mailer, the evangelist of the apocalyptic orgasm. Styron takes cognizance of the contemporary sex-cult, the mystique concerned with the Dionysian release of instinctual energy. This cult has been carried to a point where many among the beat generation suffer from the very malady which D. H. Lawrence diagnosed – and damned – as sex on the brain. One woman is not enough for them. Nor is promiscuity sufficiently satisfying. They wish to engage in communal orgies.

William Styron, in *Set This House on Fire,* introduces an amoral character, Mason, who has sex on the brain. The actual hero of the novel is Cass Kinsloving, who is aware of Mason's peculiar fixation on sex and cynically discounts it. He assumes that because Mason talks continually of sex and virtually nothing else, he must be impotent. As he says:

Forever distrust a man who *celebrates* anything too much. Get a man who's got sex on the brain, one of those types who's always whooping it up about enor-

[44] *Ibid.,* p. 218.

mous thighs and mystical copulation and frenzied orgasms and such, and then in Mason's case combine that with an overripe interest in such distractions as dirty pictures, and you've got a man who is without a doubt hard put to be of real service to a woman.[45]

His estimate of Mason's character proves utterly wrong. Mason is cruel, calculatingly cruel, to Rosemarie, his beautiful, voluptuous mistress. He does not sleep with her because he has other erotic interests and sources of satisfaction. Glib, highly verbal, he is capable of morally rationalizing his inordinate lust. He is wholly absorbed in the subject of sex. He believes that sexual freedom, in his sense, provided the basis for a new morality. Cass reports that Mason, who has spent some time in Greenwich Village fraternizing with the beat generation, looked upon sex as the last frontier. "He wanted all the arts to embrace complete, explicit sexual expression . . . He said that pornography was a liberating force, *épater le bourgeois,* and all that crap . . . ."[46]

He will not listen to the alcoholic but fundamentally humane Cass, who tries to explain the physiological function pornography is made to serve. Pornography, he tells Mason, is fantasy made real and therefore satisfied some need or it would not exist, much less thrive. Cass saw nothing particularly sinful in letting our desires be aroused from time to time, but how account for the curious incontrovertible fact that all cultures have frowned on or banned pornography.

Why? I asked. It wasn't really a moral issue at all. A dirty book can't corrupt, or a dirty picture either. Anybody who wants to get corrupted is going to get corrupted, even if they have to write or draw their own. Then why had there always been rules against it? It was simple. First, it was to keep sex the seductive and wonderful mystery that it is. And it was to keep the fun in it, too – because most pornographers are so *solemn* about it. But mainly – mainly it was to keep sex from becoming commonplace, cheap, and therefore a merciless, catastrophic, almighty bleeding bore.[47]

Peter is the friend in Italy who tries to understand the complex tissue of events and the tangle of personal involvements that culminated in the rape and the murder of the beautiful peasant girl, Francesca. What was driving Mason, what furies pursued him to his horrendous undoing? Why his compulsion to lie, to make himself out to be a wounded war hero when, actually, he was a draft dodger? Why did he pose as a talented playwright when he was nothing of the sort? Why did he collect the most obscene books and

[45] William Styron, *Set This House on Fire.* New York: Random House, 1960, p. 441.
[46] *Ibid.,* p. 442.
[47] *Ibid.,* pp. 442–443.

photographs of erotica? Mason generalizes brilliantly, devising ingenious theories that support his sick sexual appetite. He is convinced that art is dead. Science is the new Messiah. Determinism rules the universe of matter and the mind of man. His collection of erotica contains the traditional items plus some rarities, all concentrating their art on depicting the act of love in all its varied human and bestial postures.

Mason is diabolically clever in justifying his taste. He tells Peter that sex is the last frontier.

In art as in life, Peter, sex is the only area left where men can find full express-ion of their individuality, full freedom. Where men can cast off the constric-tions and conventions of society and regain their identity as humans. And I don't mean any dreary, dry little middle-class grope and spasm, either. I mean the total exploration of sex, as Sade envisioned it . . . . It's what you might call le nouveau libertinage.[48]

He would redeem the animal nature of man, for man as he is and always will be is "a thinking biological complex which, whether rightly or wrongly, exists in a world of frustrating sexual fantasy, the bottling-up of which is the direct cause of at least half the world's anguish and misery."[49] He hails Sade as the great emancipator, the original psychoanalyst of the modern age,

seeing more evil in the fruitless repression of sex, and more pain, too, than in what to him was the simple answer to that repression, and the panacea – release from the fantasy world, and the working out of sex on a functioning, active level. And again that doesn't mean some tepid little convulsion in the dark. It means group interplay, for one thing – and there's no one alive who hasn't yearned at one time or another for community sex . . . .[50]

Peter laughs when he hears this fantasy about communal sex. Mason seems intent, as he tells him, on turning sex into a kind of gloomy cult. Far from denying the charge, Mason insists that sex has always been a cult, a cult of orgiastic purgation.

Peter witnesses the beginning of a communal orgy in a Washington Square apartment. The host is a famous young playwright who, like Mason, bears in some respects a striking resemblance to Norman Mailer. After his talent had gone sour on him, he devoted his waning creative energies to the writing of articles, chiefly, "in which he hymned and extolled the then burgeoning signs of juvenile delinquency, psychopaths, rapists, pimps, dope addicts and other maladjusted wretches until, finally descending into a sort of semicoherent pornography, he became unreadable . . . . He wrote much

[48] Ibid., p. 151.
[49] Ibid., p. 151.
[50] Ibid., pp. 151–152.

about the solemnity of the orgasm, its lack and its pain, and its relationship to God."[51] Here is a writer who wastes the talent he indubitably possesses by concentrating his attention exclusively on sex and by identifying it with all that is disgusting and horrible. And Mason, too, the nihilist, derives his inspiration from this source. William Styron, in both *Lie Down in Darkness* and *Set This House on Fire,* portrays with compassionate insight the tragic failures in love and sex of his principal characters, but he is definitely no devotee of the sex mystique of his age and land.

5. Leslie A. Fiedler: Literature as Satiric Pornography

Twice discovered for America (just after World War I, and again after World War II), Freud has come to seem too timid, too puritanical, and above all too *rational* for the second half of the twentieth century . . . . It is Wilhelm Reich who moves the young with his antinomianism, his taste for magic, and his emphasis on full genitality as the final goal of man.[52]

It is true enough (at least, I cannot doubt it) that only the sex organs and the sex act any longer provide possibilities for images of the failures or triumphs of love strong enough to blast us out of complacency or *ennui.* It is pornography which has kept open these possibilities; in its lowest, crudest, most nearly illiterate examples it has preserved sex from sentimentality and has kept vivid the sense that love lives, after all, *intra urinam et faeces.*[53]

The battle for freedom of expression in the field of sexual experience has been won, and we are now reaping the tainted harvest of victory. Writers are at liberty to deal at length with any aspect of the life of sex: perversion, satyriasis, impotence, nymphomania, homosexuality, Lesbianism, sodomy, seduction, rape, and normal copulation. When the writers are charged with flagrant immorality by the descendants of Mrs. Grundy, they generally defend themselves on the ground that nothing human is alien to the literary mind. No subject, be it disease or sex or the abnormal, is taboo. How can what Whitman calls "the procreant urge of the world" be excluded from the all-encompassing sphere of fiction? The forbidden voices must be made to speak by the poets of mankind. Whitman represents the modern mind when in "Song of Myself" he declares: "Copulation is no more rank than death is."

Precisely because the battle against the curse of censorship has been won, precisely because the writer today no longer has to apologize for his venture-

---

[51] *Ibid.,* p. 153.
[52] Leslie A. Fiedler, *Waiting for the End.* New York: Stein and Day, 1964, p. 160.
[53] Leslie A. Fiedler, "On Becoming a Dirty Writer," *The New Leader,* December 16, 1957, p. 21.

some foray into the hinterland of sex, is it time to inquire critically into the aesthetics of sex. For the familiar pun that nothing succeeds like "sexcess" is not only atrocious but untrue. A pornographic work, one that is obsessed with sex for the sake of sex, is bound to be artistically a failure. The proportions are wrong, the picture of life is perversely drawn, unbalanced, as if all of life were concentrated in the activity of the genitals. Also to be questioned is the assumption that uninhibited explicitness of detail in the treatment of the sexual theme is the mark of the enlightened mind. This preoccupation with the physiology of the sexual encounter becomes after a while utterly wearisome. The sexual mystique has of late become the opiate of the intellectuals.

Believing as he does in the value of pornography as literary shock therapy, Leslie A. Fiedler, a literary critic, has turned to the art of fiction to demonstate what he can achieve in this erotic genre. What we get in *The Second Stone* is a tale of adultery that satirizes the mythomanias, the follies and fetishism, of a group of Americans, most of them writers, in Rome. We are treated to lively discussions, spiced with high-spirited, malicious wit, of politics, love, and sex, but chiefly sex. A subsidiary theme relates to the problem of Jewishness. Specifically we hear talk of orgasm, frigidity, homosexuality, the libido. The two main characters, Clem Stone, a Gentile, and Marcus Stone (alias Stein) are former boyhood friends, radicals in their youth, who meet in Rome where a Conference on Love is to be held, with Rabbi Marcus Stone at its head. Clem, already married (to a Jewish woman, incidentally, Selma) but separated from his wife, falls in love with Hilda, a shicksa, wife of Marcus Stone. They are attracted to each other at once and the problem on which the plot hinges is: shall she get into bed with him or not?

The one satirized is Rabbi Marcus Stone together with the band of disciples he has gathered around him. We hear them holding forth on the absorbing subject of love. Marcus (Mark) Stone had been a Socialist and "was now the spokesman for a return to religion without a commitment to God." [54] He is full of new messianic ideas, schemes for the redemption through the agency of love. His disciples earnestly debate the question whether marriage and sexual passion are compatible. The theme of the second session of the Conference is "Marriage, Adultery and *Amor Purus*." [55]

Clem is the iconoclast, the skeptic, the ironist, the writer whose marriage has failed and who has given up on his novel in progress. The other char-

---

[54] Leslie A. Fiedler, *The Second Stone*. New York: Stein and Day, 1963, p. 23.
[55] *Ibid.,* p. 35.

acters are types, abstractions, embodied ideas, attitudes, or passions. Mark, the visionary, has organized a Conference on Love while he neglects his wife, practically turns her over to the care of Clem. Hilda for her part is by this time nauseated by any reference to the word "love." It is Clem, the nonconformist expatriate, who is the true, if often drunken and embittered, voice of conscience. The self-hatred that consumes him enables him to see himself and others truly. He sees the absurdity of life, the hypocrisy of people, their weaknesses, their contradictions.

Fiedler composes an hilarious, debunking satire on the modern sex-craze, some of it in doubtful taste. The "angel" who subsidizes the Conference on Love is Irwin Magruder, who calls himself a Hygienic Engineer. He is the employer of a sculptor who produces large, life-sized models of the vulva. Magruder is engaged in chemical contraceptives. He talks an insane Freudian gibberish. To his hired sculptor, who suffers chronically from diarrhea, he declares that his troubles are psychosomatic. "Feces is money ill-apprehended. Poverty is regression, diarrhoea the syndrome of an indurated Oedipus complex."[56] The Conference, according to Hilda, is part of Magruder's design to transform Mark into a saint.

Clem does not give up his pursuit of Hilda but he does not receive too much encouragement. At first she decides that she will not sleep with him, and the reasons she gives are seemingly convincing. She does not believe in adultery. She is thirty-six and four months pregnant. Besides, she knows her husband needs her. Without her he is incomplete, unreal. And if he wants her to lie with him, why not? After all, she is married to him. But Clem will not give up; he wants to possess her now, at once. To which she replies with feminine logic: "And I want you to want me, though I have no intention of satisfying you."[57]

We can readily surmise that this reluctance is partly feigned, only a delaying tactic. She is bound to yield – in time. She comes to his room and sleeps in his bed but without giving herself to him. She informs Clem that her husband has been faithful to her and cannot function sexually with any other woman. How then can she betray him? She confesses that Mark believes in love while "I only lay and get laid."[58] But events turn out as the author has led us to expect and Clem and Hilda consummate their illicit passion. She confides that she deliberately made him rape her. Portions of the dialogue at this point are absurdly overstrained. Hilda emotes like a

[56] *Ibid.*, p. 79.
[57] *Ibid.*, p. 90.
[58] *Ibid.*, p. 100.

Mickey Spillane heroine: "I'm an evil woman, dear Clem, and I love you. I'm a witch, a bitch, a Bluebeard gone to seed."[59]

In the meantime, the session at the First International Congress of Love holds a lecture illuminated by a large projected image of the female generative organ. The lecture is given by a Tantrist. The comic overtones of the scene are well handled. The satire runs wild. Later, Mark holds forth on the true meaning of love. *Coitus interruptus* he brands as a sin; he even goes to the extreme of maintaining that all intercourse with contraceptives is but another form of *coitus interruptus*.

At the end Clem decides to go back to Cleveland to his wife Selma, but before he leaves he wishes to attend the dinner Marcus is giving for his disciples. Marcus, when he hears that Clem has made up his mind to go back home, begs him to stay with Hilda, and Clem, believe it or not, replies: "Just because I screwed your wife, does this mean that I have no obligations to my own family, to myself?"[60] It is this part of the novel, the resolution of the conflict, that is highly contrived and entirely unconvincing. Fiedler adds a few more not so subtle touches of the brush to complete his satiric picture of the sex-cult. At the dinner, Hashiguchi discourses on the Japanese conception of love. For his people, he declares, there is no such thing as "love." The Japanese laugh and they copulate and they use numerous devices designed to heighten sexual pleasure. Magruder, not to be outdone, grandly announces that in America "Vulcanization was the Emancipation Proclamation of the Libido."[61] We shall allow him to have the last word. The novel provides its own commentary and stands judged by its contents, its pattern of sex-preoccupation. It would be a work of supererogation to add any further critical remarks.

6. James Purdy: The Ideology of Rape

Cabot Wright Begins, by James Purdy, is the story of a Wall Street executive, Cabot Wright, who rapes over three hundred women. Satiric in intent, delightfully comic in many of its scenes, even the rape scenes, which are mercifully not described in naturalistic detail, the novel attempts to reveal the decadence of the American dream, the deadly blight of conformity that has infected the consciousness of the American people. They are money-mad but miserably bored, fearful, leading aimless and empty lives.

The newspapers play up the violent lust of the rapist. Bernie Gladhart

[59] *Ibid.,* p. 126.
[60] *Ibid.,* p. 253.
[61] *Ibid.,* p. 295.

goes to New York from Chicago, sent there by his amorous and doting wife, to do a novel on the theme of rape. He must gather the material and as an added spice locate Cabot Wright and interview him for authentic data. Bernie settles down in a run-down rooming house in Brooklyn Heights. A publisher, Princeton Keith, reads his manuscript and immediately decides it is a major find. Thus interwoven with the satire on sex is an exposé of the publishing industry and its practice of bringing out erotic books that will sell.

Bernie locates the professional rapist, who is living in the same rooming house. He reports his progress by long-distance telephone to the encouraging Carrie, who has become restless while Bernie was away. Still a sexually hungry woman though approaching menopause, Carrie offers Purdy an opportunity for poking fun at the sexual obsessions of his time:

> Carrie had grown up in an age which practiced promiscuous coitus as an injunction, if not a duty. Marriage, she and her contemporaries felt, was easier and more sensible than the single state, though not laudable or noticeably rewarding in itself – a gray *faute de mieux*. The best thing about marriage was the increased opportunities it afforded to meet a number of men sexually in relaxed homelike surroundings.[62]

She needed "romance," as she called it, a man to sleep with, and so Bernie is displaced by Joel Carmichael Ullay, a Negro, who provides a bit of variety, a break in "her monotonous racial diet."[63]

The formal structure of the ribald plot is absurd, obviously not meant to be taken seriously. The satire is the thing: the damning criticism of American materialism, the changing ideological fashions among intellectuals, the new and strange pattern of permissive sexual morality that is emerging. Promiscuity is casual. The heart of the novel is to be found in Cabot Wright's confessions or rather his recollections of his extraordinary experiences as a rapist. Strange, the power he wielded. His women victims seldom complained. It is a doctor, Bigelow-Martin, who released the dormant sexual energy in him so that he entered, as it were, upon his full manhood, the man with the unsheathed sword, in a state of permanent erection. No respecter of age or youth, he possesses woman after woman, insatiable, never satisfied.

While in prison, Cabot Wright tries to explain to the examining psychiatrist the underlying reasons for his seemingly mad behavior. He maintains that he raped out of insufferable boredom, caused by his career in Wall Street. That is the kind of life lived in America today, anesthetized with

---

[62] James Purdy, *Cabot Wright Begins*. New York: Farrar, Straus & Giroux, 1964, p. 46.
[63] *Ibid.*, p. 48.

boredom in a culture based on commercial advertising. At this point Purdy relates the sexual motif to the theme that focuses on the shoddy and debased quality of American reality. He excoriates America as a land of obscenity and get-rich-quick schemes at the expense of a gullible public, a culture of consumers who function as suckers,

a civilization that has only noise, confusion, pumped-up virility and porno-graphy. It is a nation of salesmen, imbeciles, retired faggots, strip-tease sluts with nothing above or below the navel any more (the pathetic attempt of America to simulate sexual vigor is as unconvincing as her fame as a great hive of business organization). America's single role at present is to militate confusion, dirt, hollowness, race transvestism so that she can pass as quickly as possible into the cosmic scrap-hole of non-existence.[64]

America is the failed promise, the aborted dream, the lost cause, the country in which spontaneous pleasure died when industrialism, technology, high-pressure salesmanship, radio and television set in, the land in which people are afraid of being alone, frantic in their frustrated quest for excite-ment, in need of noise, the bigger the better. With savage strokes he strips America of its ideological pretensions: the blurt about morality when all any true, red-blooded American is interested in is money and success. In Ameri-ca everything can be bought or sold – if the price is right. He roars out the truth about the fantasy common to so many executives concerned about their virility; they must be seen in public with a woman, not in the company of men, to insure their reputation for normality. "Fear of reality, America. No country ever put on such a false front over the human mask."[65] Then Purdy reverts to the causal connection between the hysterical overvaluation of sex in present-day America and the impact of its synthetic civilization. The United States, he charges, is drained of its virility:

It's the time when the country has less virility than ever before, when the men are more faggoty than all the frogs who ever lived, and the women dyed-in-the-wool irregular anaesthetic whores, and the whole communication media devoted to sex-unsex. All America talks of nothing but sex ... and there isn't a stiff pecker or a warm box in the house.[66]

That is the low depressing level to which America has sunk.

That is why Cabot Wright found that so many of his female victims thanked him for his services. His strength is beyond reckoning, his sexual energy never depleted, always up to the mark. He is a figure of mythic proportions. His

[64] *Ibid.,* p. 170.
[65] *Ibid.,* p. 173.
[66] *Ibid.,* p. 174.

strength always returned after exertion – a freshet, a throbbing vigorous spring river of seed, turbulence, overmastering desire tore at his scrotum, sent his *membrum virile* bouncing thrashing flailing against his abdomen....[67]

He is by sex possessed. The rest of the population is dead, only he is alive, filled with the power of replenishing the earth.

That, in the last analysis, is the sustaining theme of the novel: America is dead, its people have lost the power to feel; their consuming passion is for money. Cabot Wright at the end finds relief in nihilistic laughter. In the course of spinning this *tour de force* of a fable, James Purdy deliberately uses rape as a shocking symbolic device to unmask the sex mystique that is current in America.

7. John Barth: Adultery and Existentialism

Here is a metaphysical novel that probes the question of identity and the Existentialist problem of responsibility for one's actions. Jacob Horner is the spiritually immobilized hero who does not know who he is or what he shall do with himself. He has decided to take a trip as far as twenty dollars, all he possesses, will take him, but what is his destination to be? One place is as good or as bad as another. He sits in the Baltimore railroad station like one in a trance, unable to make up his mind, until he is rescued by a mysterious Negro doctor, who recognizes the symptoms Horner suffers from. The Negro therapist, or fake psychiatrist, advises him to break out of this dangerous condition of indifferentism by getting a job at Wiocomico State Teachers College.

He lands the job and a new stage of his career begins. He becomes friendly with Joe Morgan, a member of the faculty, and his wife Rennie. Joe presents a perfect contrast to Jake. Active as a scoutmaster, he believes that his life, and that of Rennie as well, can be rationally controlled. Every motive must be acknowledged and honestly analyzed. There is a reason for everything that happens under the sun. Joe will not tolerate sloppy sentiment; he will fight off the incursions of the irrational. Life must be planned, every move calculated in advance, its consequences foreseen. It is this armored rigidity that drives Rennie, without her being aware of it, into an adultery that ends tragically. The man of disciplined will and inflexible purpose is pitted against Jake, the irresolute drifter.

Jake is a negative hero, a creature of shifting moods, whose one redeeming trait is his honesty toward himself. He is a loner, but he is drawn to Joe, the brilliant talker, the type who never acts on impulse or says anything he

[67] *Ibid.,* p. 186.

has not carefully thought out. Decisive, sure of himself, free from the vice of inconsistency, he demands an equal degree of consistency on the part of his wife. He has come to some fixed conclusions on the problem of the relative versus the absolute. Even though a value is not absolute, that does not mean it is not real, and that is the view he applies to the marriage relationship.

Here is a rationalist working out a system of values which culminates in relativism. Moral ends are subjective in origin; they represent volitions, as they do in logical positivism. Every man is right according to his lights. Joe makes up a supposititious case. Suppose he were temperamentally disposed to be jealous of his wife, regarding marital fidelity as "the subjective equivalent of an absolute." [68] How then would he react if Rennie committed adultery behind his back? For him the relationship would lose its reason for being. He would break the tie or shoot himself or his wife, whereas society would judge the matter from a different perspective: it would demand that he continue to support her. That is how conflicting points of view arise, and that is why he does not apologize for the things he does. "There's no sense in apologizing, because nothing is ultimately defensible." [69] Nevertheless, he strives to act rationally at all times, and that is where he makes his mistake.

The supposititious case turns into reality. It is Joe Morgan who in a sense is responsible for his wife's infidelity. He insists that Rennie teach Jake horseback riding while he is busy working on his dissertation. The inevitable happens. When he finds out, Joe does not react as he thought he would. Before he married her, he made Rennie agree that they would frankly reveal their thoughts to each other, hold nothing back. He expected a great deal from every personal relationship. He wanted certainty. What a contrast he offers to Jake! For Rennie the latter does not exist at all as a separate entity. He is a congeries of selves, each one canceling out the other, whereas Joe, as Rennie sees him, is always the same man.

The Negro psychiatrist, in charge of a farm where therapy of various kinds is practiced, advises Jake, on his first visit, to study the *World Almanac*. As for Jake's inability to act, the paralysis of his will, the doctor believes that this inability springs from the absence or death of the self. One must choose in a given situation. The doctor preaches the Existentialist doctrine that "Choosing is existence: to the extent that you don't choose, you don't exist." [70] He does not recommend religious faith as advisable in

---

[68] John Barth, *The End of the Road*. London: Secker & Warburg, 1962, p. 55.
[69] *Ibid.*, p. 56.
[70] *Ibid.*, p. 97.

Jake's case, but he should embrace some philosophy that will keep him going. He bids him be active.

Don't get married or have love affairs yet: if you aren't courageous enough to hire prostitutes, then take up masturbation temporarily. Above all, act impulsively: don't let yourself get stuck between alternatives, or you're lost.[71]

The introspective Jake Horner, the non-attached ironist, will not allow himself to get stuck to the fly-paper sentiment of love. He will acknowledge the need for sex but see it clearly for what it is, no more than a biological urge. Not to be fooled by chimeras, not to fool himself, not to walk blindly into a trap baited and sprung by his emotionalized libido – that is what he constantly warns himself against. He knows he is inconsistent, at the mercy of his moods, but this knowledge safeguards him against romantic folly, especially the folly of mistaking sexual attraction for love, whatever that may be. He satifies his sexual instinct when the need is upon him, but he does not make a fetish of sex. Far from it. He is amused by the far-fetched theories that have been woven around the erotic impulse. Here is a representative specimen of his cynical, deflationary view of sex:

The dance of sex: if one had no other reason to subscribe to Freud, what could be more charming than to believe that the whole vaudeville of the world, the entire dizzy circus of history, was but a fancy mating dance? That dictators burn Jews and businessmen vote Republican, that helmsmen steer ships and ladies play bridge, that girls study grammar and boys engineering, all at behest of the Absolute Genital? When the synthesizing mood is upon one, what is more soothing than to assert that this one simple yen of mankind, poor little coitus, alone gives rise to cities and monasteries, paragraphs and poems, foot races and battle tactics, metaphysics and hydroponics, trade unions and universities? Who would not delight in telling some extragalactic tourist, "On our planet, sire, males and females copulate. Moreover, they enjoy copulating. But for various reasons they cannot do this whenever, wherever, and with whomever they choose. Hence all this running around that you observe. Hence the world?" A therapeutic notion![72]

The above passage is not polemical in tone; it is a wryly amused recapitulation of psychoanalytic doctrine. Sexually aroused by the attractive young co-eds in his class, Jake goes off to meet a school teacher who will, he hopes, satisfy his physical need, but he will not pretend he cares for her and base a purely sexual relationship on a lie. A consummate actor, he achieves his ends. Then comes the act of adultery with Rennie. It happened without their knowing exactly how it happened. Now he feels guilty. Why had he engaged

---

[71] *Ibid.,* p. 99.
[72] *Ibid.,* pp. 109–110.

in this mad affair? Why had he betrayed his best, his only friend? Will Rennie tell her husband?

The most startling development occurs when Joe finds out the truth. Inexorably logical, he insists on ferreting out the reason behind the act. There must have been a reason. As he says: "What a man ends up doing is what he has to take responsibility for having wanted to do." [73] Jake cannot furnish a reason that will satisfy Joe Morgan, the stern rationalist. He addresses Jake in this manner:

Why did you do it? Do you think I care what you think about the seventh commandment? I'm not objecting to adultery and deception as sins, Horner; I object to your screwing Rennie and then trying to get her to hide the facts from me. [74]

Jake feels not only the anguish of guilt but also the stirring of self-contempt. What could he do to salvage his self-respect? The deed was done, part of the past, but his interpretation of it could alter the meaning of the past. His defence is that whatever motive he might have had in committing adultery was unconscious and therefore he could not be conscious of it. From the point of view of ethics, only conscious motives can be taken into consideration. But Joe is not to be swayed by such psychoanalytic casuistry. Each person, he contends, "has to be held responsible – has to hold *himself* responsible – for his rationalizing, if he wants to be a moral actor." [75] Jake, who is capable of playing different roles at various times, keeps on protesting that he doesn't know why all this happened.

Joe remains convinced – it stands to reason – that if Jake and Rennie went to bed together it was because they wanted to. It must mean that his wife wishes to make love to other men and so, logical to the last, he sends her back to Jake. He is bent on making her behave honestly. The analysis of this involved situation – the pain, the suffering, the cruelty, the humiliation – is brilliantly handled. Barth discloses how treacherous is the inner world of feeling. Words inevitably betray what we feel. Jake concludes that those who do not possess a unitary self but a plurality of selves suffer from the conflict of irreconcilable points of view, each self insisting on its special privileged truth. The responsible self no longer exists, and this is what Joe failed to realize.

The End of the Road is but one of a host of recent American novels which reflect a radical change of attitude toward the violation of the seventh commandment. From the time of the Greek tragedies, adultery has been a recurrent literary theme, but it is treated with a challenging difference of

[73] *Ibid.*, p. 128.
[74] *Ibid.*, p. 129.
[75] *Ibid.*, p. 135.

emphasis and moral insight in the age of Freud, Reich, and Sartre. It is no longer supposed to call forth murderous rage on the part of the cuckolded husband or a sense of guilt on the part of the "sinful" woman. The blurb on the jacket of a novel, *Pretty Leslie,* which came out in 1963, sums up the new morality:

What was once the cardinal sin of adultery has become for many a mild afflic-tion that can be rendered innocuous by reason, tolerance, or commonplace legal remedies. Pretty Leslie Daniels has been raised to believe that adultery's conse-quences are as easily forestalled as foreseen.[76]

It is all part of the sexual revolution that has broken out in modern Amer-ican literature.

For our next, and last, exhibit in this brief survey of contemporary Amer-ican fiction concerned primarily with sex, we selected *Go to the Widow-Maker,* by James Jones. This novel deserves a chapter all to itself not on the ground of intrinsic excellence but because it offers a near perfect exam-ple of the excesses of the sex mystique when it it is taken literally. Sex, as G. Legman point out, "is now becoming a sort of bandwagon, since Kinsey, in line with the new and total American materialism, and people are jump-ing on."[77] James Jones jumped on with a vengeance.

[76] R. V. Cassill, *Pretty Leslie.* New York: Simon and Schuster, 1963.
[77] G. Legman, *The Horn Book.* New Hyde Park, New York: University Books Inc., 1964, p. 259.

CHAPTER XIV

SATYRIASIS AND NYMPHOMANIA

Judged on the basis of his novel, *Go to the Widow-Maker,* Jones has earned the title of being the most sex-obsessed writer of fiction in the United States, with the possible exception of William S. Burroughs, but whereas the latter indulges in lurid homosexual fantasies of the most detailed kind, fantasies induced under the power of drugs, James Jones celebrates the glory of *normal* copulatory activities. Sex is love and love is sex, sex is bliss, Heaven on earth, if the right partner is found. Promiscuity is only natural, a sort of interregnum of experimentation, until full orgastic consummation is achieved with the ideal mate, though even then an occasional going astray is not out of the question. Marriage is a trap in that it curbs the freedom of the couple to sleep with whom they please, but, as Jones shows, there are ways of breaking the contract in secret without being caught. What Dreiser defended as varietism for the male has today become a widespread cult worshiped by both sexes. In his novel Jones undertakes to demonstrate at great length the truth of the proposition that variety is the essential spice of sex.

Yet *Go to the Widow-Maker* is not a contribution to pornography, though it comes perilously close to it at times. What saves it from being a calculated literary aphrodisiac is that Jones writes with perfect seriousness about these perpetually sex-hungry, sex-seeking characters. He is explicit in describing each sexual experience – the naked body of the female, the posture assumed, the precise method of intercourse used, the reaction felt. He stints none of the physical details and he holds nothing back. The pages are strewn thick with four-letter words. And yet there is nothing inherently objectionable in these sex-charged passages that combine blunt, earthy realism with flashes of lush lyricism. He practically outdoes Henry Miller in the frequency with which he dwells circumstantially on the varied techniques of cohabitation, but it is all done honestly, without coyness or fake touches of enthusiasm. He is, in fact, unduly solemn in proclaiming the gospel of sexual vitalism, unlike Henry Miller who possesses a unique comic gift and can laugh, and make the reader laugh, at the absurd antics of the human animal in the act of sexual intercourse. For Jones, sex is fate, sex is character; it is through their sexual inclinations and behavior that men and women betray their essential self.

Go to the Widow-Maker, then, is concerned chiefly with sex, the novel to end all sex novels. Coupled with the theme of the constant compulsive pursuit of sex by women as well as men is the subsidiary but related theme of the men striving to achieve manhood by engaging in dangerous sports and thus overcoming the emotion of fear. In other words, women are necessary for men's sexual enjoyment, but they are not enough to make up the fullness of their life. A man must have his work, his favorite sport – in this case, sea-diving and spear-fishing. Another motif that crops up, though it plays only a minor part in the novel as a whole, is the criticism brought to bear on the pressure for conformity applied by mass society, the progressive loss of individual freedom. But the preponderant emphasis falls on the hero's singular obsession with sex.

The general outline of the plot is easy enough to follow. The protagonist, a brilliant, successful Broadway playwright, has been caught in his youth in the toils of a married woman, eighteen years his senior, who supported him financially when he was in need, encouraged his creative ambition, and tried to help him in his work. She induced him to live at her home, with the willing consent of her husband, who is glad of the young man's companionship. She becomes his mistress and casts a kind of spell over him so that he cannot break away, even though she fails to satisfy him sexually. He cannot escape her dominating influence. As for the accommodating husband, he may suspect that something is going on behind his back but he has no positive proof and is not sufficiently jealous or concerned to find out: To the very end he remains ignorant of the true nature of the relationship. It is also left uncertain whether he ever slept with his own wife during this period when the *ménage à trois* was established.

The turn in the story comes when Ron, determined to break away from this married woman's control and to test his manhood, decides to leave New York City and go off to Jamaica to take up the sport of sea-diving. But before he leaves he has the good fortune to meet the woman who is the embodiment of his dreamed-of ideal – the perfect sexual partner. He falls in love with her but he is not inclined to marry her. He is not the marrying kind. He values his freedom, especially his sexual freedom, too highly. He is resolved to go ahead with his experiment and off he journeys to Jamaica, where he is taught the art of sea-diving by Al Bonham.

The scenes describing the diving expeditions at various places are excellently done. Ron admires Bonham, looks upon him and his underwater feats of strength, skill, and courage as partaking of the heroic. He drinks with him and cherishes his companionship, but what troubles him is that his mistress is waiting for him at the hotel. He cannot shake her off. The image of her as the "old mantilla-ed witch-mother" [1] haunts him, but while he was down in the watery depths exploring the cavern, she ceased to exist for him. That was one way he could get rid of the old witch. And what about the girl, Lucky, he had left behind him in New York – could he be in love with her or was it only, as with a host of other girls he had possessed, a passing fancy, an illusion. He had reached the age when he no longer believed in love.

Yet meeting Lucky – her full name is Lucia Angelina Elena Videndi – had caused a marked change in his outlook. He was famous when he was first introduced to her. "In the faster sets of girls . . . he was known . . . as a very good lay and a better diver, but a man who did not want encumbering entanglements and might therefore be half fag." [2] This describes the social world this allegedly famous playwright moves in. It also sets the tone of the novel – the focus on sex, the undisguised interest in licentiousness. What disturbs this protagonist is not his creative work, though he thinks about it on occasion, or his mortal fate, though he dwells fleetingly from time to time on the thought of death – what actually disturbs him is that he feels miserably lonely when he is without a girl to sleep with. Not that he ever had a close relationship with any of his sleeping partners. They were there – that was understood between them – to provide the pleasurable sensation of sex. The women he had intercourse with "didn't give a real damn about him any more than he gave a damn about them." [3]

Always holding him back from any serious emotional attachment, a painful drag on his conscience generating a diffused sense of guilt, was the fear of hurting his mistress, the forbidding mother-image. Lucky, however, proves irresistible. We learn that though she was brought up as a Catholic she now had no religion. Strangely enough, she felt that God hated her.

She was determined to extract every fleeting joy, beauty, pleasure from her life that she could get before God or whatever Monster it was Up There snatched it away from her. She had also twisted for her own benefit Spinoza's "Because I love God does not mean God must love me in return" to fit more the modern age: "Because God hates me does not mean I must love God in return." She also said: "The reason there is so much divorce in America today is because sex is not dirty enough in the home." [4]

[1] James Jones, *Go to the Widow-Maker*. New York: Delacorte Press, 1967, p. 37.
[2] *Ibid.*, p. 44.
[3] *Ibid.*, p. 44.
[4] *Ibid.*, p. 44–45.

Here we are given the psychological motivation and spiritual lineaments of a lapsed Catholic turned hedonist, a sex-goddess who can twist Spinoza to her own purpose, an authority on what is wrong with married life in America. She is a paragon of all the virtues a Ron Grant would admire, especially since she believed in putting these virtues into practice. She is no hypocrite, she makes her moral values known freely, she does not hide her promiscuous past. In fact, she is proud of it. Ron has found a kindred spirit. From now on Jones can devote a disproportionate amount of space to the activities of these two sexual epicures, who are not burdened by a strict sense of moral responsibility.

Lucky had understood him at once but would not yield herself to him sexually the first time they met. She has her own code of social propriety: "I never lay men the first date I have with them."[5] But why, he vigorously protests, should she hold out on him when she had frankly told him about the many men she had enjoyed in her life, no less than four hundred. This sets a new record in fiction for a heroine who is not a prostitute.

Ron Grant feels frustrated. He is now thirty-six but though he has known many women he had been deprived of one thing: the experience of love. He had never had what he considered a true love affair. As a result, he had come to believe no such thing existed – except in the movies of Clark Gable and Carole Lombard; and in that insane, complex, all pervasive spiderweb laid down over the entire American nation: the great American love song industry. Anything else was just kidding yourself. He had been considerably aided in this belief by his mistress, who for reasons of her own never tired of stating it: *There is no such thing as love.*[6]

For his part he found his mistress' analysis perfectly accurate, yet he still yearned and hunted for true love. "But he could no more stop hunting love than he could stop wanting to get laid well . . . ."[7] He did not count his sexual partners in the past as having called forth or given him love. And love, as he defines it, "presupposed a need, an allpowerful, insuperable need . . . of each party for the other which superseded everything else in life."[8] He never does find love.

He reviews his relationship with Carol Abernathy. After his success as a playwright, Carol turned to the study of Oriental philosophies but without abandoning the practice of serving his sexual needs.

[5] *Ibid.,* p. 51.
[6] *Ibid.,* p. 53–54.
[7] *Ibid.,* p. 54.
[8] *Ibid.,* p. 55.

She made it plain that she now slept with him so that he would not waste precious time from his Art chasing pussy. She even went so far as to tell him that a frustrated sex life was good for him, and all artists, all great men, because it allowed him – and them – to sublimate sex energy in work.[9]

Nearly everything in the novel – art, love, sea-diving – is reduced to the primal sex urge. Rod is weak enough to accept Carol's theory as true, though another part of him knew it was a tissue of mouldy lies. Her motive in this case was clear: she wanted to keep him as her personal possession, to dominate him, and he yielded to her influence, that was the strange part of it. All he got for his pains in this unhappy relationship was a chronic, deepseated sense of guilt. He was repeatedly unfaithful to her, he was guilty of rank ingratitude as her spiritual son, guilty, too – and that hurt his conscience badly – of cuckolding his friend, Hunt Abernathy. As Carol once told him while they were lying in bed: "Christ! You're the only man I ever heard of who got to live out his Oedipus complex!"[10]

The public was hard to fool about this relationship but they played the role of mother and son so well that he was regarded as a " 'mother'-dominated neurotic."[11] Ron had to preserve the secret in order to protect Carol and especially Hunt against the spread of malicious gossip. And yet, whatever his state of restiveness or resentment, he invariably came back to Carol, and that was because of the fear that gripped him: "Fear of being alone. Fear that every girl in his life from now on would only be a liaison . . . ."[12]

That is the mania which possesses our hero night and day. His mind, like his body, is supersaturated with sexual desire. Now he thanked his stars for having met Lucky; she had helped him get rid of this incubus of fear. What he liked about her was not only her physical beauty but the way she made love. "He had never had sex like this in his life, ever."[13] Whatever secret power she possessed, she stirred him to his depths, broke down his resistance, unified his being, and yet he has his doubts about marrying her. After marriage, suppose she turned out to be different? Why take the risk?

Here we have a heroine who has engaged in sexual intercourse with no less than four hundred men (her own statistical count) and a lover, Ron, whom one of his producers accuses of suffering from satyriasis. Ron fails to come off as a credible character. He is supposed to be afflicted with moods of despair, but this is stated rather than shown. He is supposed to be convinced that increasing bureaucratic control by the government in an indus-

[9] Ibid., p. 56.
[10] Ibid., p. 58.
[11] Ibid., p. 59.
[12] Ibid., p. 60.
[13] Ibid., p. 63.

trialized society would doom the artist to impotence, but these brief, abstract intellectual discussions are quickly passed over and the author settles down to the more congenial task of reporting Ron's sex life in intimate detail. At birth he had been named, significantly enough, Decameron, and this had helped to give him a life-long inferiority complex. "Was it also what had made him so terribly oversexed all his life?" [14] This is the kind of pat, neatly contrived motivation the author provides for his main character. Jones furnishes a blow-by-blow account of the frequent love-making of Ron and Lucky. The latter is a connoisseur of a man's sexual prowess. She had belonged to a group of girls who slept exclusively with writers. She is disconcertingly frank in her disclosures. "As she was so fond of saying at parties or wherever else she thought it might shock, her trouble was that at the age of eight she masturbated and liked it." [15] And yet, for all her unabashed and uninhibited promiscuity, she is troubled at times – but not for long – by her Catholic conscience.

Ron meets some models who led a gay, free sex life and made no bones about it. During their teens and early twenties they indulged their appetite to the full "and until they gave up the gay life and became proper wives and mothers, nothing interested them except parties, money, titles, travel and celebrities. That they would ever pay later for the sins of their youth seemed highly doubtful." [16] They engage in nude swimming. Ron becomes intoxicated as he views their beautiful young bodies, but he knows he cannot possess them, even if he copulated with them a hundred times. Instead of spending the night with one of the models, he calls Lucky and begs her to fly to Montego Bay. He had deliberately denied himself the fulfillment of his sexual desire, all for her sake. Why had he done so? He was no believer in monogamy and he knew that the Christian institution of monogamous marriage was brazenly ignored and laughed at.

But none of this helped him because he had been raised, brought up, indoctrinated and oriented in the belief that the only sexual perfection lay in the one man-one woman monogamous relationship (never mind marriage). And he couldn't shake it. And his fourteen-year experience with Carol Abernathy, and all the infidelities he had been forced into by her coldness and perhaps by his own inordinate desires, as well as the busted and unhappy love affairs and marriages he had observed around him over the years, had confirmed this.[17]

In the light of all that has happened, this is hard to believe, this sudden

[14] *Ibid.*, p. 93.
[15] *Ibid.*, p. 108.
[16] *Ibid.*, p. 235.
[17] *Ibid.*, p. 239–240.

overwhelming craving for the experience of true love. When provoked into anger, he blurts out the truth about his progress toward promiscuity, which he defends on the ground that this inclination is present in all people. It is amusing to watch Lucky and Ron as each one tries to justify his own code of behavior. For all his pretended freedom from narrow prejudices, Ron cannot thrust out of his mind the thought – horrible to contemplate – of the four hundred lovers Lucky had known sexually. Her moral justification is that she never took money; her affairs were meant for mutual pleasure. At bottom, we discover, she detested men and their lecherous desires, though she insisted that the only way to know a man was to have sexual intercourse with him. That is how she had learned of the sexual peculiarities of the men in her life. And Jones is methodically explicit in describing her form of sexual enjoyment, leaving little to the imagination.

Consider the following passage of introspection by Lucky: its concreteness of functional detail, its deliberate use of the four-letter word, its interest in the techniques of coitus. Compare it with the pagan interior monologue of Molly Bloom in *Ulysses,* and the startling difference in quality of insight and style becomes immediately apparent. Jones is giving us sex for the sake of sex, without any redeeming features.

After they had made love – (God, she loved fucking, loved it so much it was almost enough, it almost was enough, it *was* enough, most of the time, the weight on you pressing you down making you helpless holding you with your legs wide open, that big red angry thing filling you up and moving inside you [they were all big when they were inside of you, unless they were actively deformed], slowly at first and then the increasing rhythm, increasing tension, the red face and bared teeth and crossed unfocused eyes as they came, came in you, you own them then, at that moment they belong to you) – after they had made love, she lay awake a long time thinking.[18]

What this stresses is the purely physical function, the mechanics of sex, the physiological reaction, the narcissistic preoccupation with the pleasure one's own body is receiving. There is no tenderness, no upsurge of love. Fundamentally Lucky hates men. How they lied to her! Not one, she feels, is to be trusted. This is the first time, according to her, she has been in love, but, as the above passage would seem to indicate, love for her means sexual gratification. Sex is the be-all of her existence. When Ron learns that Al Bonham, the man he so greatly admires, is impotent with his own wife but can function sexually with other women, he recalls what Lucky was in the habit of saying: "Sometimes I think the whole of the United States is totally

18 *Ibid.,* p. 276.

and completely sexually sick, sick to danger point."[19] And this, we are told, was one of Ron's main themes as a dramatist.

Ron breaks away from Carol, finally cuts the pseudo-umbilical, quasi-incestuous cord, and marries Lucky, but the marriage unfortunately complicates matters. He is more than ever jealous of the hundreds of men in her past. It is, he realizes, a ridiculous feeling, especially considering his own promiscuity, but he cannot reason the pain away. The pain becomes acute when he meets one of her former "lovers." Suspicion rankles in his mind.

Was he marrying himself to some kind of a damned little hustler? Was he letting himself be caught by some kind of goddamned twobit whore of a nymphomaniac? But he loved her. An of course the old clincher: if she liked sex that well with him, with Grant, why wouldn't she like it just as well with somebody else, with anybody?[20]

Ron had drifted into the marriage; he had not actively desired it but had failed to oppose it and so he found himself wedded. Even Lucky at the last moment is reluctant to give up her freedom.

The strange thing was, and they had both discussed it – both before and after – they were fooling the whole world by getting married. Because getting married could not – and did not – legalize their sex life. That would – and it did – remain just as dirty and good as before.[21]

But why, D. H. Lawrence would ask caustically, associate sex with "dirt?"

In this novel the sex mystique emerges full blown, anarchic in its advocacy of sex divorced from love. Sex is hailed as the basic instinct, the primordial motivating force in life. At one point in the story Ron thinks: "it was really where the screwing was that mattered in the end. It was where you were getting laid, and who was laying whom. People Who Fuck Together Stay Together."[22] One hardly expects this cynical – and naive – bit of psychologizing to come from a brilliant contemporary playwright, but it fits in with the author's ideological intention. Sex is the universal passion transcending all other interests and activities. Those who deny this pragmatic truth are either self-deluded hypocrites or liars. Love is an illusion. And in sex, each man to his individual taste. There is nothing perverted in any form of sexual behavior so long as it yields pleasure. This is fictional

[19] *Ibid.*, p. 321.
[20] *Ibid.*, p. 364.
[21] *Ibid.*, p. 372.
[22] *Ibid.*, p. 449.

pansexualism that attempts to make its elaboration intellectually respectable by covering it with a specious smattering of Freudian complexes. *Go to the Widow-Maker* has virtually exhausted the subject of heterosexual love. Sex is God and James Jones is its newly appointed prophet.

PART IV

CONCLUSION

CHAPTER XV

CONCLUSION

For two thousand years or more man has been subjected to a systematic effort to transform him into an ascetic animal. He remains a pleasure-seeking animal. Parental discipline, religious denunciation of bodily pleasure, and philosophic exaltation of the life of reason have all left him overtly docile, but secretly in his unconscious unconvinced, and therefore neurotic. Man remains unconvinced because in infancy he tasted the fruit of the tree of life, and knows that it is good, and never forgets.

Norman O. Brown [1]

In the union of the sexes, love reveals its most particular character. Sexual gratification may be sought and is possible without love.

Clemens E. Benda [2]

There is not the slightest doubt that the monogamic relationship between man and wife is the best attainable for the co-existence of the two sexes, the form best suited to develop the deepest, richest, and most enduring emotional ties between two people who are not neurotic.

Samuel Lowy [3]

The slogan has been sexual intercourse at any cost, even among young people, when, on the contrary, sexuality should be permitted to mature tranquilly and to advance toward a healthy and meaningful eroticism consonant with human

---

[1] Norman O. Brown, *Life Against Death*. Middletown, Connecticut: Wesleyan University Press, 1959, p. 31. Psychoanalysis takes its stand firmly on the theory of instincts. Man cannot hope to transcend his animal nature by taking refuge in some doctrine of the soul. But man is not an animal and therefore suffers from conflicts which result in neuroses. "It is the privilege of man to revolt against nature and make himself sick." (*Ibid.*, p. 84.) The solution, according to Brown, lies not in instinctual renunciation but in the resurrection of the body. He exalts Dionysian as opposed to Apollonian (or sublimation) mysticism.

[2] Clemens E. Benda, *The Image of Love*. New York: The Free Press of Glencoe, Inc., 1961, p. 14.

[3] Samuel Lowy, *Men and His Fellowmen*. London: K. Paul, Trench, Trubner & Co., Ltd., 1946, pp. 31–32.

dignity, eroticism in which the sexual element is the expression and crown of a love relationship.

Viktor B. Frankl [4]

We moderns are faced with the necessity of rediscovering the life of the spirit; we must experience it anew for ourselves. It is the only way in which we can break the spell that binds us to the cycle of biological events.

C. G. Jung [5]

Sex may be a hallowing and renewing experience, but more often it will be distracting, coercive, playful, frivolous, discouraging, dutiful, and even boring. On the one hand, it tempts man to omnipotence, while on the other, it roughly reminds him of his mortality.

Leslie H. Farber [6]

1. The Literary Eros

Toward the turn of the twentieth century something happened which destroyed in many writers the sense of unity with their fellow men. Anarchy was let loose, the center could not hold. The philosophy of relativism worked havoc with the traditional assumption that men shared common aspirations, values, and beliefs. Henceforth the writer would struggle desperately and in isolation with the effort to give voice to the inner man, his striving for self-realization and transcendence. A century ago Emerson still cherished a noble idealism, a humanism that believed in the innate goodness and even greatness of man, but in our time, when the forces of the world proved too threatening, there arose the temptation to embrace the cult of the irrational, the fetishistic worship of Nature. The call was sounded: one must revolt at all costs against the coercive, dehumanizing pressure of industrialized mass society.

Thus society is resisted in the name of the solace that mindless Nature can provide. Here is the source of freedom that authoritarian society renders impossible. Here is a welcome avenue of escape from the curse of regimented labor, the banality of bourgeois culture, and the tedium of homogenized life among the masses. Once the writer came to suspect that society was in a conspiracy against his ideal of creative self-fulfillment, he clung all the more tenaciously to his vision of Nature as offering him the boon of biological happiness he craved. It was a vision, a paradisal dream, in which he could release his instincts unchecked by the insidiously frustrating pressures

---

[4] Viktor E. Frankl, *The Doctor and the Soul*. Translated by Richard and Clara Winston. New York: Alfred A. Knopf, 1955, p. 193.

[5] C. G. Jung, *Modern Man in Search of a Soul*. Translated by W. S. Dell and Cary F. Baynes. London: Kegan Paul, Trench, Trubner & Co., 1941, p. 140.

[6] Leslie H. Farber, *The Ways of the Will*. New York and London: Basic Books, Inc., 1966, p. 54.

of the social world. In short, Nature was the one retreat where inhibited man could come into his own.

The greater freedom obtained in the selection of themes, the revolt against all forms of censorship in the sphere of art, the campaign energetically waged and with increasing success against the suppression of literature on moral or legal grounds, the attack in some libertarian quarters on the societally enforced "tyranny" of marriage, the demand for equal rights for women, the insistence that woman be regarded and treated as an individual with her own needs for independence and fulfillment – these furnished modern writers from Theodore Dreiser to the latest beat or Hip insurgent with a challenging body of new material and powerful incentives to create. They had a world of new experiences and human relationships, hitherto condemned as immoral, to explore, and they were free to experiment with new techniques and new forms.

Yet all this in itself offered no guarantee that this new material, so authentically modern, so liberating in its effect, would promote great art. For it is not the subject *per se* that is the foundation stone of literature; what counts is what the writer does with his material, how deeply he penetrates it, how profoundly his imagination succeeds in transmuting it, how organically he incorporates it within the confines of form, how well he develops universal motifs out of immediate problems and historically conditioned conflicts. For the thesis novel, the problem play, the propagandistic tract in literature, despite the excellent intentions with which they are produced or the exemplary courage with which they defend their unpopular cause, have as a rule no claim to permanence. Once they achieve their objective, they vanish into the limbo of the past, to be recalled only as footnotes to the evolution of taste and the sociology of literature. Who today reads *Uncle Tom's Cabin* or Chernyshevski's *What Is to Be Done?* or the plays by Brieux or *The Jungle* by Upton Sinclair. They have served their purpose and are largely forgotten. In the long perspective of time, the present-day battle over the meaning of love and its relation to sex (which was not, of course, confined to the literary arena), may, to future historians, well seem like a curious, long-persisting aberration.

We have seen how the battle against Puritanism was fought in the twenties. Writers demanded the right to freedom of expression, the right to portray honestly the sexual behavior of man, and their cause triumphed. But the victory, however fruitful it proved under the leadership of such talented writers as Sherwood Anderson, Fitzgerald, Hemingway, and O'Neill, did not result in a continuing renaissance of letters in America. What it produced in the fifties and sixties was an aesthetic rooted primarily in sex. This aesthetic was based on the stated or implied assumption that the subject matter of sex in itself could regenerate the moribund body of American literature. What it needed was a generous shot of testosterone. Sex was not only the palladium of freedom, it was the gateway to salvation. The new categorical imperative read: what was formerly kept fearfully in the dark must be brought to light; the taboo on sexual knowledge and sexual experience must be lifted; the sacred cause of truth must be served.

As it attracted a loyal, enthusiastic band of adherents, this aesthetic became transformed into a mystique, a veritable cult. The reaction against the ethic of repression ran to the other extreme. The sexual instinct, it was charged, had been stifled and warped to a point where it produced neurotic creatures, "grotesques" deprived of their manhood; they were ashamed of sex and therefore rendered afraid of life. To save them from this sickly feeling of guilt, to remove the chains of repression – that is the mission the beat and Hip writers set themselves. They engaged in a crusade to liberate the body and mind of man from the inherited curse of Puritanism.[7]

There is *prima facie* nothing wrong with the treatment of sexuality as the theme of a novel, a poem, a play. Ancient literature, including the Bible, did not avoid this vital aspect of experience. Nothing human is alien to the artist's vision. He is free to deal with religious mania, schizophrenia, incest, perversion, metempsychosis, the resurrection, fantasies born of drug addiction, if he can invest this material with the significance and order of art. Everything, then, depends not on the subject chosen but what the writer does with it, how he handles it in relation to the rest of the universe of experience. If he chooses to write about the theme of sexuality, from what perspective does he view it? Does he accord it an overriding importance, in the manner of James Jones, to the exclusion of everything else in the world? Does he make it the be-all and end-all of existence, interpreting it as the highest rapture, the crown and consummation of felicity, a form of ecstasy that is mystical, almost religious, in character, what Norman Mailer calls with blasphemous unction the apocalyptic orgasm? This is the mystique

---

[7] In his chapter on Mabel Dodge Luhan, which he subtitles as "Sex as Politics," Christopher Lasch makes this revealing comment on the sexual revolution that broke out early in the twenties: "The modern world in its ignorance of the past believed that it had discovered sex, had rescued it from the grip of 'Puritanism'; but what had really happened was that sex for the first time had come to be seen as an avenue of communication rather than simply as a means of mutual pleasure. By insisting that sex was in fact the highest form of love, the modern prophets of sex did not so much undermine the prudery against which they seemed to be in rebellion . . . as invert it. In effect, they took the position that sex, far from being 'dirty,' was more 'spiritual' than the spirit itself . . . ." Christopher Lasch, *The New Radicalism in America*. New York: Alfred A. Knopf, 1965, p. 109.

which, in one guise or another, has become fashionable in much of contemporary literature.

How far can this movement go? In primitive as well as civilized societies, men have had to face the issue of how best to regulate the sexual instinct which makes for the propagation of the species.[8] Instinct is the force of Nature that man has to reckon with at all times. Western civilization established the institution of marriage and attempts, not always successfully, to enforce the monogamic ideal. It requires that the young sublimate their sexual hunger until such time as they can assume the reponsibility of marriage. Today, however, the monogamic ideal has been challenged and is openly or covertly flouted, as we have seen in the fiction of Mary McCarthy, John Barth, and James Jones, thus creating a crisis in morality.[9] The rebels against convention and covenant deny the injunction that sexuality should function solely to serve the procreative purpose. Now that contraceptive devices have been perfected to a point whereby pregnancy can be safely avoided, many see no reason why sex should not provide a legitimate source of pre-marital and extra-marital pleasure. The private sex life of people, so long as they do not interfere with the rights of others, should be their own concern.

Modern literature, in its obsession with the theme of sexual love, is reflecting a profound cleavage in our culture. The drive toward unrestricted instinctual gratification is in conflict with the cultural demand for sublimation. The writers whose work we have examined ran the whole gamut of revolt. Dreiser, in his work that began with the dawn of the twentieth century, argued that while marriage was indispensable for the perpetuation of the species, the fact would have to be recognized that man was essentially a promiscuous animal. Dreiser's naturalistic fiction exposed the glaring disparity between the publicly professed Puritanic ideal and the actual behavior of men and women in America. During the twenties, largely under

---

[8] "In every human society known to us there are always some women to whom a man cannot have access and some men who are denied to every woman." (J. D. Unwin, *Sex and Culture*. London: Oxford University Press, 1934, p. 28.) Unwin holds that those societies which enforce compulsory monogamic relationships reach the highest point in the cultural scale. Another student of the subject of love declares: "Thus no society exists – or has existed – where general promiscuity is the norm." (Fernando Henriques, *Love in Action*. New York: E. P. Dutton & Co., Inc., 1960, p. 186.)

[9] In much of modern literature, marriage is supposed to result in the death of love. Love and marriage stand diametrically opposed to each other. The man becomes enslaved by a marriage into which he freely entered and in which his wife soon ceases to be an object calling forth intense passion. As Simone de Beauvoir writes: "He is taken in the snare set by nature: because he desired a fresh young girl, he has to support a heavy matron or a desiccated hag for life." Simone de Beauvoir, *The Second Sex*. Translated by H. M. Parshley. New York: Alfred A. Knopf, 1953, p. 187.

the growing influence of Freudianism, the sexual revolution broke out in full force. Somewhat later Henry Miller became the prophet of a new religion of sex, and the cult gained more extreme devotees in the fifties and sixties in the members of the beat and Hip generation, who deified sex without benefit of God. There is no taint of asceticism in their outlook; they may be drawn to Zen Buddhism but they have no intention of withdrawing from the world nor are they at all interested in the ideal of sexual abstinence as facilitating the quest for salvation. Their conviction is not that sexuality degrades man by reducing him to the animal level but that the animal is the region of the divine. The Kingdom of Eternity is to be found in the orgiastic present, and Heaven is synonymous with the orgasm.[10] Lawrence Lipton, the ideological spokesman for the rebels, announces that the sexual revolution is in fact already upon us and is making steady strides forward. A review of his recent book, *The Erotic Revolution,* will show that the sexual revolution of our time is not confined to the literary domain but has its underground social roots and ramifications.

2. *Lawrence Lipton and the Erotic Revolution*

A new world, he assures us, is giving birth to a new iconoclastic sex ethic. The emphasis is now on complete sexual fulfillment, the enhancement and intensification of sexual union, whatever form it takes. Sex, the basis of life itself, is the key that will unlock the gates of the Earthly Paradise. All this can be enjoyed without suffering any aftermath of guilt. In forbidding this natural enjoyment, it is society which is sick, neurotically repressed. Sex is good, sex is holy. Morality does not enter into the picture. Each one must decide for himself how he will experiment with sex, premaritally or otherwise.

He is a staunch advocate of sexual freedom. There is no reason why premarital sexual relations should be outlawed. Legal marriages should be optional. No forms of the sexual act should be branded as unnatural. "Nature knows no unnatural sexual acts." [11] He would legalize the use of contraceptives and the right to abortions. He defends the right of man to

[10] According to Max Weber, "The intoxication of the sexual orgy can ... be sublimated explicitly or implicitly into erotic love for a god or savior. But there may also emerge from the sexual orgy ... the notion that sexual surrender has a religious meritoriousness .... Yet there can be no doubt that a considerable portion of the specifically anti-erotic religions, both mystical and ascetic, represent substitute satisfactions of sexually conditioned psychological needs." Max Weber, *The Sociology of Religion.* Translated by Ephraim Fischoff. Boston: Beacon Press, 1963, p. 237.

[11] Lawrence Lipton, *The Erotic Revolution.* Los Angeles: Shelbourne Press, Inc., 1965, p. 11.

experiment freely in the field of sexuality. He believes that it is one of the inalienable prerogatives of man to establish any kind of sexual relationship with the female that they both find satisfying. He speaks, of course, for a dissenting minority that has been forced to go underground.

Sexual morality based on the Judeo-Christian ethos has produced a race of the frustrated, and many are revolting against its mandates. The sex culture of the United States is undergoing radical changes, even though these changes cannot be statistically measured, since the rebels have no intention of running afoul of the law. Despite the ever-present threat of legal persecution, a new ideal of the place of sex in life is emerging and being increasingly adopted by the younger generation of the disaffiliated and secretly by many who belong to the Establishment.

Lipton's criterion of value is summed up in his statement that "There are no amoral societies and no amoral persons. There are only differing moral systems, societal and personal." [12] The double standard is a fraud and a mockery. Its stringent enforcement accounts for the high rate of adultery in this land.

If extramarital sexual relations were not frequently rewarding to the husband, the wife or both, if they were not life-enhancing in themselves and marriage-preserving in their effect in many cases, who would care to risk the legal, social, economic and sometimes psychological dangers involved? [13]

In most instances, adultery is kept carefully hidden while the transgressor pays sedulous lip-service to the old moral code. Lipton deplores the need for this cowardly ritual of deception and deceit. But the "two-party, single standard adultery, when it is carried on by mutual consent of husband and wife, is worthy of respect." [14] Lipton is eloquent on the subject of those who, fearing no divine wrath visited upon them for their transgression, are "happily" experimenting with intermarital sex by participating in a switch club and swap-mating.

One chapter is entitled "The Ancient and Joyous Art of Community Screwing," a glorification of the orgy. Here is the sexual revolution being acted out in complete disregard of the laws of the land and the negative injunctions of the Church. The orgy disposes of the shibboleth of romantic love. "It is in violation of the cult of Romantic Love because it presupposes the validity and value of fucking without love, faithfulness or the presump-

---

[12] *Ibid.*, p. 39.
[13] *Ibid.*, p. 47.
[14] *Ibid.*, p. 47.

tion of permanence."[15] With no other aim except that of direct and immediate enjoyment, the orgy "makes sex an end in itself."[16]

What Lipton calls for is the introduction of the element of change in the
sexual mating of human beings. The bugaboo of original sin must give way
to a sexual life based on sane standards. Experimentation should be encouraged rather than forbidden, even experiments which the public now condemns as abnormal. Lipton insists "that anything which heightens sexual
excitement and adds to sexual enjoyment is a legitimate and healthy part
of the act of coitus."[17] There is nothing "unnatural" in sexual activity,
however widely it departs from community standards. The sexual rebels
reject "the system," the fraudulent ideals of the Establishment, what they
call "the Social Lie." Even on the campus the college youth are giving
expression to a rebellious sex ethic, "that sex is its own justification, without
so much as a thought to marriage or any expectation of marriage."[18]

These revolutionaries, and Lipton among them, swear allegiance to
Wilhelm Reich; they are determined to seek total orgasm as a good in itself.
There is no substance to the theory, they argue, that sex without love is evil
and abhorrent while sex with love is permissible and morally right. Lipton
presents his "facts" and then shows that they are in flagrant contradiction
to the assumptions on which the official morality and the Christian religion
are grounded. According to him,

the outstanding fact of sex life in our time is the increase of unmarried sex, not
as a preparation for marriage but as an end in itself. In effect, it does, of course,
prepare boys and girls for a more successful life in marriage, but only if they
succeed before marriage in wriggling out of the straitjacket of guilt, fear and
psychological armoring. Permissiveness is no guarantee of sexual freedom on
the sexual level. . . . It is not the frequency of the orgasm but the quality of the
orgasm that matters.[19]

Lipton's main attack is directed against the moral inhibitions Western
civilization has erected. His undisguised aim is to break down all barriers
and permit the orgy and the total orgasm to reign. It is evident that he articulates the views held by the *avant garde* sexual radicals. We have already
encountered some of the ideas he advocates in the work by those novelists
who subscribe to or sharply satirize the contemporary sex mystique.

As far as literature is concerned, the ideology of sexual monism reaches
to the heart of the matter. It projects a *Weltanschauung* that is radically

[15] *Ibid.,* p. 100.
[16] *Ibid.,* p. 100.
[17] *Ibid.,* p. 125.
[18] *Ibid.,* p. 135.
[19] *Ibid.,* p. 187.

incomplete, for it ignores for the most part the metaphysical dimension, the existential conflicts generated by the human condition, the nostalgia for the Absolute, the hunger for transcendence, the continuing quest, however often disappointed, for the experience of permanence in love. It represents a simplistic and cynical conception of the nature of man, stripping him of the kingdom of spirit and reducing him to a biological function. Despite what the apostles of sexual freedom preach, copulation is not the alpha and omega, the aim and end of existence.

There are signs and portents, however, even within the writings of such proponents of uninhibited sexuality as Jack Kerouac and Norman Mailer, that the reaction against such excesses is already setting in. The passage of the year ages these heroes of sex, their instinctual energies exhaust themselves in drink, promiscuous sex, and drugs, and they begin to behold the end of time, the coming on of the night of death. They struggle to heighten the pleasures of instinct, but even their sexual adventures after a while begin to pall, and then they are brought face to face with the ultimate question: what are they to do with their life? Nature is not enough to satisfy the infinite hunger of the heart. Not the womanly, but the vision of the eternal, however unattainable, lures them on. The sexual partner that was supposed to provide the beatific experience is only a body that is never completely possessed. Love is the mystery.

3. The Power of Sex and the Theme of Love

Our concern in this book is not primarily with the shifting patterns of sexual morality in modern times but the different ways in which the power of sex and the theme of love are interpreted within a large, representative body of American literature. There is, we must point out, a fundamental semantic difference between the experience of sex and the theme of sexual love as it finds expression in fiction. If a rose is not a rose, sex is not sex. Sex as it appears embodied in the novel is in a sense sex recollected even if not in tranquility, sex psychically distanced, sex transcended, sex as part of an ongoing literary tradition. Certainly the beat cult of sexuality and the Hip mystique of the apocalyptic orgasm owe as much to literary antecedents and the force of tradition as the cult of romantic love. Both forms of love reflect the nature of man and his values at a given time.

As Ortega y Gasset points out, the phenomenology of love almost resembles a literary genre. Sex as pure instinct does not and cannot exist in a state of culture; it is inevitably transformed into eroticism. Each age shapes its own myths, and the emphasis today is not on spirit or even Eros but on sex as pure instinct. But love, whether it be frankly sexual or "romantic" in character, is a commitment. No two people react to the experience of love in the same way. A man reveals himself – his sensibility, his quality of imagination, his nobility or coarseness of spirit – in the manner and object of his love.[20] Whereas the sexual instinct is not particularly discriminating in its choice of an object, love is not to be satisfied with any woman but the uniquely chosen one.

If a man's love is as he is, then it is logical to assume that as a society is so is its conception of love and the ritual of love it practices. The literary interpretation of the sexual motif is conditioned inevitably by a number of variables: the culture, the milieu, the economic background, the historical situation. Nor can the analysis of sexual love in literature be carried out in isolation, cut off from the rest of society and its activities. The study of sexual behavior is of interest not only to literature but to the natural and social sciences as well: psychology, psychoanalysis, biology, anthropology, and medicine. Under the impact provided by the investigations of Havelock Ellis and Freud, the emphasis was for a time placed on the abnormal, and literature reflected this interest in homosexuality, Lesbianism, and the psychopathological.[21] Not that the writer simply responds to the ideological determinants of his age, but he is bound to be influenced, consciously or unconsciously, by its demands. Henry Miller first circumvented the restrictions of censorship by having his novels published in Paris until the current of taste in the United States changed and *Tropic of Cancer* and *Tropic of Capricorn* could be legally published in this country. Norman Mailer and James Jones may be in revolt against the sexual conventions of American society, but the point is they cannot, as writers, entirely divorce themselves from that society and the public for which, presumably, they write. They know that sexual love is still an emotionally charged theme, and it is difficult for them, in the heat of their rebellious protest, to preserve the balance, especially in a native culture that still looks upon sex outside of the marital union as shameful, if not sinful. Victorian prudery has been overcome, but this victory has led, as we have seen, to a reaction that grossly overestimates the importance of sex.[22]

---

[20] "A man's love is as he is . . . . A man's way of love expresses his total constitution – his vital energy, his perceptiveness, his intelligence, his ability to communicate." (John H. Schaar, *Escape from Authority*. New York: Basic Books, Inc., 1961, p. 128.) Ortega y Gasset, too, feels that love expresses the intrinsic nature of man. "As one is, so is his love." (Ortega y Gasset, *On Love*. Translated by Tony Talbot. New York, 1958, p. 192.

[21] See Jeanette Foster, *Sex Variant Women in Literature*. London: Frederick Muller Ltd., 1958, pp. 240–341.

[22] "The easing of the restraints of Victorianism has led to an equally irrational

If the twentieth-century writer champions freedom in matters of sex expression and challenges the official ethic that sexuality is to be confined only to reproduction or to married partners, he owes a great debt to a number of predecessors, particularly to the work of the scientists who traced the animal ancestry of man. Though American society still condemns certain forms of sexual behavior as anti-social and immoral, modern science, notably the work of Kinsey and his associates, has led the writer to adopt a different, more tolerant set of norms. As a result, literature today reveals the emergence of new sexual attitudes, a new iconoclastic love ethic, even though in the main the older values still prevail. At any rate, a new sex morality is in the process of being formulated, so "that nobody now displays the slightest interest in the morality or immorality of the sexual conduct of another person."[23] If literature is in large measure a function of society, even when it rebels against the regnant social order, then the sexual morality that literature portrays tends to reflect the changing mores of a culture, its framework of acceptance and rejection, its conflicts and crises.[24]

Invariably, however, the question of morality crops up whenever literature touches upon the controversial problem of sex. Basically interested in regulating the sexual impulse so as to maintain unimpaired the institution of the family, the State is prepared to proscribe literature that seems to be guilty of subverting public morals. The sexual problem is complicated, as

reaction in literature and thought, to philosophies that treat sex as a *mystique*, and to an exaggerated estimate of its importance." (Alex Comfort, *Sexual Behavior in Society*. New York: The Viking Press, 1950, p. 13.) An American sociologist angrily deplores the current exploitation of the sexual instinct at the expense of the spiritual factors that should govern human behavior. "*Homo sapiens* is replaced by homo sexualis, packed with genital, anal, oral, and cutaneous libidos. The traditional 'child of God' created in God's image is turned into a sexual apparatus ... preoccupied with sex matters, aspiring for, and dreaming and thinking mainly of, sex relations. Sexualization of human beings has about reached its saturation point." (Pitrim A. Sorokin, *The American Sex Revolution*. Boston: Porter Sargent, 1956, p. 18.)

[23] Ottakar Nemecek, *Virginity*. New York: Philosophical Library, 1958, p. 87. According to Gerald Heard, the past fifty years have witnessed "a greater revolution in sex morality than in any of the other moralities. Sex morality has declined from being morality *per se* to being regarded as little more than a crabbed prejudice, as ignorant, cruel, and indeed as unhealthy as any other savage superstition." Gerald Heard, *Morals Since 1900*. New York: Harper & Brothers, 1950, p. 96.

[24] "It has often been noted that advanced industrial civilization operates with a greater degree of sexual freedom – 'operates' in the sense that the latter becomes a market value and a factor of social mores." (Herbert Marcuse, *One-Dimensional Man*. Boston: Beacon Press, 1964, p. 74.) But contemporary sexuality, as voiced in literature, is frustrated and twisted. Its expression is unrestrained, orgiastic, but it is without consequences. Nothing really happens. One sexual encounter leads to another that is equally disappointing. Industrial society "turns everything it touches into a potential source of progress *and* exploitation, of drudgery *and* satisfaction, of freedom *and* oppression. Sexuality is no exception." (*Ibid.*, p. 78).

we have seen, by the fact that Nature and man pursue different ends. Biologically the aim of sexual union is to perpetuate the race whereas th human couple seek to derive pleasure from the act. Such a separation – th divorce of sex and its increment of pleasure from the reproductive process – highlights the necessity for imposing some degree of control on the releas of the sexual instinct. In order to control the process of reproduction, societ is compelled to use the instrument of repression.[25] Every civilized societ must draw up and apply its own code of sexual morality.

But the attempt to censor literature – and we are speaking in this con text of literature, not of hard-core, commercialized pornography[26] – o prescribe what is for or against the public good is predicated on the assump tion that literature can become, if not supervised and regulated by the au thorities, a potent source of moral contamination. It is not that at all. It i not books that corrupt the minds of men and attack their moral fibre. It i life itself that generates the multiple evils which beset mankind. It is neces sary for men to know the meaning of evil before they can proceed t strengthen the foundations of virtue. If men are to be safeguarded agains the taint of evil, then not only literature but life as a whole must be purified Literature cannot be legitimately judged by the criterion of dogmatic moral ity. It is absurd to restrict literature only to "pure" and "morally safe subjects. As Chekhov pointed out: "Artistic literature is called so just be cause it depicts life as it really is. Its aim is truth – unconditional an honest."[27] The writer cannot afford to turn his eyes aside from the un pleasant aspects of life, to ignore dirt and disease, ugliness and evil, murde and rape.[28] Objective in his delineation of reality, he must reveal the whol truth, knowing "that dung-heaps play a very respectable part in a landscape and that evil passions are as inherent in life as good ones."[29]

This is in the main the aesthetic outlook in relation to sex that inform the work of writers like Dreiser, Sherwood Anderson, Hemingway, O'Neill

[25] See Abram Kardiner, *Sex and Morality*. Indianapolis and New York: The Bobbs Merrill Co., 1954.

[26] See Appendix.

[27] Anton Chekhov, *Letters on the Short Story, the Drama, and Other Literar Topics*. Edited by Louis S. Friedland. New York: Minton, Balch & Co., 1924, p. 275.

[28] These are, in substance, the grounds on which *Tropic of Cancer* has been de fended against the charge that it is pornographic. "To charge a book like the *Tropi of Cancer* with pornography is like charging life itself with pornography. Is ther anything pornographic about a man defecating? Anything pornographic about th sexual act? Anything pornographic about the sexual organs? All such processes jus are ... Life is ..." Michael Fraenkel, *The Genesis of the Tropic of Cancer*. Berkeley California: Ben Porter, 1946, p. 26.

[29] Anton Chekhov, *Letters on the Short Story, the Drama, and Other Literar Topics*, pp. 275–276.

nd Faulkner. Nor does the persistence of the sexual theme in the body of wentieth-century American literature indicate the presence of an abnormal nterest, a sex-obsessed mentality characteristic of the age of Freud and Vilhelm Reich. Everything depends, as we have said, on *how* the theme is reated, what role it is made to play in the total structure of the work. The *·ita sexualis,* as both D. H. Lawrence and Faulkner demonstrated, each in is own imaginative way, grows out of man's relation to Nature, society, nd God. In the twentieth century, the sexual instinct, no longer feared or ontemned, found a number of inspired and some intemperate literary inter-reters.

Scientific investigations revealed that there were marked variations in)atterns of sexual behavior among different nations and ethnic groups. Such variations in sex behavior occur even among primitive societies.[30] English nd American literature initiated a restless search for new modes of creative expression that would do justice to the sexual life of man in all its diversity. [n the twenties the question whether sex was a legitimate subject for the vriter was no longer at issue. What was very much at issue was the question low far the writer was justified in going when he dealt with the vagaries of he sexual instinct. In England the writer who violated the taboos surround-ng the literary handling of the sexual theme had to run the same gauntlet)f abuse and prosecution as his American counterpart. As far as English society was concerned, portrayal of sex and particularly of the abnormal vas intensely disapproved, but it was all right to develop such themes if the vriter did not dwell on revolting details and never explicitly mentioned the physiological facts. That is to say, English society was willing to yield ground but only on condition that the writer observe certain rules of the art)f circumlocution.[31] Whereas *The Rainbow,* published in 1915, was con-sidered too shocking for public taste, other novels of the time concerned, though less openly, with perversion were allowed to be published. But the rising tide of interest in the sexual theme could not be stemmed.[32]

[30] See Margaret Mead, *Male and Female*. New York: Morrow, 1949.

[31] Richard Hoggart makes the point that the English working-class people are not more sexually licentious than the others, but they talk about sex more freely, "and sexual experience in the working-classes is probably more easily and earlier acquired than in other social groups." (Richard Hoggart, *The Uses of Literacy*. London: Chatto and Windus, 1957, p. 83.) Despite all this, they are remarkably shy about some aspects of sex – "about discussing it 'sensibly,' about being seen naked, or even about undressing for the act of sex . . . ." (*Ibid.,* p. 83.)

[32] Postwar Britain is enormously interested in vice and sex. "The English are, on the whole, an inhibited people. They have a basic prudery and gaucheness in sex matters which sets them apart from almost every other nation in Europe . . . . In England, the realization that many of the restraints and taboos of Victorian times are unnatural and even psychologically harmful, combined with the decline of organized religion has led

If American writers waxed indignant because of the envenomed opposition that greeted their efforts to be completely honest and truthful in their
portrayal of the life of man, they seemed to overlook the fact that it took a
scientist like Freud a relatively long time before he could gain recognition
for his heterodox views.[33] Come what may, however, the writers refused to
hold their tongue. Neither Henry Miller nor Norman Mailer would be intimidated by the mobilized hostility of public opinion. Despite the restrictions
of censorship, American writers continued to trespass on forbidden grounds
and decade by decade the legal barriers erected against the publication of
their work had to be removed. In his autobiography, *A Child of the Century*
Ben Hecht notes the extraordinary progress that the present age had made
in its treatment of the theme of love.

> The modern novelist, rid of asterisks, has lifted biology from under the counter
> where Fanny Hill and Justine blushed in secret. His heroines are nude as eels.
> Their legs fly open like compasses; and he is expert at a sort of bimanual exami
> nation phraseology.[34]

Thoroughly versed in the science of physiology as well as the fine art of
love-making, the modern novelist is supported in his undertaking by his
psychological understanding of the perversities of sex. Hecht's complaint
about novels of this type is not that they are wicked but that "they have
substituted gynecology for romance."[35]

The most gifted novelists, men like Stendhal and Flaubert, Balzac and
Tolstoy, Hardy and Marcel Proust, D. H. Lawrence and Faulkner, were
always aware of the fact that sex is not a matter of the senses alone, an exclusively instinctual process. The imagination plays an essential role in the
complex drama of the relationhip of the two sexes. Even the Church Fathers
recognized the profound part that imagination plays in kindling sexual

---

to considerable laxity in sex matters, particularly since World War II. This, in turn,
has brought about a morbid interest in vice and low life." Alan Simpson, *Beckett and
Behan and a Theatre in Dublin*. London: Routledge and Kegan Paul, 1962, pp. 185–
186.

[33] The medical profession was inclined to be cautiously conservative in matters
relating to sex. In the early part of the twentieth century in the United States, professors
of medicine and neurology made it a practice to avoid any discussion of the topic of
sex, even though the clinics were then crowded with cases of men and women infected
with venereal disease. One medical historian reports: "Only on two occasions, as far
as I remember, did any of the instuctors make reference, and then only in passing, to
those powerful sexual drives which impelled men and women to run the risk of exposure
to the ravages of two of the most dreaded and devastating infections of the time, syphilis and gonorrhea." C. P. Oberndorf, *A History of Psychoanalysis in America*. New
York: Grune & Stratton, 1953, p. 63.

[34] Ben Hecht, *A Child of the Century*. New York: Simon & Schuster, 1954, p. 161.
[35] *Ibid.*, p. 162.

desire.[36] Yet these gynecological explorations in fiction that Ben Hecht condemns could not be checked; the writers would not listen to reason or heed the demand for moral restraint. The more fiercely they were attacked on moral grounds, the more determined became their rejection of the doctrine of original sin. Insisting that sex was a perfectly natural and wholesome impulse, they proclaimed their own unconventional code of sexual morality.

As we have already shown, some of these writers went to extremes. Their worst mistake lay in failing to distinguish between sex and love, in looking upon sexuality as solely an instinctual function. To compare the physiology of sex with the physiology of eating or drinking is to reduce love to a mechanistic basis. According to this "realistic" biological logic, the sexual act no more needs to be justified than the intake of food in response to the call of hunger. Sexual freedom is defended on the ground that it does not concern society but only the two people directly involved. Each one is entitled to pursue happiness in his own way, and sex is, of course, taken to be the royal road to happiness.[37]

This gospel of sexual anarchism did not meet with much favor either in England or the United States. Though the energies implanted by Nature cannot be abrogated by legal or moral fiat, they must in society be subjected to some measure of regulation. Moreover, the sexual instinct cannot, in the context of human experience, be separated from the organic network of other emotions that enter into the sexual act. These emotions cannot be dismissed as irrelevant simply because they are subjective, for their presence determines whether sex is for the individual simply a discharge of physical tension or a positive mode of human relatedness. It is not the discharge of energy that is the decisive factor, but the encounter itself and the relatedness or communion in love it brings about.[38]

Love is not to be confused with the sexual instinct, which can function

[36] For a discussion of this point, see "Sex and the Imagination," in Colin Wilson, *The Strength to Dream*. Boston: Houghton Mifflin Company, 1962, pp. 157–188.

[37] Those who associate psychoanalysis with promiscuous sex indulgence have not read their Freud aright. Genital love is mature love, and it definitely points to love as a desideratum and not genitality alone. Erikson admits that psychoanalysis "has on occasion gone too far in its emphasis on genitality as a universal cure for society . . . ." Erik H. Erikson, *Childhood and Society*. New York: W. W. Norton & Company, 1950, p. 230.

[38] Schachtel takes vigorous exception to the crude psychology of sex as detumescence, a physiological reflex. "If discharge of tension were the only source of sexual pleasure it would neither be understandable why the sexual pleasure of sexual intercourse is preferred by most people to the pleasure of masturbation, nor why individual variations of the sexual act are a source of pleasure." Ernest G. Schachtel, *Metamorphosis*. New York: Basic Books, Inc., 1959, p. 68.

without it. Love exists because people believe in it.[39] It is specifically a human sentiment, a vital fiction, a creative effort, as D. H. Lawrence maintained, on the part of man to transcend the boundaries of the self. The act of love is fundamentally an expression of spirit. The sexual instinct does not exist in a "pure" form, as an absolute. The literary rebels, however, were convinced that the process of sublimation could not be carried far without producing harmful effect. Love, they contended, is but a polite euphemism for sex. Nature wears no verbal fig-leaves. The sexual energy resident in man is a mighty force which can be transmuted into creative achievement, but this triumph of transcendence, they argued, must not be gained by the suppression of instinct. Morality must be placed at the service of Nature, not the reverse. The sexual experience brought one closer to the natural world, the primordial source of life. The history of our era, Lawrence said, "is the nauseating and repulsive history of the crucifixion of the procreative body for the glorification of the spirit, the mental consciousness."[40] Yet Lawrence believed in the permanence of marriage and had no use for libertinage or infidelity.

Despite the assaults made on it by the Bohemians of the twenties or the radicals of the thirties or the sexual militants of the fifties and sixties, the institution of marriage did not go bankrupt.[41] The experiment of "free love" ended in nervous breakdown or in a belated, rueful recognition of the desirability of the married state. In his controversial book, *Marriage and Morals,* Bertrand Russell was old-fashioned enough to believe that love has a definite and enduring place in human life. For all his iconoclastic views on occasional instances of infidelity in marriage, he did not agree with those who naively assumed that if their sex life functioned satisfactorily, then happiness would automatically be theirs. On the contrary, Russell maintained that love is something "far more than desire for sexual intercourse;

[39] It cannot be too strongly emphasized that the call of sex goes beyond the realm of the physical; it represents a search for human relatedness, a way out of existential loneliness and isolation. It is transformed in character when it is supported by a feeling of love and responsibility. As Dr. Benda says: "The image of love which has been dominant for two thousand years is not a mere 'feeling' that can be experienced wherever man exists in time and space, but it is based on a concept of man as a unique being who occupies a position between beast and God. This form of human relatedness does not evolve merely from instinctual behavior but is an act of the freedom of man." Clemens E. Benda, *The Image of Love,* p. 20.

[40] D. H. Lawrence, *Phoenix*. Edited by E. P. McDonald. New York: The Viking Press, 1936, p. 569.

[41] See such works as the following: V. F. Calverton and S. D. Schmalhausen (eds.), *Sex in Civilization.* Garden City, New York: Garden City Publishing Co., 1926; and Samuel D. Schmalhausen and V. F. Calverton (eds.), *Woman's Coming of Age.* New York: Liveright, 1931.

t is the principal means of escape from the loneliness which afflicts most men and women throughout the greater part of their life." [42] What the Bohemian rebels and members of the beat generation did not sufficiently take into account is precisely this point, namely, that a civilized person cannot truly enjoy the experience of sex unless it is accompanied by the feeling of love. To shatter the false dualism between the body and soul, Nature and spirit, is not the same thing as denying the reality of love or engaging in a communal orgy. But the movement for greater sexual freedom in America, once it gained momentum, could not be stopped. [43]

The consciousness of sex begins to pervade every walk of American life, public as well as private. As is documented in a book like *Mass Culture,* those who provide popular entertainment find that they can best appeal to the masses through the exploitation of sex beguilingly camouflaged. [44] Even the advertizers play shrewd and not too subtle variations on the sex motif. [45] The Americans seem to be thoroughly ambivalent in their views on sex. They adopt inhibitory, anti-sexual attitudes, though, as Dreiser and others have pointed out, there is little correspondence between their professed moral ideals and their actual behavior. [46] And this split in the human personality, which is a marked characteristic of the culture of the West, creates serious difficulties in the sexual life of the people. [47] Psychologically, as a study of literature designed for mass consumption shows, [48] this introduces a decidedly neurotic cleavage in consciousness. On the one hand, there is among the mass of people this fearful repudiation of sexual indulgence outside the sanctions of the officially approved moral code; on the other, there is this covert but pronounced tendency to revel in sexual imagery and consume licentious, if on the surface morally correct, literature. Sex, in short, is fascinating and pleasurable – but illicit. In American public life sex has

[42] Bertrand Russel, *Marriage and Morals.* New York: Liveright, 1929, p. 122.
[43] As Max Lerner declares, "every gain in sexual freedom in America has generated the appetite for further gains and has widened the gap between code and conduct." Max Lerner, *America as a Civilization.* New York: Simon and Schuster, 1957, p. 678.
[44] See Bernard Rosenberg and David Manning White (eds.), *Mass Culture.* Glencoe, Illinois: The Free Press, 1957.
[46] See Albert Ellis, *The Folklore of Sex.* New York: Charles Boni, 1951, pp. 283–284.
[46] See Albert Ellis, *The Folklore of Sex.* New York, 1951, pp. 283–284.
[47] "Sexual deviations and disturbances of potency must . . . of necessity run high in our Western culture, because sexual functioning is associated with fear." Abram Kardiner and Lionel Ovesey, *The Mark of Oppression.* New York: W. W. Norton & Co., 1951, p. 14.
[48] See G. Legman, *Love and Death.* New York: Breaking Point, 1949.

become a form of big business, a veritable industry and profitable mode of exploitation, as well as a national obsession. Sex is now a mental intoxicant, an end in itself.

The trouble with much of modern American literature is not that it is sexualized; the sexual life of man has always been a central preoccupation of the writer, though it has been disguised beneath layers of idealistic rhetoric. Nor is it the unparalleled frankness with which the sexual theme has been treated that is the root of the trouble. What is wrong is the ever increasing emphasis placed on the mechanics of sex, the technology of sex. This is wrong on human and therefore also wrong on moral grounds, for it is guilty of isolating the sexual function and making it the touchstone of happiness, the supreme desideratum. What is apparent in the literary productions which celebrate the triumph of the sexual revolution is that they purport to derive their inspiration and justification from Nature. To turn against Nature is to act "unnaturally," to suffer the ravages of neurotic frustration, to become unhappy, unfulfilled. Instead of advocating ways of defeating the bondage of the flesh, they yield to Nature's will, and that will – the will to sex – is now rampant. The sentiment of love, the wholeness of the self, its emotional needs and spiritual aspirations, all this is ignored as irrelevant. What counts is the intensity, the completeness, and frequency of the orgasm.

But however important the sexual instinct is, it is not the sole or supreme passion in life. As one literary historian sensibly sums up the matter: "Man has never been governed exclusively by his loins." [49] The human being is so constituted that he cannot, without falling into despair, concentrate all his energies on sex. On the whole, the literary revolt in America underlined the need for unhampered freedom of expression and for a relationship between men and women based on the indefeasible craving for love as well as the importunate hunger for sex. Each generation of writers struggles to interpret life anew, to preserve what is viable in the cultural heritage of the past and to slough off what is dead. In striving to resolve the conflict between Eros and the cultural demand for sublimation, American literature of the twentieth century affirmed in a number of ways the spiritual aspirations of the race. Despite the polemics of Lawrence Lipton or the fictional diatribes of Norman Mailer and James Jones, the obituary announcing the death of love is altogether premature. The quarrel over the manner in which

---

[49] Frank Luther Mott, *The Golden Multitudes*. New York: R. R. Bowker Co., 1947, p. 249.

ove should be interpreted is no mere literary issue; it stems fundamentally
rom the ongoing debate over the complex nature of man. Perhaps the future
of American literature will bear witness not to the demise of love but to the
triumph of the spiritual principle in man, giving birth to a humanism that
will affirm "sexual love as the supremely redemptive form of love." [50]

[50] Dorothea Krook, *Three Traditions of Moral Thought*. Cambridge: The University Press, 1959, p. 296.

THE PROBLEM OF CENSORSHIP

Once more but now for the last time we must tackle the problem of censorship and attempt to pin down as best we can the meaning of the two sinful categories – pornography and obscenity – against which the laws of censorship are directed.

Though some unscrupulous literary hacks may cash in on the craving of the middle class, chiefly, for works of deliberately concocted pornography, the guardians of public morality do not make the necessary distinctions and look with undisguised suspicion, if not downright condemnation, upon any novel or play that deals too frankly with the theme of sexual love. Denying that there is anything inherently indecent about the subject of sex, the American naturalistic novelists fought against the obscurantist and repressive policy of State censorship. The work produced by Dreiser, Sherwood Anderson, Hemingway, James T. Farrell, and Henry Miller brought to a head the old and troublesome problem of what constitutes pornography in literature and how the people, especially the young, can best be safeguarded against the plague of commercialized, hard-core pornography. Obscenity and pornography – these terms acquire their objectionable emotional connotation only in relation to the context in which they are used. They are a timebound function of the complex of events, the pressures and the passions, that called them forth. In the United States, the public is periodically whipped, by self-appointed watchdogs of moral purity, into a frenzy of indignation over the alarming state of immorality prevailing in the world of books. The charge of obscenity obviously covers a wide-ranging spectrum of meanings. After all, what cannot be included under the rubric of sex? The sexual instinct is tied up with all our human concerns, and language can easily be manipulated to give off suggestive overtones and ingenious *double entendres*. As soon as the free discussion of sex is muzzled, society offers in effect a premium for underground camouflaged sex expression. What is not released as a normal erotic outlet is converted into violence, the lurid exploitation of sadism. And this is precisely what has taken place. The American people give vent to their frustrations vicariously by indulging in homicidal fantasies. An anti-sexual morality is responsible, directly or indirectly, for generating an obsession with sadism and death. As Legman points out:

Sex is not a crime. Describing sex *is*. The penalty for murder is death, or lifelong imprisonment – the penalty for writing about it: fortune and lifelong fame. The penalty for fornication is . . . there is no actual penalty – the penalty for describing it in print: jail and lifelong disgrace.[1]

American society devotes a disproportionate share of attention to sex and at the same time engages periodically in orgies of righteousness and public rituals of purification. But sexual mores change, the times change, and the moral standards applied to literature perceptibly change. American writers in the twentieth century struggled to preserve and extend freedom of thought and expression. It is true that freedom must be balanced by some measure of restraint, for every culture from primitive to modern times imposes its own set of taboos, but there is today no universal agreement as to what should be tabooed. What the Victorians stigmatized as immoral is now regarded as tame and innocuous. As Eric Larrabee quips: "A nation gets the pornography it deserves."[2] And Heywood Broun, in an essay on censorship, wittily remarks that after all "it was not the novelists, not even the modern ones, who invented sex. Both the fundamentalists and the evolutionists agree that the scheme has at least the merit of antiquity."[3]

The writers whose work fell afoul of the powers of censorship fought courageously for what they considered the fundamental right of freedom of expression, the right to explore all apects of life, including the sexual behavior of man. The literature they produced was intended to vindicate this movement for greater freedom of expression. In our dicussion of Norman Mailer we showed that he refused to delete six lines of his novel, *The Deer Park,* even if this meant that the publisher would turn it down. What was wrong with the rigid Victorian system of morality was that it was externally imposed, a discipline clamped like a straitjacket on the live body of man. Now that the old taboos have largely been overthrown, the social attitude toward obscenity and pornography in literature can be rationally re-examined. A more tolerant and enlightened philosophy of love is in the making. The proposal that sexuality is to be used exclusively for procreative pur-

---

[1] G. Legman, *Love & Death.* New York: Breaking Point, 1949, p. 94.

[2] Eric Larrabee, "Morality and Obscenity," in Frederic J. Mosher, *Freedom of Book Selection.* Proceedings of the Second Conference on Intellectual Freedom, July 20–21, 1953. Chicago: American Library Association, 1954, p. 39.

[3] Heywood Broun and Margaret Leech, *Anthony Comstock.* New York: Albert & Charles Boni, 1927, p. 274.

poses ignores the elementary fact that human sexuality, unlike sexuality among animals, knows no seasonal cycle. The woman is not to be reduced to a child-bearing machine. Writers like Dreiser and Sherwood Anderson kept on insisting that life would be not only freer but also happier if man accepted the functioning of his body without a false sense of shame and guilt. Though the battle still rages over the proper treatment of sex in literature, the controversy is at bottom caused by opposed views as to the basic character of man and his place in the universe.[4]

As we have tried to show, the defence generally made by the champions of sexual freedom in literature rests on an appeal to Nature. In practice, however, it proves extremely difficult to devise an objective and reliable method for detecting the obnoxious presence of obscenity in literature.[5] If pornography is to be construed as comprising anything which tends to arouse sexual desire in the reader, then there is no limit to what might conceivably fall within the scope of this loose definition. What, then, is pornography? "The genre pornography," says Marcuse, "is distinguished above all by its unreality: existence is reduced to the vital region – and then further to the one which may not be mentioned in public . . . ."[6] Since the forthright portrayal of sex in literature is frequently and without much justification branded as "immoral," the subject of sex tends to acquire the fascination of the forbidden. But what one generation damns as offensively "immoral" or "indecent" is hailed as an artistic masterpiece by the next.[7]

[4] Lawrence K. Frank points out "that the older teachings about sex were sanctioned by the older conceptions of the universe and man's place therein which have asserted that man was outside of nature and therefore must despise and reject his organic impulses and sexual functions." Lawrence K. Frank, *Nature and Human Nature.* New Brunswick, New Jersey: Rutgers University Press, 1951, p. 155.

[5] One legal authority in the field declares that it is impossible to define obscenity since it is subjective in nature. The obscenity is discovered by the mind of the reader who injects the offending element into the book. To allege that a book contains obscene material "conceals a deduction based on certain unstated premises, the code of manner prevalent in a community at any particular time." (Norman St. John Stevas, *Obscenity and the Law.* London: Secker & Warburg, 1956, p. 2.) There is a difference between the obscene and the pornographic. It is the latter which presents a danger. The problem is how to deal with the professional purveyors of pornography, which is "a type of communication devoted almost exclusively to arousing sexual hunger by presenting vivid sexual scenes and descriptions." (Robert W. Haney, *Comstockery in America.* Boston: Beacon Press, 1960, p. 67.)

[6] Ludwig Marcuse, *Obscene.* Translated by Karen Gershon. London: Macgibbon & Kee, 1965, p. 22.

[7] It is instructive to note that a novel like *Madame Bovary,* when published serially in the *Revue de Paris,* created a scandal; legal charges were preferred against the author, the publisher, and the printer on the charge that the novel offended against public morality and religion; the defendants were acquitted. When the novel came out

There is a deep-cutting difference between those literary works that are clearly pornography in content and those that, because they deal explicitly with the theme of sexual love, avoiding the time-honored strategy of using euphemistic circumlocutions, are alleged to be obscene. One of the tests that can be applied in this case is to examine the writer's values as they emerge in the total structure of his work. If his aim is solely or principally to concentrate on sex as an end in itself, if his object is to depict sexual passion to the virtual exclusion of all other aspects of experience so that what we get is a sexualized universe of discourse, then his production affords an example of pornography, even when the words he uses are not obscene. For he turns out a caricature of man, a grotesquely distorted animalian version of human beings in action. His protagonist is a "hero" in quest but the quest, as in *The Rosy Crucifixion,* consists in his obsessive search for varied forms of sexual consummation. The compulsion of instinct overrides all other interests. The sexual hero of our time is the personification, often comic in character, of insatiable carnal appetite.[8] He tends to look upon woman – and that holds true of Henry Miller's male characters – as simply a receptive vessel, a more than willing partner in what the Elizabethans called the dance of the sheets. What we get then is the picture of Caliban as the representative of humanity.

While rejecting the imputation of pornography, Henry Miller cheerfully admits that his writing is obscene, but what of it? It is difficult to define the obscene in a way that will satisfy everybody.[9] Even the problem of legally defining obscenity has never been definitively settled. If a novel is to be examined for its obscene contents, is an isolated passage – say, the last section of *Ulysses,* the interior monologue of Molly Bloom – to be sufficient damaging evidence or is the book to be judged as a whole? Though in the

in book form, it was attacked in the press as immoral, brutal, vulgar, and morbid. See Philip Spencer, *Flaubert.* New York: The Grove Press, 1953, p. 130.

[8] Edward Dahlberg laughs to scorn the ridiculous antics of this human ape suffering from a perpetual sexual itch. Man is "the most ridiculous beast on earth, and the reason for this is his mind and his pudendum." (Edward Dahlberg, *The Sorrows of Priapus.* Norfolk, Connecticut: New Directions, 1957, p. 10.) Governed tyrannically by his organs of generation, man exalts sex into a mystique.

[9] "For society to judge a work of art obscene, there must be in evidence a conflict of values between those of the society whose existence is threatened and another, divergent system of values espoused by the author of the obscenity. Perversion is obscene to a society of 'normal' heterosexuals; extreme cruelty is obscene to a society of 'charitable' Christians. Any value may be perverted, and hence any deviation from the accepted standards of value may produce a different variety of obscenity." Eugene F. Kaelin, *An Existentialist Aesthetic.* Madison: The University of Wisconsin Press, 1962, p. 128.

past the courts singled out specific passages as proof positive of obscenity, the practice at present is to judge the work of art as an organic whole.[10]

A healthy, sexually satisfied people will not manifest any particular interest in the consumption of pornography.[11] It is, strangely enough, the affluent members of the middle class who are the most avid patrons of pornography and at the same time the most diligent supporters of the campaign for "the purification" of literature.[12] Foolishly they identify the symbolic substitute, the imagined indecency, with the thing itself. The result is that pornography becomes mechanical, brutal, and even pathological. The stereotyped aphrodisiac formula wears thin after a while, and prurient cravings must be gratified by other means. In his search for novelty, the specialist in the production of pornography must try to titillate the jaded imagination of his clientele with more audacious scenes of passion by adding stronger ingredients and by romanticizing the life of vice.[13]

Publishers recognize, of course, that if they have a responsibility to literature, they must also carry out their responsibility to society. If they issue the wrong kind of book, they may be haled to court and the book possibly be forced out of circulation. If they refuse to accept a brilliantly original novel that tells the uncomfortable truth about the life of the two sexes, then they are betraying the cause of letters. Maxwell E. Perkins, the gifted editor for Scribner's, believes that an editor must consult his own taste and follow his own judgment in disputed matters of this kind, even though he is liable to make costly errors. It is not the function of the publisher to censor morals.

But as a businessman who has no desire to lose money on his investment, the publisher knows full well that in a given society at a given time, certain

[10] In his essay on "Moral Censorship and the Ten Commandments," Farrell declares that meanings must not be torn out of context but should be judged in relation to the rest of the work. "The meaning of any passage in a literary work must be discovered by taking that work as a whole. The notion that a certain passage in a work of art will necessarily stimulate some to so-called promiscuous sexuality is nonsense." James T. Farrell, *Literature and Morality*. New York: The Vanguard Press, 1947, p. 95.

[11] Pornographic fiction, despite its supposedly vivid and exciting subject matter, is incredibly dull. "It is a substitute for experience and nothing more. Its appeal is to the repressed and the thwarted who are unable to satisfy their sexual desires in the world of reality ... and seek satisfaction in a world of fantasy." Alec Craig, *The Banned Books of England*. London: G. Allen & Unwin, 1937, p. 154.

[12] Peckham holds that "the market for true pornography, the purveying of pornography unredeemed by style, of pornography for its own sake, is primarily the well-to-do middle class." Morse Peckham, *Beyond the Tragic Vision*. New York: George Braziller, 1962, p. 317.

[13] G. Legman points out with irrefutable logic that erotic literature exists because it satisfies an important need. "This need is twofold: the education of the inexperienced young, and the excitation of the impotent or old." G. Legman, *The Horn Book*. New Hyde Park, New York: University Books, Inc., 1964, p. 71.

expressions are taboo and to protect himself against expensive law suits he may be tempted to eliminate them from the printed text.[14] If he succumbs to this temptation, he is guilty of exercising a form of censorship that any self-respecting writer is bound to resist. If so-called objectionable expressions belong organically in the context of the work, then there is no reason why they should not be used. It would be dishonest, Maxwell E. Perkins declares, to leave them out.[15] A responsible editor should have the courage of his convictions and make every effort to support freedom of expression. In the long run, censorship (who is qualified to administer it?) is dangerous. In the final analysis, the answer to the question whether society has the right to enforce its ethical standards in the domain of letters depends on the kind of culture it wishes to cultivate. "Sex itself cannot be suppressed, and the efforts to do it, it seems to me, generally result in greater damage than it can do itself. After all, it was not the invention of man, but of God." [16] Perkins' wise words may be allowed to end this brief discussion of censorship: *Sex itself cannot be suppressed!*

---

[14] Wayland Young writes a fascinating but misguided disquisition on the semantic vagaries of meaning used to describe the act of sexual intercourse. "Here is our love-scene: what shall the couple do? Shall they *copulate*? Over our picture of them slides a suggestion of two dogs in a laboratory, observed by biologists. Shall they *lie together*? They may do so in siblike companionship a night long and have nothing to show for it . . . . Shall they *make love*? They may indeed, but what does this love look like when they have made it? It is a pretty phrase, and at least they are making something, but *love*? Is that really what they are making? . . . If they have really made anything, it is not so much love as a child . . . . Or shall our couple *have intercourse*? They will certainly be said to have done so if the circumstances are adulterous and if they fetch up in court afterward. But where did they find the intercourse they were going to have? There was intercourse; one minute they were not having it, the next moment they were. The same if they *have sex*. Shall *intimacy take place*? They may have been extremely intimate in the sense of being conversant with one another's most inward desires and ambitions . . . without so much as touching little finger to little finger . . . . Shall our couple have *carnal knowledge* of one another?" (Wayland Young, *Eros Denied*. New York: Grove Press, Inc., 1964, pp. 33–34.) And the same strictures are applied to a host of other circumlocutions and euphemistic slang terms. "The only word," Young concludes, "which has no other meaning whatever is *fuck*." (*Ibid.*, p. 36.) Young disregards the unpleasant connotative resonances of this obscene word, its implications as an expression of hostility and aggression. As David Bakan remarks: "There is a great discrepancy between its actual use in conversation and in print. It is the principal 'dirty word' of the English language, suggesting its connection with anality . . . . It has strong hostile meanings . . . ." (David Bakan, *The Duality of Human Existence*. Chicago: Rand McNally & Company, 1966, p. 135.)

[15] Maxwell E. Perkins, *Editor to Author*. New York and London: Charles Scribner's Sons, 1950, p. 82.

[16] *Ibid.*, p. 281.

INDEX

810